G000122260

TEWKESBURY

Abbey Cottages.

TEWKESBURY

Anthea Jones

PHILLIMORE

1987

Published by
PHILLIMORE & CO. LTD
Shopwyke Hall, Chichester, Sussex

© Dr. Anthea Jones, 1987

ISBN 0 85033 631 7

Printed in Great Britain by
BIDDLES LTD
Guildford, Surrey

Contents

List of Plates

The photographic illustrations were planned as an integral part of the book. They are all, purposely, contemporary with the period of research and writing, most of the photographs being taken between 1985 and 1987, and a few in the early 1980's. Many of them have been paired in the hope of making interesting conjunctions by comparison or contrast, by continuing a theme or showing complementary views.

Their theme might be called 'visible history'. The photographer has had four particular objectives: to provide a record, to guide the visitor, to converse with the resident and to engender an awareness of the connections between what we see now and the past. He hopes that the photographs will suggest to the reader other ideas to explore.

G. Jones

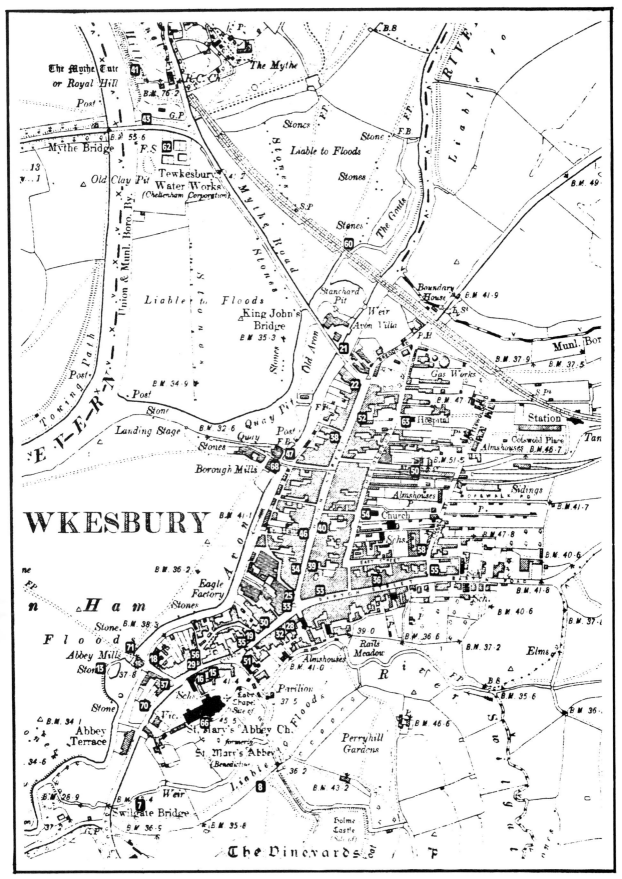

Early Ordnance Survey Map showing the locations of subjects of plates.

List of Line Illustrations

Frontispiece: Abbey Cottages

List of Maps

Acknowledgements

Throughout the book, a big debt is acknowledged to James Bennett, who either published in full or summarised a number of documents relating to Tewkesbury's history, including many of the charters. Equally important to the modern researcher is volume 8 in the *Victoria History of the County of Gloucester* which makes available, particularly for the medieval period, material which is in national record repositories. Personal research has been carried out in the original records deposited in Gloucester Record Office. Any researcher appreciates how much less progress could be made without the expertise of the archivists and their help is gratefully acknowledged. The Librarians of Gloucester City Library and Cheltenham Library are also thanked for their willing cooperation in the search for materials and the Vicar of Tewkesbury, Mr. M. A. Moxon, for the loan of material, and for permission on numerous occasions to go to the top of the abbey tower.

There are many debts to individuals who have pointed the way over several years. I would like to mention particularly Mr. Charles Hilton, for personal encouragement and for the pointers provided by his book of postcard views of Tewkesbury; Mr. R. Mulcock and Mr. M. Eyles for help in the abbey; Mr. J. Henderson, the first chemist and bacteriologist to the then Cheltenham and Gloucester Water Board; Mr. Malcolm Foster of Tewkesbury Borough Council for arranging access to maps and photographs; Mr. Mark Healing, for permission to copy the portrait of his great-great-grandfather, Mr. Samuel Healing; Mr. Nick Gill of Hammill Photo Services Ltd. of Cheltenham for skilful attention to detail in developing and printing photographs used in the book; Mr. John Cooke, the artist of the Hill Studio, Dent, Cumbria, who has spent some extremely fatiguing and wet hours tramping round Tewkesbury to capture visual aspects of its history.

My husband has been researcher, assiduous reader, critic, companion in repeatedly walking streets and fields, photographer, and constant encourager of the venture. The book is dedicated to him. It tries to answer some of his questions about 'how it happened'.

Preface

'Tewkesbury', as the title implies, is a history which starts from the town as it is today; exploration of the documentary sources and of the physical shape of the town have proceeded in step. Interest has been encouraged by others concerned with the history of the town, while the challenge of explaining history to school pupils led to a first short essay. Research stimulates further inquiry; as more information is acquired earlier ideas are modified, and exploration is always continuing. I hope that readers will tell me of further evidence which contributes to the interpretation.

The history of one particular town is clearly 'local history', and has led to reflections on the nature of this genre of historical enquiry. It does not start from an historical source, which tends to shape the enquiry, but from the more difficult task-master of a particular locality; for this, many different sources, often fragmentary, have to be pressed into contribution.

'Tewkesbury' is, in part, a history of a 'typical' town; at the same time any town is unique in its exact combination of physical characteristics, its survivals from the past and its individual experience of national events. In part this book is a history of the country seen through the eyes of inhabitants of Tewkesbury; yet only in catastrophic events like a civil war do local perspectives coincide with national ones. Nonetheless, in all periods, the story of Tewkesbury has been found very illuminating of national events. Perhaps this study can best be described as an attempt to show how history happened, in the experience of this one town. For this reason, the book is not an exhaustive compilation of material. Bennett provided this type of resource and in recent times the *Victoria County History of Gloucestershire*, volume 8, has created another substantial record. It is hoped that the reader will find points of illumination and explanation and that this account of Tewkesbury's development will also help understanding of the larger story of English history.

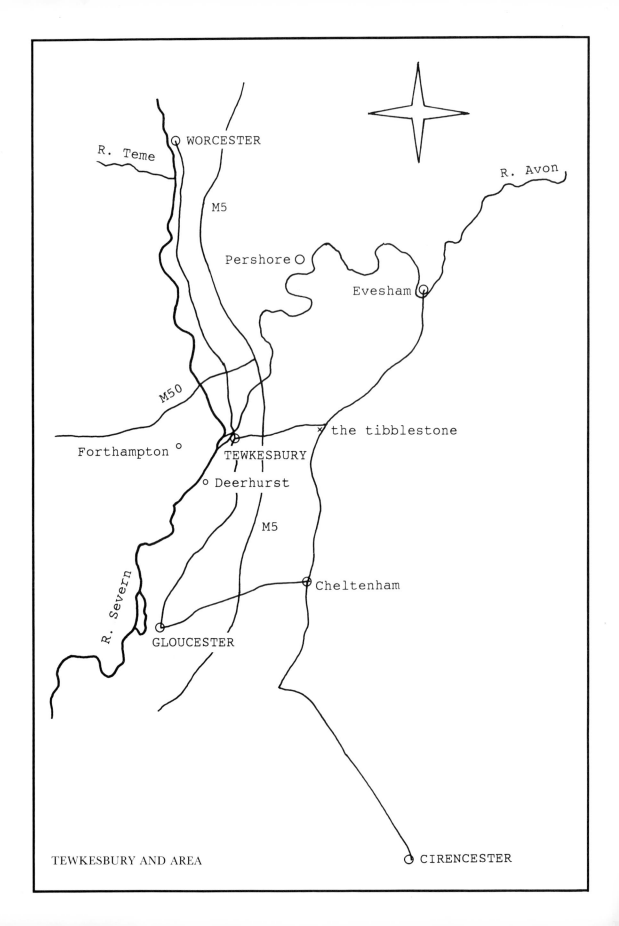

TEWKESBURY AND AREA

A Brief Guide to the Town

The traveller arriving at the Cross along one of three very old roads meeting there, from north, east or south, is at once aware that Tewkesbury is a town of vivid historical character. The first impression is of an unusual number of timber-framed buildings fronting the streets; interspersed between them are the brick facades of the 18th and early 19th centuries. The abbey church is close by; though it may not be immediately visible, the Norman tower is often glimpsed behind the houses, and from many points of view provides a satisfying focal point. It is one of the largest and most impressive parish churches in the country.

After a brief exploration, the enquiring traveller finds the rivers and bridges, the corn mills, the great meadow called the Severn Ham and tantalising snatches of a life hidden away down narrow alleys and courts. The long thin profile of the town is evident, and modern development is apparently distanced from it. The traveller may then wonder what has shaped Tewkesbury, what past events or experiences made the town as it is today. How did the inhabitants of Tewkesbury earn their livings and how much of the town which was familiar to them in previous centuries still survives?

The oldest building, as in so many English towns and villages, is the church – all that remains of an abbey founded during the reign of William Rufus, son of William the Conqueror. The nave, tower and transepts were built in the early 12th century: a clear demonstration of the simple but massive Norman style of architecture. In the early 14th century, the choir and chapels were added or rebuilt. Few other buildings in the town are as old as this, though there is a late 13th-century cellar or undercroft beneath a house on the corner of St Mary's Lane, and there may be other buildings which incorporate ancient fragments.

The abbey dominated the town for 450 years, until 1540 when, with all the large monasteries of the country, it was dissolved by Henry VIII. In the two periods of major building works, the town would have been full of masons, carpenters and glaziers, so that the fabric of the monastery was a pervasive influence. The monastic community also required of the inhabitants of Tewkesbury regular work in provisioning and service, while the abbey owned much of the town's land and houses. The timber-framed houses, dating from 1450 to 1500, and now known as Abbey Cottages, were originally shops built by the monastery as a speculative venture. They were saved from demolition in 1967 and one of the houses, the Little Museum, has been restored to show what living conditions were like at the time they were built. Since the destruction of the monastery buildings, the land on which they stood on the south of the church has remained undeveloped, though the site was levelled in 1830. Only the church remains as a visible reminder of this important aspect of Tewkesbury's history.

The main pattern of streets is probably earlier than the Norman period. Often the lines of the principal streets are the oldest feature of a town, especially as many sites were chosen for occupation centuries before the Norman Conquest. Tewkesbury's street pattern was determined by the ancient land route along the eastern side of the Severn, which crossed the Avon immediately to the north of the town. Other routes from the east converged at Tewkesbury. These form the basis of the modern Church Street, High Street and Barton Street. The rivers of Severn and Avon, and the lesser stream to the east of the town called the Swilgate, have been a constant determinant of Tewkesbury's shape and size, so that the main development has been confined to the 'Y' shape formed by the three streets.

The closure of the abbey in 1540 did not adversely affect Tewkesbury's economy. It continued to be a thriving market town – one of the three chief towns in Gloucestershire. (The other important towns at this date were Gloucester itself and Cirencester.) The prosperity of the town is obviously reflected in the number of timber-framed buildings which survive from the 15th and 16th centuries, their massive timbers speaking of considerable wealth and surviving many alterations in the succeeding centuries. There was also tremendous pressure on land suitable for building, so that the characteristic alleys developed, as houses were built one behind the other down the long narrow garden plots of the original townsmen's dwellings. Since the alleyways were insanitary by modern standards, some were demolished from the early 20th century when general reform of urban conditions was being undertaken. Nonetheless, a remarkable number survive and can be explored. Old Baptist Chapel Court opposite the Abbey Cottages is easily accessible.

After a period of relative stagnation, a further surge of prosperity in Tewkesbury is clearly evident in the large number of Georgian facades in the main streets. Some merely disguise older timber-framed houses, but many are replacement buildings in the fashionable style. Tewkesbury was still, in 1800, one of Gloucestershire's principal towns. Coaching traffic passed through its streets; the surrounding roads were turnpiked; the market, mills, breweries and stocking-knitting all provided employment. A small group of stocking-knitters' cottages at the corner of St Mary's Lane has recently been restored. They were built at the end of the 18th century with specially large windows in the first storey probably to facilitate work at the frames. The atmosphere of the town is perhaps most governed by this period in its history, with its restrained and simple building styles, which intermingle happily with the surviving timber-framed buildings.

So much of Georgian Tewkesbury remains because, in the later 19th century, the town lost its bustling importance; it was still a market-centre for the agricultural area around as it had almost certainly been since Saxon and possibly Roman times nearly 2,000 years before, but it hardly shared in later Victorian prosperity as the other Gloucester downs did. The stocking-knitting industry in Tewkesbury collapsed due to mechanisation in the Midlands. The railway killed the coaching and the river trade; it also by-passed Tewkesbury itself, taking away the town's importance on the older lines of communication which had sustained it for so long. Almost the only prominent building from the period before 1939 is the public library, formerly the grammar school – a vividly red brick edifice opposite the abbey gateway. There are, however, many small unobtrusive houses and workshops dating from this time, especially in the area of the Oldbury, which had for centuries been an arable field shared and cultivated by the townsfolk. After enclosure in 1811, this area behind High Street and Barton Street was developed piecemeal and in a more humble fashion than the main streets.

In the middle 20th century, the decision was made to encourage light industry to come to the town, to save it from its dependence on a small-scale agricultural market. This has led to much new building, but, fortunately for the visitor's interest, demolition of old buildings had barely begun before the unfortunate examples of Gloucester and Worcester led to a strong move for conservation and a realisation that old unfashionable buildings could be renovated to provide an atmosphere and attraction that were irreplaceable.

Thus, Tewkesbury today is thriving again, while its town centre is one of the remarkable concentrations of old buildings in the country. In the following chapters, the history of the town in each of these periods is expanded, with attention drawn to features that the visitor may observe for himself.

Tewkesbury from across the River Severn.

Chapter 1

Before the Normans: B.C. to 1066

Rivers and Roads

Rivers and roads are basic determinants of many settlements. The key to Tewkesbury's siting and development is the Severn and the road running north and south parallel to it, which crosses the Avon immediately to the north of the town. For early explorers and settlers, a river provided a sure guide through unknown countryside. Following the east bank of the Severn, travellers were able to ford the Avon at Tewkesbury, possibly because at this point it was wide and shallow. The general line of the modern Gloucester to Worcester road follows this almost certainly pre-Roman route, passing through Tewkesbury along Church Street and High Street. The Avon joins the Severn on the farther side of the great meadow or Ham. This river, too, was a guide to the early traveller, so that a path struck off along the east bank, in a north-easterly direction, at a safe height above the flood plain. It linked Tewkesbury with Pershore and Evesham. A modern road to Bredon follows this route, which seems to be a continuation of the north-south axis of the town, but has been less important historically.

A third road goes in an easterly direction, taking the traveller over the Cotswolds. It has been suggested that this is part of an ancient route to north-east England. From Barton Street, Tewkesbury, the road follows the Carrant brook, a tributary of the Avon, while again avoiding low-lying ground. It leads directly to the Tibblestone at Teddington Cross Hands. The guide post perhaps dates from the 16th century, but the Tibblestone is much more ancient; it was a sufficiently notable feature to give its name to an administrative area in Saxon times. From here, the traveller from Tewkesbury could proceed to Sedgeberrow and thence to Mickleton or, by another Cotswold crossing, from Stanway to Stow-on-the-Wold. This easterly road was also important in the development of Tewkesbury, and its intersection at the Cross with the north-south road determined the position of the market.

While these ancient ways have changed their courses many times, modern roads often follow their general direction. Minor roads, paths and hedgerows of today also provide clues which suggest where an old road lay. The present-day position of Tewkesbury's main roads was only fixed about a hundred and fifty years ago by the work of the Turnpike Trusts, but nonetheless these three ways have been determining factors throughout Tewkesbury's history.

As well as the rivers and roads, Tewkesbury also has a man-made feature of almost equal importance in its development, the Mill Avon. No-one knows when this cut was made, linking the waters of the Avon with the much smaller stream called the Swilgate. The cut brought a good flow of water close to the habitable higher ground. It was used for hundreds of years to drive the corn mills. The Abbey Mills existed before 1102 when they were assigned to the newly-founded monastery, so that the cut may be Saxon

1. The Mill Avon provided water-power for the mills. Today it is used mainly for leisure boating. Near the river new buildings are replacing the builder's yard of Collins and Godfrey and Nailors' Square.

2. A road sign near the *Royal Hop Pole Hotel* shows the Y of the main streets. The canopy was formerly over the carriage entrance.

or even Roman. It could have been defensive in origin, providing a barrier against attack by marauders coming up the River Severn. No doubt it has been widened and deepened since it was first dug by hand. It now provides anchorage for many small pleasure craft. The Mill Avon has been an integral feature of Tewkesbury for perhaps a thousand years.

Many English towns owe their foundation to a conjunction of river-crossing and converging roads. In Tewkesbury, the Y-shape formed by the original lines of communication has remained to the present day the visible basis of the town. The three roads follow narrow slips of land which are above the level defined by the 40 foot (12 metre) contour, and are surrounded by low-lying marsh and watermeadow. Development has therefore been very restricted, except between the two arms of the 'Y'. Even so, flooding has been one of Tewkesbury's recurrent dangers and dramatic tales of the town's inundation have been told at all periods right up to the present. Looking towards the Severn across the Mill Avon and the Ham, it is not difficult to imagine water covering the meadow and spilling over onto the road. It is more difficult to envisage the danger from the very tiny streams, the Carrant and the Swilgate, which flow east, north and south of Tewkesbury. The Carrant joins the Avon just north of the town: the Swilgate flows from the south and then loops round close to the Abbey, and with the Mill Avon joins the Severn. Both these tiny streams carry floodwater, turning Tewkesbury effectively into an island. The causeway linking Tewkesbury with its modern extension towards Ashchurch is just discernible today, pointing to the low-lying nature of the ground here. Modern residential development both to the north-east and to southwards is necessarily beyond this band of meadow. The old market centre of Tewkesbury is thus still, as it would have been in former times, surrounded by green fields.

Four rivers, or two rivers and two streams, have thus contributed to Tewkesbury's history, forming barriers in some respects but also providing in themselves a means of communication. The Severn has always been navigable beyond Tewkesbury, and the Avon was made navigable in the 17th century. The Avon and the two streams were not too difficult to ford or, in later times, to bridge. In the 16th century, 300 years after the Avon was bridged, a field was still known as 'Avonford'. The Severn, however, was more hazardous to cross and proved an impossible task to bridge before the 19th century. From Tewkesbury, two ferries, at the Upper and the Lower Lode, carried the traveller across the river.

Earliest Settlements

Exactly when a settlement grew up at the Avon crossing is not known. Ancient traditions concerning the founding of Tewkesbury Abbey, and more significantly the Saxon name of the town, seemed to imply an origin in the fifth century A.D. or later. More recently, archaeological discoveries have shown that people were living on the site at a much earlier date. Some Neolithic pottery found in the north-east part of Tewkesbury would place habitation about 2500 B.C., and this accords well with the date of the many Cotswold long barrows which seem to suggest more intensive settlement in the area than has been demonstrated by archaeology. Many of our villages and towns are perhaps built on top of settlements as old as this.

Nothing is known of Tewkesbury between this remote date and the Roman conquest of Britain in the first century A.D. At this time, the Gloucestershire area was the territory of a group of people called the Dobunni, who were willing to co-operate with the Romans and whose capital was at Bagendon, just north of Cirencester. A new capital of the province was founded by the Romans at Cirencester, then called *Corinium Dobunnorum*. An early military camp at Kingsholm was soon converted to a colony called *Glevum Colonia*, now Gloucester, one of only four places with this status in Britain, where retired soldiers were given grants of land. From both these Roman towns, a network of roads was constructed.

It would have been practical for one road to be based on the older route following the Severn, which now linked the colony of Gloucester with Droitwich, an important source of salt. Margary in his book *Roman Roads in Britain* published in 1957, identified a Roman road going through Tewkesbury and Worcester, which joined the Ryknield Way near Birmingham. He found evidence in modern road and field boundary alignments south of Worcester, and, a few miles north of Tewkesbury, in the name Stratford, a Saxon word which usually indicates Roman road construction. Subsequently, a section has been dug across Shuthonger Common just to the north of Tewkesbury, which confirmed his suggestion. Roman use of both Severn and Avon riverside routes gains support, too, from the discovery of a number of Roman sites nearby, some of which were found in the course of hurried excavations during the construction of the M5 motorway.

It is now accepted that Tewkesbury was occupied in this period. Finds of Roman coins in and near the town, and also the remains of stone structures under the ground which were probably Roman, were reported by Bennett in the three volumes relating to the history of Tewkesbury, published between 1830 and 1849. Recently, when demolition and development was proceeding along Tewkesbury's main streets, a scattering of Roman finds was recorded, and some systematic excavation has produced evidence from the first to the fourth centuries. There is also evidence of Roman settlement just to the south at Southwick Park.

Could Tewkesbury be *Argistillum*? Two as yet unidentified names, *Argistillum* and *Vertis*, placed between Gloucester and Droitwich, occur in one of the lists of towns in the *Ravenna Cosmography*. The *Cosmography* was an enumeration of countries, towns and rivers made in the seventh century; the British section was based on Roman road itineraries which by this date were some centuries old. One subsidiary route started from Gloucester, and after Droitwich proceeded to Cirencester and Silchester. It included *Argistillum* and *Vertis*. The only explanation for the name *Argistillum* at present is that it is a Latinised form of a Welsh word, possibly meaning 'white and gleaming'. Could it refer to the flood water which often covers many acres round the town, and from a distance does shine? If it is identified with Tewkesbury, then it has not influenced at all the Saxon name for the town which we use today. *Vertis* may mean 'a turn', and perhaps describes a river loop. It could have applied to the Avon where it makes a particularly large loop at Evesham. Many Roman finds have been made in the Vale of Evesham to support at least the possibility, while a route from Droitwich to Cirencester could certainly pass through Evesham, as the chief salt way did in medieval times.

As well as archaeological evidence of Roman occupation of Tewkesbury, there is also a local place-name which may show Roman influence on the town to the present day. The name Oldbury is first recorded in 1257; Oldbury Street was the name for the present High Street. The Oldbury was an open field of more than seventy acres to the

3. & 4. Tewkesbury is seen across the Ham from the rising ground of Cork's Hill, which is west of the River Severn and near the Upper Lode. The Mill Avon is at the far edge of the Ham, and marks the limit of building; the land in many places is only about six feet above the level of the floods which frequently cover the Ham with 'shining' water.

east of High Street, and north of Barton Street. The name suggests that Saxon inhabitants saw mounds and ditches, or even the ruins of masonry, perhaps hundreds of years after the end of Roman rule which they recognised as an old fortified place or 'bury'. Bennett reported Roman finds in the area, and recent excavation has produced further evidence of Roman occupation. The Saxons left the site unoccupied, building their houses a little to the south on the same spit of higher ground; it remained an open field shared amongst Tewkesbury residents until the 19th century. The traveller who walks from Barton Street into the Oldbury area can see at once the untidy Victorian development of brick houses, churches, factories and warehouses; here was the obvious place for gasworks and railway station. Yet this was the logical site for settlement: the only part of Tewkesbury above 100 feet (30 metres), with useful deposits of gravel for dry foundations. The causeway across the Avon Ham from Mythe Hill, where the route of the Roman road is known, leads directly to the Oldbury; southwards, the obvious route would be across the Swilgate to Perry Hill, and the alignment of many 19th-century field boundaries may preserve its course.

Though Tewkesbury had some Roman settlement, in comparison with Gloucester and Cirencester it was not important and does not appear to have had either walls or public buildings. It may have been larger in area than Gloucester, which was planned on 45 acres, but it lacked the special status that being a *colonia* gave. Tewkesbury also had a less favourable crossing point of the Severn. At Gloucester, the river divided into two channels, making the crossing easier; moreover, from there the Romans could quickly reach the valuable resources of iron and coal in the Forest of Dean, which were extensively exploited. Cirencester was much larger: an area of 240 acres laid out as befitted the capital of the Province. In time, it became the second largest town in Roman Britain. Two great Roman roads, Ermin Street and Fosse Way, intersected at Cirencester. Tewkesbury commanded less important routes, in only three directions not four. For many centuries, Cirencester and Gloucester were the only two sizeable towns in the area of present-day Gloucestershire.

The Saxon Period

The Romans abandoned the defence of Britain early in the fifth century, and at least two hundred years of political uncertainty and intermittent warfare followed, at first between the native Britons and invaders, and then amongst different groups of the invaders themselves. The towns were no longer sustained by Roman commerce and control, and their buildings were destroyed in the fighting. We may suppose the Britons struggled to maintain their farms and livelihoods, though Bede in his history of the English church, written in the eighth century, speaks of great famines.

The Saxons, penetrating into this area from the south, were the first threat to the British inhabitants but, after a great British victory at the end of the fifth century, the Saxons were held for 50 years. Gloucester, Cirencester and Bath were all capitals of small British provinces prior to 577. In that year, the Saxon advance was resumed; a battle was won at Dyrham near Bath and both Cirencester and Gloucester were taken. The Saxons' hold on the area, however, was fragile, and Tewkesbury may have been beyond their influence. For this reason, it is suggested, there are very few early forms of Saxon place-names in the district.

The Saxons were soon challenged by another group of invaders, the Angles, who were approaching down the Avon from the Midlands. The Angles were creating a great kingdom controlled by Mercian rulers from a base around Lichfield and Tamworth. After a victory at Cirencester in 628, the Mercian prince Penda created a large kingdom of the Hwicce, under Mercian control. Four years later, Penda became king of Mercia; eight members of his family in succession ruled the kingdom. The Wychwood in Oxfordshire was the wood of the Hwicce, and a little later Worcester became the centre of the Christian church of the Hwicce. Their territory included Worcestershire, south-west Warwickshire and all Gloucestershire east of the Severn, with a small amount of territory on the right or west bank. The diocese of Worcester mainly comprised this area; the division into shires is rather later. Tewkesbury was now firmly within the Anglian kingdom of Mercia and remained so until Mercia itself was broken up in the ninth century. It remained within the diocese of Worcester until the 16th century.

From the time of the conquest by Penda, the Angles began to settle in north Gloucestershire, filling the countryside and leaving us, to a surprising extent, the present-day place-names on our maps, which were their farms, hamlets, villages and towns. There is a remarkable concentration of place-names with the same construction within a short distance of Tewkesbury. The names are formed from a personal name, with the suffix '-ing' meaning 'belonging to' and finally the word '-ton' meaning farm. Teddington, Taddington, Toddington, Wormington, Frampton, Alderton, Woolstone, Gotherington, Timbingctun (now Bishop's Cleeve), Kemerton, Fiddington and Pamington all lie a short distance off the Tewkesbury-Stow road. Tredington, Boddington, Elmstone, Evington and Uckington are all south of Tewkesbury, off the road to Gloucester. Although modern usage has obscured the '-ington' form in some of these names, all are derived this way. It suggests a large number of individuals settled on suitable sites at about the same time, and perhaps under the initiative of one landowner. We cannot tell for sure if the Angles merely renamed existing British or even Roman farms, or were creating new settlement sites; most likely it was the former.

A surprising proportion of these places was later within the same administrative areas: the hundreds of Tewkesbury and Deerhurst, which probably originally formed one large estate, not two. Most interestingly, the only '-ington' name west of the Severn is Forthampton (the 'ton' belonging to Forthelm). Forthampton was part of Tewkesbury manor, and it was also one of the few Gloucestershire territories on the west bank of the Severn in the diocese of Worcester. Other territory west of the Severn was in Hereford diocese, when these administrative areas were defined in the ninth century.

What happened to the British inhabitants of the area we do not know. Some fled westwards. Some lived in semi-independence within their own areas, perhaps on land specially allotted to them, for example at Walton Cardiff and Deerhurst Walton. 'Walton' often means the 'ton' of the 'wahls' or Welsh, as the Angles called them. The same word gives us Wales. Some stayed on completely under the control of their new masters, the ancestors of the 50 slaves in Tewkesbury in 1066 recorded by Domesday Book, and of the scattering of slaves in many of the outlying villages.

The Angles renamed nearly every settlement, only accepting from the British the names of natural features like the rivers Avon and Carrant. Sometimes they anglicised a Roman name, like Severn for Sabrina, and perhaps Southwick from the Roman 'vicus', often applied to a dairy farm on the edge of a wooded area as this would have been, and often also associated with a Roman road or settlement; but generally their language

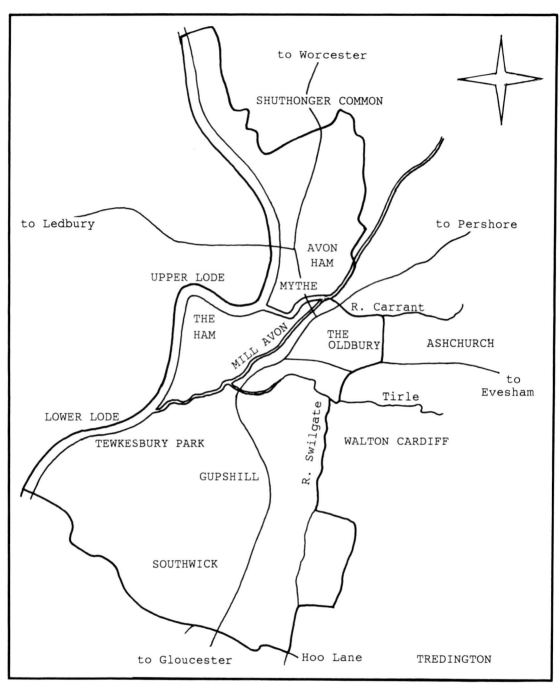

THE BOROUGH AND PARISH BOUNDARIES OF TEWKESBURY
based on Lewis's *Topographical Dictionary*

seems all-pervading. Their place-names, when their meaning is elucidated, often reflect observant appreciation of scenery and topography. An example is the Hoo Lane, in part the southern boundary of Tewkesbury, which runs from Tredington to a prominent rounded hill above Deerhurst, a 'hoo'. The land between the two rivers, the Severn and the Avon, is described in the name Mythe, meaning the confluence of rivers. A 'hamm', being either land almost surrounded by water or a water-meadow, is Tewkesbury's Ham of today. The Gastons was a pasture. Deerhurst was the deer forest; the Leigh a clearing within the forest. These last two names suggest new settlements, and so does Newton on the edge of Tewkesbury. Otherwise, it is reasonable to suppose that the area immediately round Tewkesbury was cleared and settled before the Angles took it over, as the number of Roman settlements would have led to fairly intensive cultivation of the land.

5. & 6. The expanse of the Ham, about 200 acres, is apparent from the abbey tower. As well as providing the burgesses with rich pasture after the hay had been mown, the Ham has been used as a racecourse. Floods sometimes prevented racing; in 1727 the Ham was flooded 20 times.

Topography can often throw light on place-names and similarly place-names can illuminate history. When the Healing family bought land for the erection of the new Borough Mills in the mid-19th century, the area where their barges are now moored was called the Pale Pill. A 'pill' was an Old English word meaning a pool or tidal creek or sometimes a harbour; it is cognate with 'pull' as in Pull Court in Bushley and is common on both sides of the Bristol Channel. The name could have preserved the memory of the first harbour, before the construction of the Mill Avon made it more convenient to have the quay a little farther down the river. The name of the river Swilgate also offers interesting ground for speculation about its derivation. A 'gate' is a road; it has an Old Norse origin and Danes certainly penetrated to this area, wintering in Gloucester in 877. An old road from Tewkesbury ran southwards close to the Swilgate before the period of the Turnpike Trusts in the 18th and 19th centuries, passing Tredington and continuing on towards Deerhurst Walton. 'Swill' may indicate pigs. Was this the road pigs were driven along to and from their winter feeding areas in the woods around Deerhurst? If so, it helps explain how Swilgate superseded an earlier name for this river, the Tyrl, which is found in an eighth-century charter; later the Tyrl is only a small stream feeding the Swilgate. 'Piggeway furlong' was in this area in 1540.

The Organisation of the Christian Church

Soon after the Angles won Gloucestershire, the Mercian rulers were converted to Christianity. The British inhabitants who had survived had not promoted their Christianity in any way, if indeed it was still alive. Bede described their failure as an 'unspeakable' crime. Augustine had arrived in England in 597. Paeda, the son of Penda, became a Christian in 653 before his father's death, and once he was ruler of Mercia he facilitated the work of Roman church missionaries amongst his people. The eastern part of Mercia was tackled first. Missionaries reached the Hwicce through the patronage of two earls or 'under-kings' and Bede says they were baptised sometime before 685.

About this time, too, Mercia was divided into five dioceses; Worcester was the centre, or 'head minster', of the diocese of the Hwicce. The bishop of Worcester then had the task of persuading landowners to give suitable endowments for the establishment of 'ordinary minsters' – lesser centres from which the work of conversion could be carried on. Enough land was needed to support a community or college of several clergymen, who at first probably lived together, though not monks. This provided the framework of parishes. Simultaneously, monasteries of monks and nuns were founded, not necessarily through the initiative of the bishop. In some cases, the bishop resented the affluence and power of monasteries like Evesham and Pershore, and tried, often unsuccessfully, to establish authority over them. By the beginning of the ninth century, minsters or monasteries existed in the Tewkesbury area at Beckford, Bredon, Cheltenham, Cleeve, Deerhurst, Twyning, Winchcombe and Withington. The number of religious foundations certainly indicates some density of settlement in the area.

In the late 15th century, a monk of Tewkesbury Abbey wrote a chronicle of his monastery's history, starting from its foundation at the time of the Hwicce's conversion.

In the Times of the Most Illustrious Princes and Kings of Mercia, Ethelred, Kenred and Ethelbald, there flourished in Mercia under those Kings, two great Men truly noble, to wit, Oddo and Doddo, Persons of very honourable Parentage, and eminent in themselves for their great Vertue, and what was their greatest Praise, they were pious Men and honoured God, and loved him above all things, and worshipt him with sincere Devotion. Their true Zeal for the Service of God, and unfeigned Love for him, did evidently appear; for thro' the Inspiration of the Holy Ghost, they granted many Estates to divers Monasteries built by themselves or their Ancestors, for the sake of Religion, and for promoting Divine Service.

These two Noblemen, amongst other Acts of Piety and Charity, founded in the Year 715, a Monastery, to the Glory of God, and the Honour of the Virgin Mary, on their own Estate, near the Severn, 7 Miles distant from Gloster, in the Place where a certain Hermit called Theocus, had made his Abode, and therefore called Tewksbury. These aforesaid Noblemen had a certain Brother named Almaric, whose Body was buried at Deorhurst, in a little Chapel over against the Gate of the Priory. This Chapel was formerly part of a Royal Palace, and his Sepulchre is shewn at this Day, with an Inscription on the Wall over the Gate, That Duke Dodo caused this Royal Palace to be consecrated into a Church, to the Honour of the Virgin Mary, for the Love which he bore to his Brother Almaric.

This story has been accepted and repeated, especially as this translation of the monk's chronicle was published in 1712 in Atkyn's *Ancient and Present State of Gloucestershire.* Careful research into Anglo-Saxon England, however, in the late 19th century began to raise doubts. Oddo, who was buried at Pershore, although certainly associated with the small Saxon chapel at Deerhurst, lived in the 11th century. Doddo perhaps lived in the ninth century, giving his name to Dudstone Hundred and less certainly to Dowdeswell, or 'Doddeswelle' as in Domesday Book. Neither of these men lived in the right century for the chronicler's story. Once undermined, the reality of Theocus the hermit was also questioned – his name looks suspiciously like a deduction from the name Tewkesbury. Finally, it was noted that the earlier and simpler *Annals* of Tewkesbury Abbey, written in the late 13th century, made no mention of the monastery before 1102. The most recent account of Tewkesbury's history, in the *Victoria County History,* rejects all Saxon origins for the monastery and starts from the undoubted foundation by the Norman, Robert Fitz-Hamon, about 1102.

There is nonetheless some truth in the monk's story. An early minster church was established near the beginning of the eighth century on the area of Tewkesbury between the Severn and the Avon river confluence. The area is now called the Mythe but at that time was called *Tweoneaum,* meaning precisely 'between the rivers'. The prioress in 740 was probably the princess Aethelburg, daughter of the royal family of the Hwicce, and later prioress of Withington. From Tewkesbury minster a number of 'field churches' were established which continued as late as the mid-16th century to be subordinate to Tewkesbury, until Henry VIII reorganised the church after the dissolution of the monasteries. The group of chapels dependent on Tewkesbury included Forthampton and Bushley west of the Severn, and Ashchurch, Tredington and Oxenton east of the Severn. The first element in the place-name 'Tewkesbury' may reflect the siting of this important church, 'twixt' the rivers. Other explanations of the name rely on a person to whom the 'bury' belonged, Theocus the hermit in the monk's chronicle, or Teodec a landowner in more recent place-name studies; neither really matches modern pronunciation 'Tyuksbry'. On the other hand, half of Leland's spellings of the name, of which there are 12 variants in the course of a few pages of notes, do support the topographical explanantion: Twexberye, Twekesbyrie, Twekesbyry, Twexsbiri, Twekexberye, Twexsbyri (used several times). The other six variants are: Tewkesbury (he used the modern spelling at least three times), Tewkesburie, Tewxbery, Theokesbyri (quoted a number of times from the monk's chronicle), Teokesbyri and Theukesbyri.

About a century after the minster's foundation, Coenwulf, King of Mercia, compensated the bishop of Worcester with some alternative sources of revenue and took from him the minster's lands. He probably wanted the superb look-out position on the tip of Mythe Hill, which commanded the ford across the Avon and the confluence of the Avon and Severn. Ditches may have been dug to make the look-out more secure. Mercia was fighting Wessex for supremacy; after Coenwulf's death, his successor was defeated and Wessex became the dominant kingdom. The monk in his chronicle referred to these civil wars, and said that Tewkesbury Monastery was often plundered and twice consumed with fire. He perhaps had good evidence for his statement, now lost to us, or perhaps he guessed because of what was known generally about the history of England.

Invasions of Danes and Normans

The fortifications dug by Coenwulf were soon needed for defence against the Danes, who began to plunder and also to settle in England. The Danes were famous for the lightning speed of their marches. About a hundred years later (c. 995), a chronicler named Aethelweard, a relative of King Alfred and of sufficient education though a layman to write in Latin, described this time of disruption:

> Anno 887 The barbarians . . . devastate the kingdom of the Mercians and drive out all the free men. They erect their tents in the town of Gloucester.
> Anno 909 The lands of the Mercians are laid waste on all sides by the hosts aforesaid, as far as the streams of the Avon, where begins the frontier of the West Saxons and the Mercians.

Neither the chronicler nor later historians can speak more definitely of Tewkesbury. Perhaps the Mill Avon was dug at this time. Tradition associates the Mythe Tute with the Danes. The man-made tumulus on the tip of the hill certainly increases the value of the look-out position, but it is more likely to have been Normans than Danes who constructed it. The view today is partly obscured by trees, but a public path to the Tute has been carefully preserved. The tumulus has been much eroded by the action of the Severn on the soft red marl, so that approximately half only of the original mound now exists. The defensive ditches on the tip of Mythe Hill account for another element in the name of Tewkesbury – 'bury' meaning fortified place. We can only guess at the bury's occupants – Mercian, Wessex or Dane – in the 10th century.

By the time Edward the Confessor died without an heir in 1066, the English state had been unified and, stimulated by the need to organise defences against the Danes, the former area of Mercia had been divided up into shires. The boundary between Gloucestershire and Worcestershire was drawn very close indeed to Tewkesbury; though nearly all Tewkesbury minster's lands were included in Gloucestershire, it had scattered estates placed in Worcestershire. Gloucester was rather more powerful and managed to secure all its estates within the county. The shire boundary was artificial, yet its intricacies lasted until very recent times.

Within each county there were smaller administrative units known as 'hundreds'. Each hundred was probably at first an area which could supply a proportion of money and men for defence. It is possible that some of the hundreds were based on Roman land divisions, which had survived despite the many upheavals of the Saxon period. It is notable that the more important places on the east side of the Severn – Berkeley, Gloucester, Deerhurst and Tewkesbury – all had within their hundreds the areas immediately across the Severn, so that they had complete control of their crossing points.

This was the Anglo-Saxon administrative framework which was taken over by the Normans in 1066. Only an already well-developed state could have undertaken the survey of all the land of England which forms Domesday Book. The Normans imposed new lords over the land, but only small numbers of ordinary Norman folk followed the Conqueror to settle in England, unlike the great migrations of Saxons and Danes. Six hundred years separate the ending of Roman control early in the fifth century from the arrival in England of William the Conqueror. In these centuries, many features of our present-day landscape were established: much of the waste land was cleared and settled, place-names which we still use were created, boundaries of county and parish were drawn. Throughout this period, too, written records steadily became more plentiful.

The last Saxon lord of Tewkesbury was called Brictric, a name that had been borne by a king of Wessex in the past. We would know Brictric's name from the Tewkesbury Abbey chronicle, but we know more about him and his lands because Domesday Book included a retrospective survey of all who owned England's land in 1066. Brictric was an important man in the south of England. As the chronicler said, he was probably descended from the royal family of Wessex, and he and his family seem to have owned a very large amount of land. Brictric witnessed Edward the Confessor's foundation charter of Westminster Abbey in 1062, styling himself 'princeps'. It is likely that if the Conqueror had not arrived, Brictric would have become an earl, which was in effect a position of semi-kingship within a locality. Brictric's estates were concentrated in Gloucestershire, Somerset and Devon, though he had much land scattered through all the southern counties and possibly even in East Anglia, but the single largest estate which Brictric controlled was Tewkesbury.

Tewkesbury was by any standards an enormous manor. The centre of the estate was a compact stretch of country of approximately twenty-two square kilometres or fourteen square miles, bounded on the west for more than two miles by the River Severn and stretching eastwards five miles to the Cotswold scarp. It covered 8,800 acres. Within this area there were farmsteads or small settlements at Southwick, Tredington, Fiddington, Pamington, Natton, Walton Cardiff, Aston-on-Carrant and Oxenton – all places which exist today. Brictric had a hall or chief residence somewhere in Tewkesbury itself, and another at Oxenton. This was a great agricultural enterprise requiring considerable labour and equipment of ploughs and oxen. There was enough arable land for 58 plough teams, each one ploughing up to 120 acres, though the amount ploughed by a team varied considerably according to soil and to custom. There had to be plenty of pasture to feed all the oxen, each plough normally requiring eight oxen; 144 acres of meadow were recorded by Domesday Book in Tewkesbury. Brictric farmed directly about a third of the area, perhaps two and a half thousand acres, and had 50 slaves (male and female). The rest of the land was divided into 59 farms or smallholdings of varying size. The manor was a unit providing self-sufficiency. It contained woodland '1½ leagues long and as wide'. A league was one and a half miles, so that there were about 3,240 acres of wood. This is such a large area that it suggests it was the forerunner of the Park defined in the early 13th century, and was land over which the lord had particular rights, rather than an area covered with trees. There were also two mills, a fishery, a salt-house at Droitwich, and eight burgesses in Gloucester, the latter providing the Tewkesbury landowner with a guaranteed and convenient market for products. The impression is of a well-developed farming enterprise, in which the landscape would have looked not very different from today. There could not have been many waste areas, though there was more wood. As to the site of the present-day town, there was probably no more than we would recognise as a hamlet – a little group of 16 smallholders clustered round the great hall of the lord. Only Gloucester and Winchcombe were recognisably towns in 1086.

In addition, there were other townships owing service to Tewkesbury manor, bringing Brictric revenue and prestige. These were Forthampton, Shenington, Clifford Chambers and Hanley Castle. The church of Tewkesbury was within the manor, and it too controlled estates at Stanway and further afield on the Oxfordshire and Warwickshire boundaries. Altogether another 10,500 acres was part of the manor. Much of the land was tax-free, a privilege indicating the antiquity of the land grants and the status of the owners. In the surrounding area, a number of landowners had found it wise to 'put themselves and their lands in Brictric's power', which underlines his influential position in late Saxon society. Only one other manor in Gloucestershire was anywhere near as large or wealthy as Tewkesbury and that was Berkeley, which had been taken over by the mighty Earl Godwin, father of King Harold, and which therefore became King William's at the Conquest. No wonder Tewkesbury became the central estate of the Norman 'honour of Gloucester', and one of its early Norman owners was created Earl of Gloucester.

William the Conqueror did not allow Brictric to remain in possession of all his widespread estates for long. He was named with two others in a writ from the king soon after the Conquest, concerning land in Wiltshire and Gloucestershire, and he probably attended the coronation of William's queen, Maud, in 1068. However, then, as the Tewkesbury chronicler says:

> Afterwards the Scene was changed, in the Year 1066, when Duke William conquer'd England, he brought with him a certain young Nobleman named Robert, the Son of Herman, Lord of Astreme-Ville in Normandy; and Maud the Queen, Wife to the Conqueror, hated that Nobleman Brictric Meau, Lord of the Honour of Gloster; because when he was publick Ambassador beyond Sea he wou'd not marry her: But she being afterwards married to William the Conqueror, taking an opportunity, she gets Leave and Authority from the King to seize him in his Manor of Hanley, and sends him Prisoner to Winchester, where he dyed and was buried, leaving no Children behind him.

> The King gives Brictric's Honour to the Disposal of the Queen, who retained the whole Honour of Gloster, which had belonged to Brictric, to her own Use during her Life; but the Queen dying in the Year 1083, in the Month of April, the King takes the Honour into his own Hands. William the Conqueror dying in the Year 1087, his Son William Rufus succeeds him. This William, some time afterwards, gave Brictric's Honour to Robert Fitz-Hamon, freely and intirely as his Father or Brictric did ever hold the same; and he did this in reward of the great Labours and Perils which he had undergone for his Father.

The truth of this story cannot be vouched for, though there are some facts which support it. Domesday Book records that Queen Maud had acquired much of Brictric's land. Hanley Castle, where he was supposedly arrested, was one of Brictric's estates. It is true that Robert Fitz-Hamon was later granted Tewkesbury manor, and quite probably William Rufus was the king who made the grant because Fitz-Hamon was one of his companions; but the colourful story of Brictric, when he was an ambassador abroad, slighting Maud and so making, as it turned out, a most unfortunate enemy is more difficult to verify. The story first appears in written form in the continuation of the Chronicle of Wace, some two hundred years after the events it describes. The

Tewkesbury chronicler may have learned the story from this source. It is possible that Brictric was still alive in 1086 when Domesday Book was compiled, and still a landowner with a much-diminished estate; there is a Brictric described as one of the king's thanes in Somerset. William the Conqueror dispossessed nearly all the Saxon lords; he needed no particular excuse to humble Brictric. On the other hand, it looks possible that Brictric had been involved in the revolt against William in the west in 1075, led by Roger, Earl of Hereford; this could explain why Domesday Book says Tewkesbury had been 'destroyed and dismembered', while the value of the manor had been reduced from £100 prior to 1066 to £12. By the time of the Domesday survey, its recovery was underway and the value had risen effectively to £50. Thus ended 600 years of Saxon lordship of Tewkesbury. With the Norman lord, Robert Fitz-Hamon, and the building of a great new abbey, another chapter in the history of Tewkesbury begins.

Jetty bracket, corner of Tolsey Lane.

7. & 8. The river Swilgate enclosed the abbey precinct to the south; to the north there was a boundary wall. The Swilgate often carries flood water, but only in exceptional years has the abbey church itself been flooded. The monastery buildings were mainly on this south side; the end wall of the transept shows marks of a fire and the effect of the dissolution.

Chapter 2

Monastery and Market: 1066-1400

From the Norman Conquest, Tewkesbury became a town of increasing importance through the establishment of a successful market. It was also dominated from 1102 by the Benedictine abbey, until its dissolution in 1540. For over four hundred years, Tewkesbury's history was woven round these two features. But it was still close to the countryside, as all medieval towns were; the townsfolk cultivated their long crofts or gardens and had shares in the Oldbury field and the Ham meadow. The rhythm of the agricultural year and the abundance or otherwise of the harvest was a matter not merely indirectly of economics but of daily survival. As written records became steadily more plentiful in the medieval period, much more is known about the town than in the centuries before Domesday Book. There are buildings, too, to speak directly of the life of the time.

The Norman Influence

The market was legally established before 1086 by William the Conqueror's queen, after she obtained the estate from Brictric. Domesday Book tells us this and also that there were 13 burgesses or town-dwellers living in Tewkesbury at that time. Queen Maud also established a market at Thornbury, another Gloucestershire estate she acquired from Brictric. In all likelihood, there were markets already in existence in these places, which the queen's grant merely formalised; their commercial importance perhaps explains why the queen retained control of these particular estates when Brictric was dispossessed. Markets in Gloucestershire were also recorded in Domesday Book at Gloucester and Winchcombe, Cirencester and Berkeley.

The legal grant of a market had several benefits: it bestowed on the townsmen the right to buy and sell products which the lord could then tax, and it freed the burgesses who lived in the market area from the normal round of farming services. They paid instead a fixed rent to the lord for their land; in Tewkesbury the rent was one shilling for each whole burgage plot.

Not all market grants were equally successful; in some cases the hoped-for trade never came to the town. In Tewkesbury, however, the market flourished. The 'bishop's quarter at Tewkesbury' was referred to as a standard measure of grain in a Worcestershire charter of 1180, and so extensive was Tewkesbury's trade by 1337 that the townsfolk were exempted from paying tolls for the carriage of goods anywhere in the kingdom. This right was successfully defended in the 16th century to give Tewkesbury men toll-free passage over the bridges at Gloucester and Worcester, and was a valuable privilege.

The charters granted to Tewkesbury by its lords in the early 12th century tell us something about the market. Agricultural produce such as grain, pigs and sheep, and iron and linen are all mentioned specifically. Purchasers had to pay to the crown a toll of a halfpenny on a cartload of corn or pease and a penny on a cartload of other wares.

There were no tolls on goods worth threepence or less. The chapman, who travelled from market to market with a small cartload of trinkets or household articles, had to pay one farthing to set up his stall, which was simply a place in the market for an animal and cart to stand. Market days were a busy time of carts and animals jostling in the streets for an empty place, and goods being sold from the cart.

For hundreds of years the centre of the market was at the south end of the High Street, at the meeting of the three roads; the present-day war memorial is close to the site of the original market cross. Gradually, some men set up more permanent shops, often encroaching on the market place to do so. A tenement was described in 1540 as 'within the market place'. The space at the Cross became more and more congested with buildings, including two market halls. There are probably still some buildings today which stand in the area once used as a market place.

Very soon after the Conquest, the Normans constructed the motte at the north end of the town, on Mythe hill. Known as the Tute, this mound increased the effectiveness of the look-out position between Severn and Avon and, as has been noted in Chapter 1, it still provides a good point from which to see the town and the Ham. The Normans were great castle builders – it was one of the ways in which, despite their small numbers, they overawed the native Saxon population. The earth mound was quickly and cheaply constructed; it was placed in a symbolic position near the old minster. In many places it was later improved with stone buildings. Tewkesbury was not selected as the site for a stone castle, as Gloucester and Bristol provided more useful positions for the control of the land, whereas the Mythe's importance had been in controlling river raiders. The tip of the Mythe was also not a very good spot for a castle, as the soft earth cliff is constantly being eroded by the Severn. However, at the time of the dissolution of the abbey in 1540, a pasture in this area was called 'Great Baylye' and in the 19th century 'Great Baylies' and 'Little Baylies' were two closes of seven acres immediately to the north of the motte. These names are a direct link with the bailey of the early Norman castle. The fields adjoined Mythe manor house; an earlier building was demolished in mid-18th century and replaced with the existing Mythe Court. It is possible that the Norman lords of Tewkesbury first built a house on this site, in the vicinity of the motte, but later moved their residence nearer the new abbey to the south of Tewkesbury.

Much uncertainty surrounds the site or sites of Tewkesbury manor house, both before and after the Conquest. Domesday Book says that, in 1066, 16 smallholders lived round the 'hall'. The 13 burgesses of 1086 seem likely to be the successors to the 16 smallholders of 20 years earlier, so that the hall may well have been in the present town centre. We might expect the Norman lords of Tewkesbury to build themselves a new and more impressive house, and perhaps the old house was then used simply as a farmhouse, or perhaps it provided the first living quarters for the monks. By the mid-13th century, the 'barton' or working centre of the abbey farm had given its name to Barton Street which may, therefore, be a clue to the former manor house's position.

Soon after the death of Queen Maud in 1083 and William I in 1087, William II granted Tewkesbury to Robert Fitz-Hamon, a Norman noble who had proved a very staunch supporter. Robert Fitz-Hamon decided to found an abbey there, and in 1102 the first monks arrived to take up residence. Robert Fitz-Hamon planned a mighty church, on the scale of the abbey being constructed nearby at Gloucester. The architectural style of both buildings was based on Worcester, which had been completed about ten years previously. In 1105, Fitz-Hamon made provision for the maintenance of his foundation, transferring a number of his estates as well as the property of Tewkesbury minster. He did not live to see his church completed, but died in 1107. The church was consecrated in 1121. (The Abbey annalist says 1123 but the Worcester chronicler's date is now accepted as correct.) A large proportion of the early 12th-century fabric survives in the nave, transepts and tower.

Robert Fitz-Hamon was one of the most powerful Norman nobles in England. His father had come over with William the Conqueror, and both Robert and his brother Hamo helped William II besiege Rochester in 1088 when Odo rebelled; it is suggested the grant of Tewkesbury was a reward for this service. Robert Fitz-Hamon was with the king on the hunting expedition in the New Forest in 1100 when he was killed; Fitz-Hamon shed tears when his lord's body was discovered, and covered it with his new mantle. An accident was to end his own life not many years later. William of Malmesbury, a monk who obviously knew the family and dedicated his chronicle to Robert Fitz-Hamon's son-in-law, described the circumstances. Henry I, the next Norman king of England after William Rufus's death, was fighting to gain control of Normandy. In the battles, he was finally successful

> but lost many of his dearest associates. Among these was Roger of Gloucester, a tried soldier, who was struck on the head by a bolt from a crossbow, at the siege of Falaise; and Robert Fitz-Hamon, who receiving a blow on the temple, with a lance, and losing his faculties, survived a considerable time, almost in a state of idiotcy. They relate, that he was thus deservedly punished, because, for the sake of liberating him, king Henry had consumed the city of Bayeux, together with the principal church, with fire. Still, however, as we hope, they both atoned for it. For the king munificently repaired the damage of that church: and it is not easy to relate, how much Robert ennobled, by his favour, the monastery of Tewkesbury; where the splendour of the edifice, and the kindness of the monks, attract the eyes, and captivate the minds of the visitors.

Fitz-Hamon was buried in the chapter house of his new monastery, but later his body was moved to the church itself, and in 1241 the chantry chapel which can be seen today was built to glorify his memory.

The abbey brought with it a great demand for goods and services. A market was often founded at the gate of a monastery. In Tewkesbury the market was already established, though its expansion and prosperity were encouraged by the abbey's success. The accounts of the kitchener Robert Carsyntoun for the ninth year of the reign of Richard II, that is 1385, which by chance have survived, show the enormous demands for provisions made by the abbey. In one year, 73 bullocks, three cows, 18 calves, 216 sheep, 135 hogs, 29 porkers and 60 sucking pigs were consumed. Besides this quantity of meat, the kitchener accounted for 96 geese, 24 ducks, 61 capons, 225 fowls, 1,675 pigeons, two-and-a-half tons of cheese, 210 gallons of milk and 70,180 eggs, and an immense quantity of fish.

The monks did live well, and were reproved for it by the Bishop of Worcester after a visitation. The abbot was told he should discipline his monks against 'gluttony and drunkenness and against drinking elsewhere than in the refectory, according to the philosophical doctrine that they should eat to live and not live to eat'. On the other hand the abbey had to provide hospitality to travellers, especially to the wealthier and more important, for whom monasteries provided the equivalent of a modern hotel.

The Normans imposed on the whole country an apparent uniformity of organisation, which they called the 'manor' (from *manerium* in Latin and *manoir* in French). The manor

9. & 10. The Norman tower of the abbey was described by Sir George Gilbert Scott as one of the finest in the country. It was intended to be open inside and the ceiling hides more arcading. The unusual six-arched west front is one of the abbey's major Norman features. A seventh arch was destroyed when a perpendicular-style window was installed.

was an area of land held or controlled by a lord. Within the manor the lord had responsibility for law and order, but also received benefits in the form of money payments or, more likely in the early Middle Ages, in practical work-tasks performed by the inhabitants. As a large agricultural estate, Tewkesbury could thus be called a manor; there was a manor court which gave judgement on local matters, registered transfers of land, and decided on farming practices for the area. Manors could be large or small, and Tewkesbury was such a large one that it also had its own hundred court, instead of being grouped with other manors to form this second tier of organisation.

The services required of the inhabitants by the custom of the manor varied. In the early 14th century, the farmers in Tewkesbury manor numbered 56, and they had to work, winter and summer, ploughing, harrowing, sowing, carrying, threshing and making malt for the lord as well as for themselves. Some of the work required was in the lord's vineyard. They each paid one penny for carriage of salt from Droitwich, and provided grain for seed and four hens at Christmas. There were also 17 men called 'Enches', or ploughmen, and they were in effect labourers employed six days a week on the lord's estate but having a plot of land of their own. They likewise provided four hens at Christmas. Finally, there were cottagers each with an acre or two. In 1307 Nicholas the smith, in return for his land, had to make the ironwork for the lord's nine ploughs, and was given four shillings a year for coals. By 1375, a large part of these services had been commuted.

As well as being a manor, Tewkesbury was also called a 'borough' throughout the medieval period. For instance, in 1206-8, rents and dues to the Crown were described as the 'farm of the borough'. Like the word 'manor', 'borough' has several shades of meaning, but also can be used in a very precise way to define a town with a charter, which has the right to govern its own affairs free from the authority of a lord. Tewkesbury did not acquire this full legal status until it received a charter from Queen Elizabeth I in 1575, but in many respects it had the attributes of a borough. First and foremost, it had the market. In the 12th century, the lords of Tewkesbury granted charters of privileges which made the area of the town effectively a separate unit from the agricultural manor. These privileges were confirmed more than once in the following century. There was a separate court, the borough court, and the town's inhabitants did not have to attend the manor court. The borough court dealt with the regulation of trading, and appointed a number of officers: bailiffs, constables, serjeants, meat inspectors and ale-conners. The town had its separate money chest, and was granted rights of pavage by the Crown in 1324 and subsequently, allowing it to collect money and improve the streets.

The life of the townsman or burgess was much freer than that of his rural contemporaries. The charters said that he could buy and sell his property or lease it 'to whomsoever he pleases' without needing the permission of his lord, and he could pass it on to his heirs when he died. No death duty had to be paid to the lord on inheritance. Children could be married without obtaining the lord's permission. The burgess did not have to take his corn to the lord's mill, nor take his cloth there for dyeing or fulling. He could sell wood, or his horse 'or any other article he legally holds, without licence of the lord'. He could brew ale or bake bread freely, and have his own hand or horse-mill and his own dovecote. Restrictions like these applied to the countryman even though he ploughed a large number of acres which, in today's legal system, he would be described as owning. Despite all these privileges, men did not flock into the towns. They were taking a large risk in early medieval England in disassociating themselves from farming and relying on an income from trade.

Tewkesbury was thus both borough and manor. When a new tax on moveable property was introduced in 1334, Tewkesbury paid at the lower agricultural rate of one-fifteenth of the assessed values rather than the higher urban rate of one-tenth, because of its large rural area. The distinction between the town and the agricultural area only gradually evolved. The process of differentiation started in 1205, when for the first time Southwick and the Mythe were individually named in tax returns, though still part of Tewkesbury, and was not completed until 1575 when the borough received a charter which drew clear boundaries round the urban area.

During the medieval period, Brictric's great manor of Tewkesbury gradually shrank in size. Its various constituent settlements, like Ashchurch and Tredington, became accepted as separate manors. Ashchurch had its own church, serving a group of hamlets, about 1145, and Tredington's church is about the same date. Even Southwick and the Mythe could eventually be called manors. This was part of a process of sub-division which occurred generally. In the same way, the abbot built up a manor of Tewkesbury Barton within the town. His claim to separate jurisdiction over the monastery's property in Tewkesbury led to fierce disputes with the bailiffs about who should punish offenders, but in the end the abbot established his position. In one respect, though, the abbey kept part of the manor together, because only after the dissolution of the monastery did Ashchurch and Tredington become separate parishes.

The Development of Tewkesbury's Town Plan

The characteristic of Tewkesbury's town plan is the long, thin plots of land which stretch back in narrow parallel lines from each of the three main streets. It is impossible to say at what date these streets were established and the burgage plots were laid out. There were likely to have been several phases of development. It was usual for the lord fostering the development of a town to allocate plots of sufficient size to allow each burgess some self-sufficiency and accommodation for his animals. As the townsman also needed a frontage to the street to sell his products, this led naturally to long, thin plots of land. In Tewkesbury, space for burgage plots near the central crossing point of the roads was limited by the rivers, so that plots could not be very much more than 200 feet deep; this fact helped determine the position of the streets.

All three of the main streets which exist today were probably deliberately planned, and the various lanes in Tewkesbury may represent the pre-existing road structure of the town. Looking at the present-day map, it seems possible that St Mary's Lane, Tolsey Lane, and perhaps Red Lane are remnants of the original road which twisted its way towards the Avon ford. Tolsey Lane used to be called Salters Lane, a name which indicates both its direction and its antiquity. Droitwich, near Worcester, was said in Domesday Book to supply Tewkesbury with salt. Salt ways and salters' ways are usually of considerable antiquity. Gander Lane, with Church Street from this point, marks the boundary of the abbey precinct. These lanes governed some aspects of the final layout.

Barton Street and probably Church Street were laid out before High Street. The boundaries of the plots on the north side of Barton Street have been modified to accommodate the line of High Street. There are regular-shaped plots on the south side of Barton Street continuing along Church Street as far as Gander Lane. These two roads follow a fairly uniform distance from the river Swilgate. They may have been designed on a new straight line to overlay whatever was there already, though the loop of St Mary's Lane apparently survived. Liability to flooding limited the amount of land wich could be developed along Barton Street. Barton Road, as Barton Street becomes beyond Chance Street, remained open until the mid-19th century.

The oldest domestic buildings which survive in Tewkesbury are in Barton Street and Church Street. The cellar of 89-90 Church Street is late 13th or early 14th century; 81-2 Barton Street is a 14th-century cruck building (not fronting the street). There are two early 15th-century buildings at 105 Church Street and 27 Church Street (Newton

House); on the latter site, the old building is behind the much more modern one fronting the street. Though all these are rather later than Queen Maud's market grant of the late 11th century, they may point to the original nucleus of the town.

A bold stroke of planning laid down the long line of High Street, which existed by the mid-13th century. At that time, High Street was called Oldbury Street, which suggests that it had been carved out of the Oldbury field. On the east side, the plots all abutted onto the Oldbury field. On the west, they reached nearly to the Mill Avon. A map of the Oldbury made before it was enclosed in the early 19th century showed two main sections or furlongs, one called Upper Furlong and the other Middle Furlong, separated by an access lane which forms the basis of Chance Street today. Each furlong was divided into about a dozen long, thin strips of land of about two acres each, mainly running east-west. Another access lane, now called Oldbury Road, divided the High Street back gardens from the field; similarly East Street is on the line of a lane which ran at the back of Barton Street gardens. It seems reasonable to deduce that, when the High Street was laid out, the burgage plots on the east side were carved out of the original Upper Furlong and followed the boundaries of the strips; at the same time each burgage had an area for the house squarely fronting the street. Thus the odd deflection in the lines of the plots which is such a strong feature of them today; it can be seen particularly clearly in the side boundary of Hereford House, at the north end of the High Street.

By 1327 there were 114 burgesses in Tewkesbury. If we assume that the plots were of similar size to those in Stratford-upon-Avon or Thame in Oxfordshire, that is 60 feet wide, then the entire length of frontage available in the three main streets was developed. More likely, however, the older plots near the Cross were smaller or already sub-divided, because at the top of High Street the plots were close to one hundred feet in width. This implies that there was still room for development. By the beginning of the 16th century, there were at least 28 more burgages. The larger size of the plots in High Street would have encouraged its development as the 'chiefest' street, as Leland described it about 1540.

Burgage plots could differ considerably in size. In Stratford each plot was 60 feet wide and 200 feet long, that is a quarter of an acre, and the rent was a shilling – the same as in Tewkesbury. In Thame, the plots were much longer, though the same width, and approached an acre in size, for the same shilling rent. The less certainty of success a town seemed to have, the larger the plots. Tewkesbury's plots of a quarter of an acre or less point to fair confidence in the attractiveness of this market town.

All the buildings fronting the streets today are from the 16th century or later. They do not give us a good impression of the town in the early medieval period. Undoubtedly, the streets were much wider than they are today; householders have steadily encroached on the road to build more modern premises or add fashionable fronts onto their existing houses. There would have been spaces between houses, especially in High Street, and behind each house we may imagine vegetable gardens, pigsties, stables and barns. The distinction between town and countryside was naturally more blurred than it is easy to imagine today. In later times, the plots were filled with more and more buildings, as the need for both workshops and domestic accommodation grew. As early as mid-12th century, half-burgages counted with whole ones in entitling the holders to full urban privileges, and by 1500 some of the plots were divided into quarter burgages.

11. (*above*) & 12. (*opposite*)   The shape and layout of the town can be studied from the abbey tower. Healings' mills and the Mill Avon can be clearly distinguished at the town's western boundary. Church Street is seen between the open ground of the Bull Ring and the Cross, with long, narrow burgage plots stretching nearly to the Mill Avon.

Tewkesbury's Lords

One of the reasons for Tewkesbury's success was the status of its lords. From the time of Queen Maud, Tewkesbury manor was in the Crown's hands on a number of occasions. Apart from the Crown, three powerful families controlled it during 400 years following the Norman Conquest, and through the female line they were all indirectly descended from Robert Fitz-Hamon.

Yet Fitz-Hamon died leaving no son to succeed him, despite having been on pilgrimage to Glastonbury to pray for an heir. He had a daughter, Mabel, who married Robert Fitzroy, the son of Henry I. Robert Fitzroy was illegitimate, so could not be heir to the throne, but Henry I created the Earldom of Gloucester for him – the only earldom he created in his reign. One story says that Mabel persistently refused Robert's suit until Henry I was persuaded to give him this honour. Through his wife, Robert became lord of Tewkesbury. Like his father-in-law, he was a benefactor to Tewkesbury Abbey and he issued a charter of privileges to the townsmen, as did his son, William. Unfortunately, Robert was deeply involved in the struggle for the Crown after Henry I's death. He had been present when Henry had nominated his daughter Matilda to succeed him; but before Matilda could arrive from the Continent, Henry's nephew Stephen had seized the throne.

During the civil war which followed, known as the Anarchy, the manor house at Tewkesbury was destroyed in 1140 by Waleran, Earl of Worcester. Robert kept his promise to Henry I and supported the Empress Matilda as the rightful heir, but the Earl of Worcester supported Stephen. A monk at Worcester Abbey who continued the chronicle of Florence of Worcester described Waleran's raid like this:

> In 1140, king Stephen arrived in Worcester, and while he marched from thence to reduce Hereford, Waleran fell upon Tewkesbury, with a great multitude of armed men, and took immense spoils, sparing only the goods of the church of Tewkesbury, being overcome with the importunity of the abbot and friars: he burnt the magnificent seat of Robert Earl of Gloucester, and all things round about, and pillaged or laid in ashes all the houses till he approached the city of Gloucester, within the distance of a mile. On the return of the earl with his army to Worcester, he protested with an inhuman glee of triumph, that 'neither in Normandy nor in England had he ever burnt more villages and houses in one excursion'.

This manor house could have been on the Mythe, and its destruction have prompted the move to the south of the town, where the lords of Tewkesbury certainly had their seat in the next century. Stephen finally won the civil war, but with his death in 1154 the rule of Norman kings was ended. His successor was Henry II, the first of the Angevins.

Only two generations of Earls of Gloucester held Tewkesbury, and then when William died in 1183 there was again a failure of the male line. Each of William's three daughters in turn brought Tewkesbury to her husband. Isabel married John, one of Henry II's sons, and later King of England, but had no heir; after John divorced Isabel, the second daughter's husband became lord of Tewkesbury, and was also without an heir. Finally, in 1217, the manor passed to Gilbert de Clare, son of Amice, William's third daughter.

The period of John's lordship of Tewkesbury was one of important activity in the town. John became king in 1199. He kept Christmas in Tewkesbury in 1204: 4,000 plates and 500 cups were specially purchased from Staffordshire potteries and despatched there for the feast. John improved the manor house with new chimneys and windows in 1201, and he also created a park. Most important for Tewkesbury, he instigated the building of a bridge over the Avon.

King John's Bridge.

The tradition that John was responsible for the bridge was recorded about two hundred and fifty years afterwards by the Tewkesbury monk in his chronicle, and was later noted by Leland. Leland says:

> King John beyng Erle of Glocester by his wife caussid the bridge of Twekesbyri to be made of stone. He that was put in truste to do it first made a stone bridge over the gret poure of booth the armes by north and weste: and after to spede and spare mony he made at the northe ende a wodde bridge of a greate lenght for sodeyne lande waters, putting the residew of the mony to making of the castel of Hanley on the inheritaunce of the Erledom of Glocester.
>
> King John gave to the mayntenaunce of this bridge the hole tolle of the Wensday and Saturday marketes in the towne, the which they yet possesse, turnyng it rather holely to their one profite than reparation of the bridge.

There seems no reason to doubt this account; some confirmation exists in the note in 1205 that the bailiff of Tewkesbury was supplied with two oak trees from Bushley 'for making a bridge'.

In the eight centuries since the bridge was probably built, it has of course been repaired and rebuilt many times. The earliest known reference to repairs is in 1368, when the north part was said to be broken. Tewkesbury was held responsible for the repair. The bridge was on a major road and with its causeway was an extensive structure, so it was often a source of worry and expense. Tewkesbury's inhabitants thought it was of such benefit to the whole county that the expense of maintaining it should be shared. They continued to try to evade the responsibility until the end of the 19th century, when the county finally adopted it. A most extensive rebuilding was carried out in 1962 to accommodate modern traffic, but the medieval style of the north side of the bridge was preserved, so that it still provides for the visitor a traditional and picturesque scene by the riverside.

King John's Bridge is a relatively modern name. From at least the beginning of the 14th century, it was known both as the Long Bridge and also Mythe Bridge, as it connects the town with Mythe Hill. After 1826, the latter name was appropriated to Telford's new iron structure over the Severn at the Mythe. When Bennett published his *History of Tewkesbury* in 1830, he referred to the ancient Avon bridge as the Long Bridge. Bennett, however, published Leland's description of how King John caused the bridge to be built, so perhaps he familiarised people with its history; by the end of the 19th century, the name King John's Bridge had replaced the ancient name.

There is a local tradition, recorded by Dyde in 1798, that King John stayed at the very old house on the Mythe while the Long Bridge was being built. Dyde also says that the house was sometimes mistakenly identified with Holm Castle. The whole area, of Tute, field called 'Great Baylye', manor house, out-buildings and a former chapel, belonged to the abbey at the dissolution; it is quite possible that King John did stay on the Mythe in abbey property, perhaps while Tewkesbury manor house was being improved. The private house which Dyde was describing is now called 'King John's Castle', but was known simply as 'The Castle' in the 1820s. Like the bridge, it seems to have been given King John's name in the 19th century.

The park which John created, although not as important as the Avon bridge, has also left a mark on Tewkesbury's history. The Norman kings had set the fashion for parks, because of their fondness for hunting and for venison. A park was a practical way of ensuring a supply of deer for the household. There are references in 1185 and 1187 to the enclosure of Tewkesbury Park. The area which was then fenced round was south of the town, in what today is called Southwick, and it probably comprised between 600 and 650 acres, or approximately one square mile. This was not as large as some parks, which could be 1,000 acres, but it was a significant adjunct to Tewkesbury manor. It covered all the south-western part of the parish of Tewkesbury. We can imagine that this area was quite wooded, as it reaches to the boundary of Deerhurst, a name which proclaims the ancient existence of a deer forest. Both brushwood and charcoal were produced in 1232 from the woods. The park could also have included arable fields, and meadow; it need not have been solely woodland.

The deer park continued to exist until at least 1540, when there were 300 deer recorded, though only 80 acres of parkland. The amount of true parkland had perhaps been reduced as land was put under the plough in the 13th and 14th centuries in response to population pressure and the demand for corn. Nonetheless the whole area of the park remained quite distinct. Leland said in about 1540 that it stretched from Deerhurst to 'the old plotte of Holme Castle', which was the full length of the original park, and this area continued to be separately listed for rating purposes at least until the end of the 17th century. In the 19th century it was still usual to refer to 'Southwick and The Park'.

It is from the late 17th-century rating lists that the original area of the park has been deduced. Some of the field names survived into the 19th century and can be matched with Croome's map of the parish of Tewkesbury made in 1825. This map shows how distinct the field boundaries of the former park still were. Lincoln Green and Bloody Meadow seem to have been the northern boundary. On the west, the river Severn and then the road from the Lower Lode ferry provided the boundary. In 1519 this road was described as 'under the forest'. On the east side of the park, a long straight boundary ran from Lincoln Green, behind Southwick Park house to the Deerhurst parish boundary. The area of Holm Hill, where King John probably had his manor house, was in Southwick in the 17th-century rating lists, so that the park reached right to the edge of the manorial enclosure. To a large extent these park boundaries still exist. Today some of the park is a golf course.

John surrendered the manor of Tewkesbury when he divorced the heiress Isabel, and after a few years the lordship passed to Gilbert de Clare, who was a descendant of Robert Fitz-Hamon. Gilbert de Clare instituted a century of control by the de Clare family, lasting from 1217 to 1314, though occasionally interrupted as when an heir was under age and so a ward of the Crown.

The de Clares were one of the great noble families in England. Gilbert de Clare was involved in the arguments with John in 1215 at Runnymede over the rights and privileges of barons; shortly afterwards, a copy of Magna Carta was deposited in Tewkesbury Abbey. The de Clares, as their name suggests, came from Suffolk, but were Earls of Glamorgan and of Hereford as well as of Gloucester; thus their estates were very extensive. But Tewkesbury appears to have been a favourite manor; not only did the de Clares renew the charters and extend the townsmen's privileges, but they also chose to be buried in Tewkesbury.

During the de Clares' period of lordship, the manor house on several occasions was the scene of magnificent entertainment. Richard de Clare is said to have had 60 knights at one of his Christmas festivities there, and twice at least kings of England stayed in the house. For a number of years while the heir was a ward of the Crown, Henry III took an interest in the manor. In 1236 he stayed in Tewkesbury while negotiating a treaty with Llywelyn ap Iorwerth, and he re-stocked the park with deer in 1238. Edward I, too, stayed there in 1278, and concluded a peace treaty with Alexander III of Scotland.

A little surprisingly, there is now no trace of the de Clares' manor house, and not even the site is known precisely. There has been speculation and controversy about it at least since the time of Dyde's first guide book of 1790. The interpretation provisionally offered here links together several scattered pieces of evidence in this interesting but uncertain area of historical detective work. It is suggested that two manor house sites should be considered in the period between Waleran's destruction of a house in 1140 and the move by the Despencer family to Tewkesbury Park in the mid-14th century. The name 'Holm' was appropriate to the first of the two.

Leland's description of the ruins of the manor house has always been the starting point of the discussion. In his notes on Tewkesbury made after a visit to the town in about 1540 he said:

> Ther was at the south west ende of the abbay a castel caullid Holme. The tyme of the building of it is oncerteyne. It is certeyne that the Clares Erles of Glocester, and especially the redde Erle, lay much at Holme.
>
> Ther hath beene yn tyme of mynd sum partes of the castel stonding. Now sum ruines of the botoms of waulles appere. *Now it is caullid Holme hylle.*

He also noted that the Swilgate 'enterith into Avon at Holme castelle'. From this time, the name Holm or Holm Castle has customarily been used to describe the de Clare's manor house. Unfortunately, Leland's description of its position is not as precise as it seems, particularly as Holm and Holm Hill cannot describe exactly the same spot, as 'holm' is a very common place-name applying to low-lying ground, or an enclosure, surrounded by marsh.

The location of the Vineyard where the tenants of the manor were obliged to work in the early 14th century has always been known. Three field names recalling the vineyard continued in use into the 20th century; the fields were purchased by the Tewkesbury Corporation in 1929 and now form a recreation ground called Vineyards Park, which provides a good open space to the south of the abbey. A monument was erected on the highest part of the area recording the manor house. Below the Vineyards, outlines of fishponds fed by the Swilgate could be seen until the area was levelled in 1964 to provide playing fields. A fishpond is also associated with the manor in medieval times.

The erection of the monument in that position was probably influenced particularly by Bennett's discussion of the question. He said:

> Holme Castle stood near the top of a field, now called the Vineyard, where recently a considerable excavation remained, which had evidently been made for the purpose of procuring the stone which had been used in the foundations of the building – probably for repairing the adjoining turnpike-road. Upon levelling some of the hillocks, in 1826, a quantity of rubbish and mortar, many painted bricks, and also large solid masses of common bricks and stones, were discovered; the appearance of the latter clearly demonstrating that the edifice, of which they formed a part, had been destroyed by fire . . . the form and extent of the mounds on the two lower sides of the field . . . led to the conclusion that they were the sites of the boundary walls of the castle. In corroboration of this notion, when one of those shelving banks was cut through, in 1821, for the purpose of making a drain, hewn stones of a great size and thickness, strongly cemented with lime, sand and gravel, were found at the depth of five or six feet from the surface. Before the field was levelled, one might indeed, in imagination, have traced out in the Vineyard not only the ground plan of Holme Castle, but also the extent of the whole area included within its bounds, as well as the situation of many subordinate members of that once celebrated baronial residence.

The bricks described by Bennett show that the building on this site was not abandoned in the 14th century when the Despencers moved to Tewkesbury Park. Most likely it was the house called the Vineyard in 1553, which still existed in 1685 and at some time thereafter seems to have burnt down. Vineyard House, with orchard, gardens, moat and fishpond, is described in a deed of 1631; it was the centre of a small estate which included land called Wynyards, Gastons, and Conygree, all field names still in use in 1825 and adjacent to the site of the house marked by the monument. Together, these

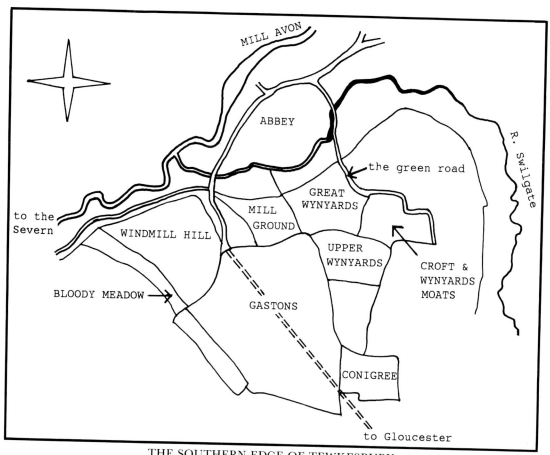

THE SOUTHERN EDGE OF TEWKESBURY
based on the 1825 Croome Map

do support identification with the manor house. The conygree was a rabbit warren which supplied food to the lord's table; the rabbit was introduced into England about the beginning of the 12th century. Moats were fashionable about the middle of the 12th century, often as a status symbol rather than for their limited defensive advantage. The dates accord well with a rebuilding in this area after the destruction of the earlier residence in 1140.

There is at least the possibility that a new manor house was first built below Vineyard House, on the nearby moated site, still open and neglected. This area was known as 'Croft and Wynyards Moats' in the 19th century, and comprised nine and a half acres. The 1885 Ordnance Survey map placed Holme Castle here. The moated enclosure was square and had an entrance to the north from the green road which was still very distinct on the 1825 map of Tewkesbury. The road led to the Gander Lane bridge. The name 'Holm' is appropriate to the site, which may have been abandoned because too wet, and a new residence, Vineyard's House, built higher up in the same area. This

13. & 14. Two mills in Tewkesbury are mentioned in Domesday Book; two were given to the abbey at its foundation. Adjacent to the Abbey Mills were the Town Mills, which belonged to Tewkesbury manor. All were part of the Tewkesbury Park estate from 1554. Town and Abbey (or Upper and Lower) Mills may be discerned from the Ham. The abbey's 'great barn next the Avon' is behind.

may even be the extensive building work known to have been undertaken by King John. Because of the importance of the Holm, thereafter the hill close to it was called Holm Hill.

Recent discussion of the puzzle of where the de Clare's manor house was has concentrated on Holm Hill itself. It was once the whole area now occupied by the Borough Council's offices and by the former workhouse. It was pasture land in the 16th century, and was sometimes called 'the great garden' or 'upper garden'; it was associated with the Park estate rather than with the Vineyards. There was a windmill on Holm Hill in the 17th century, and probably one belonging to the lords of Tewkesbury manor as early as 1291 was in the same position. At this date and later, the tenant of the Abbey Mills also held the windmill. Gradually the name Windmill Hill replaced Holm Hill.

Before the present Borough Council offices were built, an archaeological excavation revealed a complex of buildings of 12th-century date, and a later, 13th-century hall, substantially built of stone with a vaulted undercroft. The site had been occupied since Saxon times and into the 14th century. Occupation therefore pre-dates the manor house at Holm but from about 1140 the buildings on Holm Hill could have provided ancillary accommodation to the manor, for instance the guest house. The wealthy de Clares might well have built the 13th century hall here for that purpose.

It is a little surprising that a house providing the scale of entertainment of the de Clares and Despencers was wholly abandoned when they moved to the new site farther south in Tewkesbury Park. More likely, the older house provided a residence for a lesser member of the gentry. The windmill on Holm Hill was still useful to the lords of the manor. Other buildings were robbed for stone. Finally only the windmill remained. If these hypotheses are correct, the ruins of walls seen by Leland were probably on the moated site which his word 'plot' also seems to fit. No medieval source ever refers to a castle in Tewkesbury, though Leland apparently relied on popular tradition in his account. The tradition may have derived from the early Norman motte on Mythe Hill, or the moated house was commonly called a castle.

The period of control by the de Clares came to an end when, in 1314, Gilbert de Clare was killed at the Battle of Bannockburn, and his wife died the following year. Once more in Tewkesbury's history three sisters were co-heirs. For a while the Crown again controlled the estate – a short period of royal patronage which brought Tewkesbury benefit, because Edward II made the first pavage grant in 1324. This grant allowed Tewkesbury to develop its municipal administration and its civic consciousness. Then one of the de Clare sisters married Hugh le Despenser, and in 1325 the Despenser connection with Tewkesbury began.

Like the de Clares, the Despensers controlled Tewkesbury for nearly a hundred years – the last great family to do so – and the abbey church is full of reminders of this powerful family. They instigated a great rebuilding of the roof and upper storey of the church in the Decorated Style. The vaulting is splendid but perhaps does not entirely fit with the simpler, massive Norman pillars. During the rebuilding, seven windows were constructed above the choir arcade, which still contain the original glass. It can therefore be closely dated to 1340-44.

The Despensers also constructed a series of chapels, and later erected three notable memorials: two for members of the Despenser family, and one to celebrate the abbey's founder, Robert Fitz-Hamon. These are of great architectural interest, small demonstrations of the Perpendicular Style which developed from the mid-14th century. On the south side of the choir is Trinity Chapel, built for Edward le Despenser (died 1375). Edward himself is portrayed kneeling on top; he can be seen best from the choir side. Froissart said of Edward that he was the

> most honourable, gallant and valiant knight in all England, much beloved of ladies, for the most noble said that no feast was perfect if Sir Despenser was not present.

On the north side of the abbey are the Fitz-Hamon chantry chapel, built at the end of the 14th century, and the Beauchamp chapel, built for Richard Beauchamp (died 1421), the first husband of Isabel le Despenser. There are also interesting monuments in the church to people connected with this noble family. For example, also on the north side there is the tomb and effigy of Guy de Brian, who was standard bearer to Edward III at the Battle of Crecy in 1346.

The Despensers also built a new manor house. Edward Despenser, who died in 1375, lived in Tewkesbury Park, or Tewkesbury Lodge. The new manor house was situated in the deer park, which perhaps influenced the decision to move there. The alternative name 'Lodge' suggests that the house was once used for shooting parties and could have been the house of the 'parker', the official responsible for the park. Soon after it was built, Richard II stayed there when Parliament was meeting in Gloucester in 1378. Leland said of this house:

> There is a fair manor place of tymbre and stone yn this Theokesbyri Parke where the Lord Edward Despenser lay and late my Lady Mary.

Lady Mary was the elder daughter of Henry VIII, later to become queen. Henry VIII stayed in Tewkesbury Park in 1535. The existing house on this site is late 18th-century, but there are traces of a much larger house, hinting at a medieval layout. The house is now used by the Golf Club and, with fewer trees round it than once there were, is seen on quite a prominent hill.

The Early Medieval Economy

With all the building activity in the town, the 14th century must have been generally one of prosperity in Tewkesbury. It is difficult to estimate the size or prosperity of any town in the medieval period, but in the amount of tax assessed in 1334 Tewkesbury ranked fourth in Gloucestershire, after Bristol, Gloucester and Cirencester. Gloucester was considerably larger and wealthier, fourteenth in the whole kingdom, while Bristol was second, only London being larger and wealthier. The exceptional size and importance of Bristol was recognised in 1373 when it was granted the status of a separate county, and was thus removed from Gloucestershire. Apart from the county town, Cirencester and Tewkesbury were then the two most important towns. Cheltenham, for example, or Winchcombe, were rather smaller, though still market centres.

The population of Tewkesbury in the 14th century may have been about one thousand. As well as the 114 burgages of 1327, there were possibly an equal number of cottages occupied by the humbler craftsmen and labourers. Two centuries later, they outnumbered the burgesses and could well have done so in earlier times.

One of the functions of the town was to be a stopping point for travellers. Although not one of the most important towns marked, it is significant that Tewkesbury is on the very early map called the Gough Map, dated to 1360 and to be seen in the New Bodleian Library in Oxford. The map shows a road from Bristol through Gloucester and Tewkesbury to Worcester, the road which had always been important in Tewkesbury's history. The occasional visits of kings were often made in the course of their many journeys to Worcester. In medieval times kings regularly moved about the country, doing justice and impressing their authority on their subjects. Many other travellers must also have passed through Tewkesbury.

Some hints of the variety of crafts which supported Tewkesbury's continuing urban success can be gained from the surnames of the 65 inhabitants who paid taxes in 1327. Surnames were just beginning to become more general at this date. A century later they had become hereditary, rather earlier than in Ireland or in some continental countries. Like place-names, the vagaries of spelling often make it difficult to be sure of the meaning of the name. Some surnames were derived from a man's place of origin, like Walter Galeys who presumably came from Wales, or Roger de Pershore from rather nearer Tewkesbury. Others were based on physical characteristics, like Richard Suel (the Anglo-Saxon word for active), William Smale and Stephen de Longeneye. Some are clearly indicative of occupation: John Portreve and Cristina Portreve were both officials of the market or 'port'. The occupations of Walter and John Dyer, Robert Goldsmith, John Barber, Jacob, Philip and Walter Tailor, John and Henry Tanner, and John Glasswright are clear. John Lorimer made small metal pieces, particularly as used in horse harness. John Spice was probably a grocer. Edith Ferrour was an iron-worker. Gunnyld Marshall may have been a keeper of horse or a shoeing smith. William Butler looked after bottles, and was perhaps the steward of the manor house. Other names in the list are tantalising. What is the explanation for William Pyge or Richard Whyroun?

The list certainly shows some of the crafts in Tewkesbury which could lead to sufficient wealth to make their followers into taxpayers. It obviously does not include a large number of ordinary occupations which existed in the town in the medieval period. Not even all the burgesses were taxpayers. But from the surnames of those who were, the manufacture and sale of goods continued to be the justification for their special status as burgesses.

Richard le Despenser, who died in 1414, was the last of that name to hold Tewkesbury. After his death, the lordship passed backwards and forwards with bewildering frequency to men related through their wives or mothers to the Despensers, including the Earls of Warwick and of Clarence, and the Seymour family. The names of Warwick and Clarence summon up the period of the Wars of the Roses, when Tewkesbury was much affected by national events. A better-known chapter of Tewkesbury's history begins with these royal rivalries and with the policies of the Tudors, who in turn were lords of Tewkesbury.

The east end of the abbey.

Chapter 3

The Impact of National Events: 1400-1550

No great family dominates the history of the town in the 15th and 16th centuries as the de Clares and Despensers had done earlier, and the lords of Tewkesbury do not provide a guiding thread in the later medieval period. After the death of the last Despenser lord of Tewkesbury, Richard, in 1414, the lordship passed through many hands, including a succession of the husbands of female heirs. Some of the changes were the result of the political instability of the period. The lord's influence, though, could still be important, for instance in determining which side should be supported in 1471 when Tewkesbury suddenly became the scene of one of the best-known battles of the Wars of the Roses.

The struggle between the Yorkists and Lancastrians, which lasted for a generation from 1455 to 1487, only intermittently flared into battle, and probably caused little disruption to the life of a small country town, except for those dramatic days in May 1471 when the town was full of soldiers and nobility. Tewkesbury prospered, especially towards the end of the 15th century and the beginning of the 16th century, and money was spent on building the substantial houses which still survive, and on paving the streets.

The last distant successor of Robert Fitz-Hamon to hold Tewkesbury was the Dowager Countess Ann, who died in 1490. Her husband had been Richard Neville, Earl of Warwick. Warwick was known as 'the King-maker' because his changes of allegiance between the royal families of York and Lancaster apparently determined which should rule England, and his death in 1471 opened the way for Tewkesbury's Yorkist stance. Ann survived her husband by some twenty years, and was in possession of Tewkesbury at her death. Thereafter it remained a Crown manor for nearly the whole Tudor period, and members of the royal family on occasion stayed in Tewkesbury Park.

Ironically, King Henry VIII was lord of Tewkesbury when in 1540 he closed the abbey founded by his predecessor, and caused the buildings to be destroyed so that no trace of the monks should remain. Like the Wars of the Roses, the impact of the dissolution of the monasteries was probably not as great as might be expected, particularly visually as the town retained the church and tower. It did, though, bring to an end an institution which had contributed to the life of the town for over four hundred years.

The Battle of Tewkesbury, 1471

The battle was fought to the south of the town, somewhere in the countryside beyond the abbey and the Swilgate bridge. On the one side was the Yorkist Edward IV, in possession of the throne again after his return to England in March 1471; on the other side was Margaret, wife of the simple-minded and imprisoned Lancastrian Henry VI, together with their son Edward. At this point, May 1471, the town seems to have been Yorkist in its sympathies. It must have refused Margaret and her army shelter or help,

15. & 16.   The Abbey Cottages are a unique row of medieval shops. They were built towards the end of the 15th century in front of the abbey wall and illustrate the growth in Tewkesbury's trading importance. The cottages have been extensively restored by the Abbey Lawn Trust.

or otherwise she could have put the town between herself and the pursuing Yorkist army. She could then have taken up a strong position to the north on Mythe Hill, with command of the Upper Lode crossing over the Severn, which would have allowed her to join up with the strong Lancastrian forces in Wales. As it was, she took up position to the south of Tewkesbury. The town's Yorkist stance reflected the very recent change of lord. The Earl of Warwick, 'the King-maker', had been killed in March at the Battle of Barnet, fighting with the Lancastrians against Edward IV. George, Duke of Clarence, was the heir to Tewkesbury, and thus had only become lord a few weeks before the Battle of Tewkesbury. Although not very reliable in his loyalties – 'false, fleeting, perjured Clarence' Shakespeare called him – Clarence was in the Yorkist Edward's camp.

Queen Margaret had reached her position after her army had marched from Gloucester, where she had already been refused entry. She came through 'a foul country, all
in lanes and stony ways, betwixt woods, without any good refreshing'. She probably
came along the Lower Road which went close to the Severn through Deerhurst and
past Tewkesbury Park. In 1514 this was still described as a way 'under the forest'.
Edward was pursuing her from the 'village' of Cheltenham, and spent the night before
the battle three miles distant from Tewkesbury. He probably used the old road which
went from Cheltenham through Tredington and Gupshill and thence eastwards of the
modern road to the Swilgate bridge. The present-day road from Gloucester to Tewkesbury was made in the 18th century, and superseded both these old ways.

The exact position of Queen Margaret's army is a matter of controversy. Various sites
south of the town have been, as Bennett said, immemorially associated with the battle.
There is Bloody Meadow, a narrow low-lying strip of land off Lincoln Green Lane,
which preserves a memory of the blood of Lancastrians shed there; 'Blodyfurlong' is a
field name recorded less than 20 years after the battle. There is the Gaston Field, lying
east and west of the modern main road to Gloucester, which Leland said was where
the battle was fought; and there is the medieval house site known as Queen Margaret's
Camp, opposite Gupshill a little farther south on the Gloucester road. A Yorkist
chronicler of the time who may, it is true, have exaggerated the strength of the
Lancastrian position, said that Queen Margaret's soldiers were placed

> in a field, in a close even at the town's end; the town and the Abbey at their backs; afore them and
> upon every hand of them, foul lanes and deep dikes and many hedges, with hills and valleys, a right
> evil place to approach as could well have been devised.

Windmill Hill, where the Borough Council offices now are, suits the description best,
especially as the hill commanded both roads to Tewkesbury from the south as they
approached the Swilgate bridge. The moated site at Gupshill could perhaps be associated with King Edward's position, as it was beside the Tredington road.

In the event, some of Margaret's forces were tempted to leave their good position to
try to attack the Yorkists, and then found themselves strongly resisted. They were forced
back up the hill, the Yorkists fighting all the way into the Lancastrian entrenchments.
Men fled in all directions. The Lancastrian army had perhaps numbered six thousand.
A band of Yorkists stationed in Tewkesbury Park attacked those fleeing towards
the Lower Lode ferry and caught them in Bloody Meadow. Others fleeing towards
Tewkesbury itself were drowned in a millpond, presumably by the Abbey Mills. Some
accounts say the slaughter was even carried into the abbey church where a service was
in progress.

Many of the dead were buried unceremoniously in a pit near the battle-ground; the
more important were buried in Tewkesbury abbey. Two days later the people of
Tewkesbury witnessed the execution in the market place of some of the principal
captives. Enough armour was picked up from the field of battle to make a series of thick
oblong plates which were nailed to the inside of the Sacristy door in the abbey church,
held in place by diagonal metal strips. This thrifty reinforcement of the monastery's
treasury door is still in place. Also enduring is the triumphant addition of the sun, the
Yorkist badge, to the intersections in the vault of the Presbytery roof. Shakespeare made
use of this image in the first lines of Richard III, which is set in the months immediately
after the Battle of Tewkesbury:

> Now is the winter of our discontent
> Made glorious by this sun of York

The Yorkist triumph did not endure long. In 1485 Henry Tudor re-established the Lancastrian family as rulers of England, defeating Richard III, the last Yorkist king, at the Battle of Bosworth.

The Battle of Tewkesbury, as the occasion when Tewkesbury's name is part of national history, is the subject of much local tradition and speculation. Street and house names are drawn from the personalities who were engaged there. Bennett wrote in 1830 that a house in Church Street was traditionally regarded as the place where Margaret's son, Edward, was assassinated, although some accounts, which are probably more reliable, say he was killed on the battlefield. Quite recently, the writer and naturalist John Moore, in *The Blue Field*, has written of the profusion of the red cranesbill flower in Bloody Meadow, making it seem stained with Lancastrian blood.

Late Medieval Houses

The prosperity of Tewkesbury in the late 15th and early 16th centuries is seen particularly in the substantial timber-framed buildings which survive from this period and which contribute much to the visual attractiveness of the town. Houses which have survived for so many hundreds of years must have been constructed from especially large and well-seasoned timbers. They illustrate not only Tewkesbury's expansion but also the general advance in living standards which led to a great rebuilding of houses all over the country in the Tudor period, though occurring in rural areas some fifty years later than in the towns.

Most of the houses built at this time were two-storied (some have a third storey added later) with roofs parallel to the street. Usually they have a side entry incorporated into the building itself, giving access to the yard, outbuildings, and garden behind. This was necessary because there was generally no back road in Tewkesbury as in many medieval planned towns; barns and warehouses had to be reached from the front. By this date the original burgage plots had been much sub-divided, so that the whole frontage was needed for the residential and commercial accommodation, and house space could be gained by building over the sideway. There is an example of a medieval barn down Lilley's Alley, and a barn of late Tudor date exists at the back of *The Berkeley Arms* down Ancil's Court.

In High Street there is a concentration of buildings of this period towards the Cross. Numbers 154-5, 140 (Clarence House), 132, 129 and 128, and on the opposite side 9 (Keys House or the House of the Nodding Gables), 12 and 15 (The Ancient Grudge) were all either built at or have features dating from this time. Farther along High Street, numbers 117-18 and at the north end 75-6 and *The Black Bear* on the corner are of a similar age. In Church Street, proceeding northwards, there are numbers 82-3, 88-88a, the eastern end of the Royal Hop Pole Hotel, and 107-8 (Cross House); and on the opposite side 15, 16 and *The Berkeley Arms*, together with a second house at its rear. All have naturally been subject to many alterations and additions since they were built, and some have been refronted so as to disguise the age of the house behind, like 128-9 High Street. The roof and the rear reveal the antiquity of this structure, which still has a timber-framed staircase wing added at the back. Similarly, numbers 75-6 High Street have recently been refronted in Tudor style.

17.   At the end of the Abbey Cottages is the former National School; until 1786 there were five more houses between here and the *Bell Hotel*, making Church Street very narrow.

18.   Mill Bank Cottages were also abbey property, and the corner building dates from c.1500.

In Barton Street there are fewer examples of very old buildings; 29, 32-3 and 35, and a little farther along on the other side number 50, indicate a small amount of development by the mid-16th century, reaching no farther than the junction with Chance Street where a tithe barn once stood. The buildings in Barton Street are generally smaller than those in High Street or Church Street.

As well as these individual timber-framed houses dating from about 1500, there is also in Church Street, Tewkesbury, a unique medieval row called Abbey Cottages, which dates from the mid- or late 15th century. The row was recently threatened with demolition and was in a rather decayed state, but was rescued and restored by the Abbey Lawn Trust between 1967 and 1971. Built originally as shops by the abbey, there were at least 23 dwellings, of which 17 survive. Each was about 11 ft. 6 in. wide, and the row backed onto the boundary wall of the monastery itself, so was effectively built in the street.

One house in the row, called the Little Museum, has been restored to show what it was probably like when built. In front was the shop, with window shutters that could be let down horizontally to form a counter in the street. Behind was the living-room, with open fire and no chimney. Soot-blackened plaster above shows where the smoke found its way up into the roof and out. Upstairs was one bedroom. Quite soon after the original construction, a third room was added behind the living-room. At this date there was no window glass, but wooden shutters over all the windows could close out the cold and wet. These were not poor men's houses, though they were clearly not intended for those as wealthy as the occupants of the other houses already mentioned.

A surprising number of Tewkesbury houses have exceptionally large windows across the entire frontage, apparently contemporary with the building. Not all the examples visible today are from the late 15th or early 16th centuries, as houses with these windows continued to be built into the 17th century. From the medieval period, good examples of long windows at first floor level are 82-3 and 88-88a Church Street, and 117-18 High Street. The *Berkeley Arms* still has the first floor range but used also to have similar windows to the ground floor. Number 140 High Street has these windows along the first and second storey. Number 100 Church Street (The Hat Shop) and the Barton Street museum have similar ranges of windows which date from the later 16th century. The visitor will notice many later examples as he explores the town.

The Economy of the Town in the Later Medieval Period

The fenestration of the houses strongly suggests that they were originally built for clothiers, and the windows were designed to light the workrooms where looms were placed. Several hand-looms could have been placed in each room, so that a number of weavers were then employed in the clothier's own house. Written medieval sources support the architectural evidence that the textile industry was important in Tewkesbury. There are frequent references to dyers, and records also of mercers and hosiers, who both sold the cloth and stockings and also organised the manufacture. The wool was spun, woven, fulled, and dyed in the town, and a whole range of craftsmen were consequently engaged in processes which supported the industry, like card-makers, and carders who prepared the wool for spinning, wool-winders, and shearmen who finished the cloth. Walker's Lane, also called St Mary's Lane, was where the walkers or fullers were concentrated. Cappers and tailors worked up the cloth; the guild of tailors, the

19.   There is a stone undercroft of c.1300 below the building at the end of St Mary's Lane. The next house, late 15th-century, was jettied front and rear.

20.   From the abbey precinct it is possible to study the later addition of chimneys to the Abbey Cottages.

first of the guilds in Tewkesbury, was established by the late 15th century. Tewkesbury market was able to supply the neighbourhood with cloth and clothes; cloth was also exported.

The economy of the town was only partly based on the textile industry. Other important crafts and trades provided the range of goods necessary for everyday existence. For example, there were many carpenters and shoemakers in Tewkesbury. Leather-working was one of the larger local trades. Tanners and skinners prepared the leather and saddlers, glovers, and shoemakers used it. In the 16th century, guilds were formed for several of these crafts. The guild was an association of master craftsmen, which tried to regulate the standard of work and the rates of payment. The guilds formed one element in the government of a medieval town. As in the case of cloth, most manufacturing work was carried out in the house, and we should imagine a large part of Tewkesbury's population busy in domestic industry.

The marketing of agricultural produce continued to be important, as it had been throughout the early Middle Ages. Corn was conveyed by river or road but particularly to Bristol. Licences were obtained for export overseas. Naturally, food and provisioning occupied many people. References to butchers, bakers, and brewers are quite frequent. Some brewers were also maltsters, and malt was one of the items shipped down the Severn. There were several inns in the town, and at least four flour mills. There were grocers and spicers and sellers of salt.

A special trade was developed in mustard, which was ground and made up into unusually strong mustard balls, described as 'hot, biting and poignant'. Mustard-ball making, too, was a domestic craft. Bennett described the local method of manufacture:

> The good housewives here however uniformly pounded the mustard seed in an iron mortar, with a large cannon ball, or other hard substance of a similar shape and size; and after the flour had been carefully sifted from the bran, it was mixed in a cold infusion of horse-radish, and well beaten or stirred up for the space of at least an hour. It was considered that the horse-radish imparted great additional pungency to the mustard, and that the continued beating gave it that consistency and strength which were deemed essential to its good preservation.

Tewkesbury had a very particular reputation for these mustard balls. They were already famous when Camden's *Britannia* was published in 1586, the first-known written reference. The frequent recording of financial dealings between Tewkesbury inhabitants and grocers and spicers in London and elsewhere in the country may well indicate that the trade was flourishing in the 15th century. Tewkesbury's speciality was immortalised by Shakespeare in *Henry IV*: Falstaff says of Poins: 'his wit is as thick as Tewkesbury mustard'. In the Parliament of 1621, one of Tewkesbury's representatives was sarcasti-cally described as: 'this Tewkesbury-mustard-burgesse' and the reputation of Tewkes-bury mustard continued all through the 17th century. Fuller, in *Worthies of England*, an anecdotal directory to all the notable places in the country, published in 1662, said that

> the best in England (to take no larger compass) is made at Tewkesbury. It is very wholesome for the clearing of the head, moderately taken; and I believe very few have ever surfeited thereof. It is generally used in England.

Some time after this, the trade began to fade. Although Atkins, whose history of Gloucestershire was published in 1712, knew that the town was 'remarkable for making Balls of the best Mustard', the vicar, the Rev. John Matthews, wrote a doggerel verse with a different view in his commonplace book in the same year:

> The little poignant seed I will not name,
> Which lies conceal'd under a gilded frame,
> But now, alass, these famous balls less shine,
> This noble manufacture doth decline.

The vicar's information is more likely to be reliable. By 1830, as Bennett reported,

> The manufactory has long ceased to be carried on in the town, though nothing could be more easy
> than to restore it; as the mustard, which grows spontaneously in the corn-fields, and other places,
> in the neighbourhood, and which is in fact here a common weed, is of the same species as that which
> is cultivated with so much care, in the north of England, for the sake of its flour.

The Public Ways to the Town

As a market town, Tewkesbury depended on good communications; unfortunately the local roads were often in a very bad state, especially because of the wet low-lying nature of much of the land round Tewkesbury. The miry condition of the ways followed by Margaret's army in 1471 was particularly remembered by the chronicler. Tewkesbury had to look after 'four chief public ways' or 'four highways attaining to the town' and the wills of public-spirited inhabitants quite often included money for their repair. Richard Payne's will in 1507 describes these four roads precisely:

> to the highway or pavement on the east towards Aschurch; to that on the south towards Gupshill; to that on the west towards Deerhurst; to that on the north towards Mythe.

The road towards Ashchurch was called Salendine's (or Salandine's) Way and was raised on a causeway or bridge by the early 16th century. To the south the road crossed the Swilgate by Holm Bridge and then divided, going southwards towards Gupshill and Tredington, or westwards towards Deerhurst and Gloucester; the Lower Lode road remained the main road to Gloucester into the 18th century. To the north, the road crossed the Long Bridge and causeway and then proceeded round Mythe Hill. Less important but also mentioned in at least one will was the road to Mitton and Bredon.

Until 1555 the repair of the roads was left to private initiative. There must have been an increasing volume of road traffic everywhere; that year the importance of adequate roads was recognised nationally in the Highways Act, which placed on each parish's inhabitants collectively the responsibility for the roads within its area. The spate of Tewkesbury wills making provision for road repairs in the first half of the 16th century also suggests an increasing amount of traffic. In Tewkesbury's case the responsibility was particularly onerous because the Long Bridge and causeway beyond were always very costly to repair, as Tewkesbury complained. Bequests for this purpose were more frequent than for any other road. Flood damage was the most usual reason for the bridge's decay.

Including the Long Bridge, by 1575 Tewkesbury was maintaining no less than seven bridges. Some were only footbridges, like the two over the Swilgate and one over the Old Avon. Two were drawbridges by the time of the Civil War. The position of one is uncertain but may have been Quay bridge over the Mill Avon. An engraving published after its demolition, in Bennett's *Tewkesbury Yearly Register and Magazine*, suggests that it had been one. The other was Holm Bridge, rebuilt in 1601 at the same time as the

21. & 22. The rebuilt King John's Bridge over the Mill Avon has a medieval appearance. though altered many times. The *Black Bear Inn* beyond is early-16th century; its sign may relate to the Beauchamps, 15th-century lords of Tewkesbury. It has a teazle post on the corner, supporting jetties on two sides. Next to it there used to be a distillery.

Lower Lode Lane causeway was raised and presumably a drawbridge from this time if not before. Three bridges at least were of stone: the Long Bridge, the Quay Bridge built of red sandstone and Salendine's Bridge carrying the Ashchurch road.

The people of Tewkesbury also attempted to safeguard their legal right to protection in the free use of the River Severn. They secured a private Act of Parliament in 1430 to recover damages from the men of the Forest of Dean who, it was said, more than once attacked Tewkesbury 'vessels and trows carrying wheat, malt, and other corn and goods' and threw the sailors overboard. The men of the Forest were perhaps driven to desperation in a time of dearth by the sight of foodstuffs being carried down the river and away. Tewkesbury successfully defended the right of all to use the Severn freely.

The town quay was the subject of a bequest in 1519. The money was to be used for its repair, but only on condition that two new slipways were constructed. Boat-building was therefore another aspect of the economy of Tewkesbury. The town quay was situated on the old Avon; Healing's mill now occupies most of the former quayside. The Avon was not navigable above this point until a considerable amount of money was spent on making it so in the mid-17th century. After 1575, the Town Council often paved, repaired and extended the quay.

In many ways Tewkesbury was typical of medium-sized towns which were the manufacturing centres for their rural areas. However, Tewkesbury's importance in its own region was considerable. By the mid-16th century it had probably overtaken Cirencester as the largest town in the county, excluding Bristol and Gloucester which were by this time county boroughs. A number of estimates point to a population of about 1,600. There were 142 burgage plots in 1540, and at least another 160 houses owned by the abbey; in 1563 the vicar said there were 396 households. One third of the heads of households were technically burgesses; they were the better-off inhabitants who formed the political community of the town.

> Memorandum, that the said town of Tewkesbury is a very great market town, where is kept market twice every week, whereunto is continual access of a great number of people, besides those (which are no small number) that [be inhabitants] within the same town . . .

This is how Thomas Sternhold described Tewkesbury, when he made enquiries concerning chantries which still existed after the monastery was closed. He went on to suggest that Tewkesbury was therefore deserving of a school, a mark of a thriving and important town.

The Dissolution of the Monastery

The threat that all the monasteries in England might be closed began to be perceived, after Henry VIII divorced Catherine of Aragon and married Ann Boleyn. At first, the abbot and the 37 monks in Tewkesbury abbey accepted the supremacy of Henry VIII over the English church, as did all the clergy in England. They signed their acknowledgement in August 1534. But submission was not enough. A year later, the king's commissioner arrived in Tewkesbury. He wrote apologetically to Thomas Cromwell, Henry VIII's chief minister:

> We have so much to do at the abbey of Evesham that we cannot attend you tonight, but will see you tomorrow. We must take Tewkesbury in our way, and peruse the inventory, appropriations and other muniments.

The results of this and similar surveys carried out all over England were collected together in the *Valor Ecclesiasticus*, which provides an invaluable account of the wealth of the monasteries on the eve of dissolution.

For four years after this visit the threat of closure hung over Tewkesbury Abbey. The abbot, John Wakeman, tried to ensure his own future by a timely gift to the powerful Cromwell. He wrote:

> I thank you for your goodness at my preferment, and your loving commendations to the king when he was at Tewkesbury, as yet undeserved of me. I had trusted to have provided a gelding for you, and I now send you one, with £5 to buy you a saddle.

The abbot was duly recompensed in 1541 by becoming the first Bishop of Gloucester, a new see which was carved out of the great diocese of Worcester. He was one of the monks who found it possible to accept the Protestant reformation which Henry had been bringing about.

Tewkesbury Abbey was one of the wealthiest monasteries in England. Only 24 monasteries out of 553 had a yearly income exceeding £1,000. Westminster and Glastonbury were the richest, with incomes approaching £4,000. Tewkesbury had about £1,500 a year. St Peter's, Gloucester, had about £200 more, Cirencester a little less. At the other extreme, some houses struggled along on less than £20. It was partly the great wealth of the monasteries, which altogether owned one-sixth of the land of England, that tempted Henry VIII to dissolve them and appropriate their property.

Over the centuries, the monasteries had been given estates in order that the monks should pray for the souls of the benefactors; in some cases there was enough endowment to provide a chantry priest specially for this purpose. Tewkesbury, with its royal and noble patrons, had obtained estates all over the western shires. The monasteries had also acquired rectories and parsonages. When the cure of a parish was granted to a monastery, a vicar (who was a substitute rector) would be paid to look after the spiritual needs of its inhabitants. His stipend came out of the church's income in that parish, that is from the tithes, which were annual payments from the produce of the land made either in money or in kind. Once the stipend was paid, the rest of the tithes could be used by the monastery. Tewkesbury had the cure of no less than 48 parish churches, some as far away as Devon and Cornwall. The abbot had pleaded in the past that the abbey needed more income to repair its buildings. Giving it another rectory was one way of increasing its income. The Bishop of Worcester had at one time protested, realising that there was a danger that the monks would not discharge their parochial duties adequately, but had been obliged to accept the position.

Tewkesbury Abbey also owned a large amount of property in the town itself, some of it part of the original endowment by Robert Fitz-Hamon. Following the dissolution, instead of paying their rents to the abbey, tenants paid the king. An Augmentations Office was specially created to deal with the administration of all the confiscated monastic estates. Accounts, rendered from Tewkesbury by Daniel Perte, 'bailiff of the lord King there', still exist written in Latin on many sheets of parchment. They show that the abbey owned property in all three streets in the town.

Church Street, Oldbury Street or High Street, and Barton Street were the three main streets, as they are today, and from them already a number of alleys and lanes branched off. Leland about 1540 noted that High Street was the 'chiefest' of the three main streets. Off Church Street, as today, was Gander Lane, the Bull Ring, Mill Street and Mill Bank, St Mary's Street, and Wayte Lane. Part of St Mary's Street was also known as

Walkers Lane. Crispe Lane, Brasiors Lane, and Long Alley have disappeared as names, though Long Alley is probably now called Old Baptist Chapel Court, its new name referring to the chapel established in the mid-17th century. Church Street ended at the High Cross. Beyond the cross were Barton Street and High Street; Key Lane and Red Lane were the only turnings off High Street on the Avon side, both existing today.

A few particular buildings are named in these accounts. The Tollbooth, the main administrative centre for the town market, stood at the junction of High Street and Barton Street, near the High Cross. The Shambles or slaughter house was in the Oldbury field. The abbey had a prison in Barton Street, and a large hospice or inn called the *Crone* (Crown) or *Newynde* (New Inn) which backed onto the Swilgate. Some of the property was very decrepit: two chambers 'have fallen to the ground and no one will have them'. Materials salvaged from the demolition of unwanted abbey buildings were allocated for the repair of tenements in the town. Some of the rooms were empty. Pigsties and cow-houses in the backyards are occasionally mentioned.

The dissolution of the monasteries involved the transfer to the Crown of all the monastic land and property, all the rectories and parsonages, all the jewels and silver in the monasteries, even the lead off the roofs. Everything of value was swept up into the king's treasury.

Tewkesbury was one of the last monasteries to be closed. The deed of surrender to the king was finally completed in January 1540. The monks left, each to be paid a pension so long as he lived. The very great status of the abbot is obvious from the pension list. He received £257 a year. Abbots were aristocrats, and some were members of the House of Lords. The prior, the immediate supervisor of the monastic community and next in importance to the abbot, only received £16 and the humblest monks £7 each. These charges were met out of the monastery's income. The keys were given to Richard Paulet, Receiver.

The abbey comprised a large complex of buildings. As well as the church, and the monks' accommodation: dormitories, refectory, cloister, kitchen, library, chapter house, hospital and so on, there were all the buildings required for a large agricultural enterprise. The abbey had its own bakehouse, brewhouse, slaughter house, tannery, dairy, malthouse, barns and workshop. There were houses and lodgings for monastic officers and for visitors. The abbot had a house to himself, on the pattern of the great manor houses, with a separate pantry, cellar, kitchen, larder and 'pastry'. There were three gates and gatehouses, and a belfry, and all was surrounded by the monastery wall.

It was the king's intention that everything should be demolished. Anything which might in future have tempted a monk to return was 'deemed to be superfluous' by the king's commissioner. Only a few buildings, useful for secular occupation, were allowed to remain, for example the abbot's house (now probably incorporated in the Vicarage) and 'the great barn next the Avon' (also partially existing in the building opposite the abbey mill).

As well as the monks' living accommodation, the church itself was scheduled for demolition. Valuable lead on the roofs was first to be taken off, and then the building would in any case gradually decay, and local people would rob it for stone. In the event, the townsmen claimed that they had no church of their own, and so they negotiated the purchase of the church and chapels for £483, an act which has won them the gratitude of later generations. The Lady Chapel at the east end was not spared.

The work of destruction was quickly under way. Payments were recorded in Daniel Perte's accounts for

> pulling down and destroying of divers houses and buildings, superfluous possessions of the king, assigned for the repair of tenements within the town of Tewkesbury, of which wood, tiles and stone are carried away to a certain house of the king in Barton called a storehouse there.

Consequently only a few scattered remains of the monastery can be seen today. There is a gatehouse, which was substantially rebuilt in the last century, and the Abbey House or Vicarage. On the south side of the abbey there are tantalising glimpses of the stonework of the cloisters, and blocked doorways and arches show the mutilation necessary to remove the main conventual buildings which stood where now is grass. In 1830 this area was an orchard which was levelled, and the foundations of the monastery exposed. Bennett says that they extended 80 yards (73 metres) south of the church transept, 12 yards (11 metres) to the east, and on the west nearly to the gatehouse. Building stone was excavated from the site before the levelling started, and Bennett regretted that the opportunity to record the layout of the monastery was lost. Six Roman coins were also found.

Part of the monastery boundary wall survives, adjoining 'the great barn next the Avon', in the gardens leading off Mill Street. This seems to show that at one time all this area was within the precinct, and the road skirted round it. In a will of 1502, money was left for the repair of the road from the Avon to Holm Hill, which does suggest that it ran from the bottom of Mill Street. Traces of the old road remained until 1897, when it was decided to create a pleasure ground to commemorate Queen Victoria's Jubilee on

> the site of what was a remaining and disused portion of the ancient road leading from Tewkesbury towards Gloucester and it had from time immemorial been known as 'the Pound Wall roadway'. It was a neglected spot, and being subject to the floods, was generally nearly or quite impassable. There were certain landing-place rights pertaining to the roadway.

Within this part of the monastery site, some new houses have recently been built on the former bowling green. When the foundations were being prepared, archaeologists found evidence of buildings probably dating from the period before the dissolution; this makes it unlikely that the bowling green itself dated from the monks' time, as local tradition has suggested. The green used to be surrounded by a yew hedge, and was owned by *The Bell Hotel*. In the 19th century, it was a well-known attraction in Tewkesbury. The bowling green provided the setting for *John Halifax Gentleman*, the novel by Dinah Mulock or Mrs. Craik, published in 1856, in which the yew hedge was associated with the monks. It was probably here that the vicar of Tewkesbury played bowls in the early 18th century. Some time after the First World War the green lost its attraction, and *The Bell* ceased to advertise it on its front board; so another tenuous link with the monastery ended.

A fragment of the monastery wall, called the Warkhey Wall, may be seen in the Abbey Lawn car park. There used to be an entrance to the monastery through the Warkhey gate, in effect the tradesmen's entrance to the workshop area of the monastery. This part of the wall formed a section of the town's boundary in 1575.

How much difference did the dissolution of the abbey make to Tewkesbury? A great many town houses changed hands. Large blocks of abbey property were sold to speculators, like John Pollard and Arthur Barte who purchased 164 houses. Nothing is known of them after this; it seems probable that they sold off the houses in smaller lots and thus saved the crown much detailed work and expense. Some better-off townsmen quickly moved in as the monks moved out. William Read, for instance, immediately occupied the abbot's lodging or Newark, and after four years as a tenant he purchased the house which was owned by his descendants for the next 70 years. He also bought other houses and land which had belonged to the abbey, in Tewkesbury and surrounding areas. The Read family were well-to-do citizens of Tewkesbury throughout the next century; it is probably Read initials which appear over the doorway of the Hat Shop in Church Street, dated 1664, and in 1682 John Read gave £50 to the poor of Tewkesbury. As far as most tenants of the houses were concerned, the dissolution made little difference to them; they simply paid their rents to new landlords. On the other hand, the disposal of so much property probably acted as a stimulus. We may guess that some new owners who had previously rented their houses were now keen to improve or even to rebuild. There are certainly many houses dating from the later 16th century in Tewkesbury.

Tewkesbury Abbey's rural estates were spread widely through Gloucestershire and beyond. In each parish there seem to have been willing purchasers; often they were the former tenants. In the villages and hamlets surrounding Tewkesbury, the same names tend to recur, as wealthier local gentry families took the opportunity to add former abbey property to their estates. Daniel and Alexander Peart, or Perte, are good examples. There were several yeoman farmers of the same name in north Gloucestershire, and Daniel Peart was the king's bailiff in charge of the Tewkesbury Abbey estate in 1542; he was therefore in an ideal position to enrich himself. The two Pearts bought a large block of abbey property; they then sold off some, while in turn buying other parcels. This was a process being repeated all over the country; the buying, selling and leasing which followed the dissolution led to rich rewards for many members of the legal profession. The Pearts acquired Mythe Manor and stayed there until 1611. Tewkesbury Park, the once important centre of Tewkesbury manor, was purchased by a stranger, Sir Henry Jerningham, Queen Mary's vice-chancellor, after he had leased the house and grounds for some years.

Economically the life of the town was by this date independent of the religious foundation which had provided considerable stimulus in earlier times. The abbey we may suppose was largely a self-sufficient enclave. On the other hand, it certainly provided employment. There were only 38 monks in Tewkesbury Abbey, but there were 144 laymen also resident or employed there. Some few were pensioners who could have bought themselves an asylum in old age; others lived wholly on alms. The majority, though, carried out the extremely varied work of a large landed estate: cooks, brewers, carpenters, grooms, thatchers, carters, shepherds, and so on. In addition, 47 men were abbey administrators, stewards, bailiffs, auditors and receivers. It was a large enterprise to sustain fewer than forty monks.

The abbey had also provided help for some townsfolk through alms-giving and the maintenance of a school. In both cases some at least of the charitable work of the monks had been required of them by Robert Fitz-Hamon when he founded the monastery. There were, for example, the 'Founder's Thirteen Almsmen', who received money from the abbey almonry every week for food and a yearly sum for house rent and clothes. They petitioned Henry VIII for continuance of the charity, which was agreed, but no provision was made for fresh nominations in future. By the time Mary came to the throne, in 1554, nine of the almsmen had died. Mary was a Roman Catholic and naturally sympathetic to the former monasteries. She issued a new charter which named nine more almsmen, and made provision for their successors when necessary. From this time the 13 were known as Queen Mary's Almsmen; one shilling a week was still being paid 300 years later, and after several reorganisations the charity continues in the 20th century.

The foundation charter was similarly said to require the abbey to feed and clothe a number of poor boys and provide them with schooling. Some details are recorded in the *Valor Ecclesiasticus*: 16 poor scholars were given alms and woollen cloth and more were given food, drink and other necessaries. Some townsmen no doubt paid for the monks to educate their sons. Tewkesbury's inhabitants, 'having many children likely and apt through good instruction to attain to learning', petitioned the king for a

23. & 24. At the south-west corner of the abbey was the abbot's house, purchased by John Read from Henry VIII, together with the abbot's gateway leading to it. The property boundary followed the south wall of the church and included the cloister area. One room at first-floor level was actually within the church until it was restored in 1883.

schoolmaster's salary to be paid 'for the maintenance of a free school there for ever'. Tewkesbury was subsequently said to be one of four places in Gloucestershire where grammar schools were to be erected, so the petition was probably granted. The free school provided secondary education; the children first learnt their letters elsewhere. In 1572 there were three schoolmasters in the town. From Elizabethan times, and in all likelihood from much earlier times, the school was in the room built on to the north side of the abbey. When all the conventual buildings were destroyed, this room escaped, though the adjoining structure did not. It can be clearly seen today from the outside, by the north transept. Tewkesbury tradition called the schoolroom the Chapter House, but, as the centre of the monastery's government, such a building was unlikely to be spared.

Tewkesbury Abbey did not have a particular reputation for scholarship, though it had had one notable scholar, the Abbot Alan, who had edited a collection of St Thomas á Becket's letters after his murder in 1170. There had also been a scholar monk who wrote the history of the abbey about 1475. When Leland visited the library he noted several valuable books and also made detailed notes from the chronicle. All the books were dispersed at the dissolution but many were not lost. Some were acquired by notable Tudor antiquarians like Francis Thynne, Lancaster Herald, who died in 1608, and subsequently have found their way into the British Library. The monk's chronicle is one example. The copy of St Thomas á Becket's letters once in Abbot Alan's possession and annotated by him is also in the British Library.

It was recognition that if the monasteries were closed the libraries would be dispersed which seems to have prompted Henry VIII to appoint John Leland 'King's Antiquary' some time in the 1530s. His commission required him to

> diligently search all the libraries of monasteries and colleges of this realm, to the intent that the monuments of ancient writers might be brought out of deadly darkness to lively light.

Most of his journeys were made after the suppression of the larger monasteries in 1540. Leland claimed to have seen every notable feature of the English landscape, whether natural or man-made, 'and notyd yn so doing a hole worlde of thinges very memorable'. He died in 1552, before he had begun to put his notes into coherent form in the series of books he planned. Fortunately his notes survived and, now published, provide us with precious details of England in the mid-16th century. His journeys mark in one way the end of medieval England, but in another way they point to the future. In Tudor times, numerous men of letters began to travel and describe the history and topography of England. The evidence for the next period in English history is much more plentiful.

John Cooke

Timber-framing in High Street from the rear.

Chapter 4

The Establishment of the Borough – Progress and Setbacks: 1550-1700

The formal incorporation of Tewkesbury as a borough was achieved in 1575 by a royal charter giving a council power to govern the town. In many ways this legal event made little difference. The charter itself specifically said that the townsmen should enjoy 'their former liberties, privileges and franchises'. The town had chosen annually two bailiffs, two serjeants at mace and two constables 'from time immemorial . . . for the better government of the inhabitants'. The charter of 1575 augmented the powers of the bailiffs, but their existence was no novelty. As in the past, the town was authorised to have markets and fairs, and 259 men who previously might have been called burgesses now took an oath of allegiance to the queen and to the good government of the town, and so became the first freemen of the borough.

In one respect, however, the charter is a turning point. From this date many more written records exist, generated by the council's administration, and maintained in nearly unbroken succession until the borough was reorganised in 1973. The first minute book, begun in 1575, is not easy to read, as handwriting has changed very much. It is in English, though Latin was used for formal records such as the admission of freemen. For a short time during the Commonwealth, when England was governed by parliament rather than by the king (Charles I was executed in 1649), the legal use of Latin was abolished and the Tewkesbury freemen's register was kept in English. In 1660 it reverted to Latin, and continued to be kept this way until 1733, when parliament again abolished its legal use. The first minute books do not contain reports of council discussions, nor of day-to-day decisions, but they do include summaries of the chief events of the year in the town. Memoranda were also included of charitable bequests, the annual elections of officers, the town's stock of weapons, and many administrative details during the exceptional period of the Civil War.

In general in Tudor times there was more record-keeping. Registers of baptisms, marriages and burials, for example, were required to be kept in 1538, and although only a few survive from this date, the parchment registers of Elizabeth's reign are quite frequently preserved. In Tewkesbury the baptism registers go back to 1559, and the burial and marriage registers to 1595. Every parish presented annual accounts concerning repairs to the local roads, relief of the poor and maintenance of the church. Some of these records, too, have survived from the 16th century. The increasing quantity of written material makes it possible to know much more about the town than in the medieval period.

For 60 years after the borough charter was granted, the council developed and improved Tewkesbury's amenities with only small indications of real cleavages in opinion on religious matters. This apparently peaceful progress was seriously interrupted by the Civil War. Politics sharply divided the townsmen. As Gloucestershire was much fought over, Tewkesbury could not escape being affected by the war, and frequently soldiers were quartered in the town. After this period of disruption, life did not immediately return to its former equable state. The charter had to be defended and reclaimed several times, reflecting the troubled national politics in the years up to 1688. Eventually, in 1698, a charter was obtained under which the town was governed for more than a century, until all boroughs were reformed simultaneously in 1835 by Act of Parliament.

1575: The Borough Incorporated

The charter making Tewkesbury a borough was granted by Elizabeth I in 1575. Cirencester had received a charter four years earlier, though there it was considered a restoration of borough status which had been lost through disputes with the abbot. Over a hundred towns became boroughs in the 16th century.

The Earl of Leicester was instrumental in securing Tewkesbury's charter, and appropriately he became the first High Steward. He was sent gifts, including 'a very fine fat ox' while he was at Kenilworth and a barrel of sack and two sugar loaves whilst visiting Twyning. He had political motives for securing the charter for Tewkesbury. Once it was a borough he could hope parliamentary representation would follow, and he could then persuade the town to elect his supporters. He attempted unsuccessfully to persuade Gloucester to do this in 1580. However, parliamentary representation was not granted to Tewkesbury until 1610.

There were administrative reasons for reorganising the government of the town. The king had taken over the monastic property which had formed the Abbey Barton manor but he had not delegated the abbot's former authority to any local official. Consequently criminals could take refuge in houses once owned by the abbey and not be brought to justice by the town's bailiffs. It was claimed that this was happening daily. The bailiffs needed clear authority over the whole town. Tewkesbury was also 'great and very populous', in the words of the charter, and so fit to have its own town council.

The charter made Tewkesbury a 'free borough consisting of bailiffs, burgesses and commonalty'. The government of the town was entrusted to a council of 14 men; the first members were named in the charter. Two, called bailiffs, were the chief officers of the town, and the others were called principal burgesses. The commonalty was not defined, but in any case played little part in the running of the town. There were no popular elections; when a councillor died, the surviving members elected his successor. The council was allowed to make bye-laws regulating the tradesmen and other inhabitants, and a weekly court for the recovery of very small debts was instituted. Tolls paid by the street traders in the markets and fairs were collected by the council, but it was not apparently the crown's intention that the council should benefit from them. The council fought to oust the queen's clerk from having any authority in Tewkesbury, and eventually established its autonomy in this respect.

Official documents were now authenticated with Tewkesbury's own seal. The first example which survives is dated 1651; the design was of an embattled gateway. Examples can be seen today at the sides of the town hall doorway in High Street, and also on the iron bridge at the bottom of Quay Lane. It is a surprising emblem in view of Tewkesbury's lack of defences – there were no great walls or gatehouses. But it symbolised the ability of the town to exclude strangers. The motif is incorporated in the modern arms of the town, granted in 1964.

Only the built-up area was in the borough, which at this date did not, as later, include the Severn Ham, the Oldbury, Southwick or the Mythe, nor even the site of the abbey church. As Bennett observed, the bounds of the borough as set out in the charter 'are not now very easily understood'. They mention Salendine's bridge and Holm bridge, and the wooden bridge over the old Avon which was the westward extension of King John's Bridge. Other points of reference were the Town Mills, the Hermitage, Quay Lane, Avonmouth, the Swilgate, Gander Lane, and the Warkhey wall. All these names except the Hermitage still exist. Responsibility for the bridges meant including in the borough long thin fingers of land along the roads while excluding the open land on either side. As the town already owned the parish church, the council also assumed responsibility for parochial affairs; in effect, as parish council its authority extended to those surrounding areas which the charter had not included in the borough.

The first meetings of the new council were most likely held in the Tollbooth or Boothall, the building which stood in 1540 at the south end of High Street on the Oldbury field side. Meetings were weekly, and members of the council were required to come in their gowns. Differences in dress distinguished bailiffs from principal burgesses. The bailiffs' gowns were faced with more expensive fur, and they wore fur tippets; the principal burgesses had to have lambskin facings and could not wear tippets. Dress not only reflected social position but also served to mark council members from ordinary citizens, and so helped to encourage the respect necessary for authority. Other town councils similarly regulated dress, and Tewkesbury was simply following the traditions established by other towns at least as early as the 15th century.

In order to maintain its position, the council needed a formal method of asserting its authority over the ordinary citizens of the town. It consequently insisted that all who worked in a handicraft, who kept shop or who made malt or traded in corn and grain in Tewkesbury, must first become freemen of the town. Initially 245 men were admitted in 1575. For the future the sons of the freemen, and those who had served a full seven years' apprenticeship to a freeman, would be admitted after paying a merely nominal fee. Others wishing to work or trade in the town had to buy the freedom to do so. In the first 25 years of the borough's existence, about sixteen men a year became freemen, of whom about a fifth had served their apprenticeship in Tewkesbury. The admission fees provided a modest source of income but, probably more important, the oath-taking required of a freeman helped to maintain the authority of the council. New councillors were drawn from the body of the freemen. Freemen did not have to pay the market tolls; they were, indeed, the proper successors of those first burgesses whose privileges were the basis of the legal market town after the Norman Conquest.

In its regulations controlling the craftsmen and tradesmen, the council was also taking over the existing organisation of the guilds. In the early medieval period, guilds had been formed in many market towns by some more important inhabitants as a means of providing a civic organisation independent of the lords of the manor. These guilds had a religious as well as social basis. In 1389 there were three in Tewkesbury, and similar organisations existed in Cirencester and Tetbury. Later, guilds of craftsmen were formed, which protected the skill and status of the men in that trade. The oldest craft guild in Tewkesbury was the tailors, in existence at least from the 15th century. Other guilds were formed by the dyers and drapers, mercers or haberdashers, glovers and whittawers (whittawers were saddlers or harness-makers), cordwainers (who were

25. & 26. Cross House was originally three houses, one at least fronting the narrow lane at the side. At one time called Salter's Lane or Geast Lane, today's name records the former Tolsey nearby. The clothier and merchant, Giles Geast, may have lived here. The Geast family was very important in 16th-century Tewkesbury.

skilled shoemakers) and weavers. The records of the cordwainers survive from 1562. The first ordinances of the Tewkesbury council in 1575 incorporate the rules of these guilds, which required tradesmen setting up in business in the town to pay an entry subscription and agree to observe the guild's rules. Apprenticeship was also regulated. During Elizabeth I's reign, further guilds were organised by the coopers and joiners, shearers and cutters, and spurriers (spur-makers). Six masters' seats were specially reserved in the abbey next to the bailiffs.

The guilds are seen generally as a brake on enterprise and innovation, tending to discourage town crafts and lead to their relocation in the countryside where there were no guild restrictions. But the guilds in the towns knew what pay a man could live on; in the countryside, employment in the textile trade was often combined with agricultural work, and so men were able to accept lower rates of pay. The guilds retained some useful functions at least into the 17th century, though they gradually became more interested in ceremonial than practical work.

In some towns, the guildhall served naturally as the town hall (as in the City of London or in Gloucester). In Tewkesbury there was no guildhall, though the tailors owned property in High Street which may have served as a meeting house. More likely, however, the guilds met in some of the town's many public houses, or in one of the market buildings. At the extreme northern end of the High Street there was a boothall, much later referred to as the butter market. Between High Street and Church Street stood the High Cross, the original focus of the market; near it was the Tollbooth, also called the Boothall, which was probably the main market building. Another building was called the Tolsey. Both tollbooth and tolsey are words which imply that traders came here to pay the fee or toll which allowed them to buy and sell in the streets. Freemen, like burgesses before them, did not pay these tolls. There was an upstairs room or 'solar' in one of the market buildings. The wool and yarn market was moved there in 1575, probably because the usual room at the Tolsey was adapted to accommodate the new weekly law court. While the alterations were being done, the Tolsey was also equipped with a clock; it was sufficiently unusual for the town clerk to note this particularly in the record book.

As is the way with newly-created councils, it was soon decided that better premises were needed. Three years after coming into existence, the council found the Boothall to be old and decayed. A new timber-framed house was begun, standing farther forward to the street than the old one. It was a substantial building which took six years to complete. One year the frame was constructed, the next year it was set up, and the year after it was roofed and provided with gutters. The glazier who put 20 feet of glass in, an expensive feature at this date, was rewarded by being made a freeman of the town. One room was wainscoted, presumably designed as the council chamber, and over it was the wool solar. Once the Boothall was completed a new tolsey was then built, taking another two years to finish. Later the name Boothall was dropped, and what was quite a complex of buildings became known familiarly as the Tolsey, or more formally as the town hall. In 1700 it was described as both market cross and town hall, and also as 'a very fair market house with a spacious town hall above for courts and public entertainments'. Thus the central importance of the market in the life of the town was epitomised in the transformation of boothall and tolsey into town hall. Unfortunately, not one of the market buildings of Tewkesbury survived the modernising enthusiasm of 18th-century inhabitants.

As well as building a new boothall, Tewkesbury council also sponsored the raising of funds for the free school, another project which added to the town's prestige. The schoolroom must have been very simple, because in 1600 a subscription was raised to repair the school by unblocking and glazing the windows, boarding the floors and constructing galleries. Window glass was only then becoming common.

The Port

It is hard today to imagine Tewkesbury as a port yet, in this time of growing confidence at the end of the 16th century, Gloucester and Tewkesbury successfully asserted their independence of Bristol, which up to this time had controlled their water-borne trade.

27. The war memorial cross is on the Tolsey site, in 'the very centre and trading part of the town'. The passage-ways on either side of Tolsey and Boothall were eight feet at their widest and much narrower in places.

28. Near the Cross is a notable late 15th-century house, the *Berkeley Arms*, with a medieval barn at its rear.

Like the grant of a market, the grant of the status of 'port' brought income to the crown but also to the port itself, through the collection of customs dues. A 'customer' or customs official would be appointed and the need to pay dues at the port also encouraged the sales of merchandise locally. As a result of the separation of Gloucester and Tewkesbury in 1580, Bristol complained that the city and its neighbourhood were short of provisions of corn, grain, butter and cheese, but did not win back control. Tewkesbury, however, was subordinate to Gloucester. Together they were required to provide a ship for the navy at the time of the Spanish Armada, which they failed to do in time, and the following year the mariners of Tewkesbury were mustered, or listed, so that they could be called up if required. In 1596 Tewkesbury contributed £40 towards the £200 Ship Money tax imposed on Gloucester.

Tewkesbury boats accounted for about a third or even a half of the cargoes passing through Gloucester around 1600. Agricultural produce, timber, coal, and malt were the main items of trade. In early charters the townsmen had been given exemption from tolls all over the country, and now successfully maintained their freedom from contributing to the upkeep of Over bridge at Gloucester when their boats passed beneath it.

Extension of the Borough's Powers

Queen Elizabeth died on 24 March 1603. News reached Tewkesbury in the evening. The town hesitated to proclaim her successor King James I until Sunday 'upon the certain report made of the like in some other places the day before'. In the early years of James I's reign, Tewkesbury twice negotiated a new charter. James I was always short of money; the issue of new borough charters brought in a small amount of income through the fees paid. One charter was obtained in 1605. The sale of crown land also raised money, and the council, taking advantage of this policy, purchased the two Tewkesbury manors, and at the same time negotiated a new charter in 1610.

The charter of 1605 gave the town a further measure of independence. The council was given the power to tax the inhabitants 'towards the necessary expenses of the borough'; as a result they no longer had to pay county rates. The charter also set up a magistrates' court. The two bailiffs automatically became justices of the peace, together with two others. Now, instead of minor crimes being tried in Gloucester, there was a court to deal with them on the spot. This in turn saved Tewkesbury inhabitants from jury service elsewhere in the county, which as Bennett said in 1830 was a worthwhile privilege. The magistrates' court continued to be held in the town until the mid-20th century. This charter doubled the size of the council to twenty-four.

Only five years after this, the town negotiated another charter, at the same time as the purchase of Tewkesbury and Abbey Barton manors was completed. The crown received £2,453 for the manors and £427 for the charter. Some of the money was raised by using the newly-won power of taxing the inhabitants. Tewkesbury claimed as a result to be too poor to mend the Long Bridge, but most of the money needed to buy the manors was in practice lent to the town. The effect of the purchase was to make the borough boundaries coincide with the parish, thus including the surrounding rural areas of Southwick and the Park, the Mythe and Walton Cardiff, as well as the Oldbury and the Ham. The residents of these areas were perhaps not very pleased to be taxed by Tewkesbury, and Walton Cardiff was eventually separated from the borough. The size of the council was again doubled by adding 24 assistant burgesses. There had probably been pressure for a more democratic council, as in other towns, but the attempt to widen its membership was not really successful. There was always a tendency for the principal burgesses to allow numbers to decline by not appointing replacements when councillors died. The council remained a select body until the 19th-century reform of municipal corporations.

The 1610 charter was particularly important because it made Tewkesbury a parliamentary borough. Only 12 boroughs were enfranchised by James I, but a large number, 62, had been enfranchised by Elizabeth I, including Cirencester in 1571. Cirencester and Tewkesbury, together with the county town, were the only boroughs in Gloucestershire to elect members of parliament until the general parliamentary reform of 1832. The first members for Tewkesbury were Sir Dudley Digges and Edward Ferrers. Sir Dudley Digges's election was promoted by Lord Salisbury, James I's chief minister, who exercised the influence the Earl of Leicester had hoped to have. Even so, Digges became a notable critic of Charles I. He represented Tewkesbury until 1626, and shows the tendency of the town from the first to elect radical members. He was not a local man – he lived at Chilham Castle in Kent – but he won the goodwill of the town by giving a small endowment to the free school. The other member, Edward Ferrers, was local. He only sat once, and his election appears to have been a token of gratitude for the services to the town of his brother, William, who lent over £2,000 for the purchase of the manors from James I. The town had later to give him the 94 acres of Tewkesbury Ham to pay off the debt, though the townsmen's rights of common were safeguarded and the council regulated them from time to time. William Ferrers was a merchant in the City of London, but his family had lived at Fiddington, a few miles east of Tewkesbury, since the mid-16th century. A monument in Ashchurch lists his charitable deeds. They included a generous endowment to Tewkesbury free school, which from this time was often known as his foundation. The schoolmaster had to educate free four children from Ashchurch. From Tewkesbury school a few scholars went on to Oxford in the later 17th century.

Boroughs were eager to have parliamentary representation because then they could hope to obtain parliament's help in dealing with their problems. In 1621, for example, Tewkesbury's members presented a Bill to compel the county to pay the cost of repairs to the Long Bridge, which had been seriously damaged in floods the previous year. It was Tewkesbury's proper responsibility but an Act of Parliament could override this. Some county members protested that they had no benefit from the bridge, which was 'in a corner' of the county, and that adjoining shires should also contribute. Tewkesbury's M.P.s won; Tewkesbury was required to find only a sixth part of the cost and the county the rest. In the election of 1624 Tewkesbury refused to have Sir Robert Tracy of Toddington in Gloucestershire but elected instead Sir Baptist Hicks. Tracy wrote bitterly to a friend in Tewkesbury about his rejection, despite, as he said, his care to serve the town's interests by not speaking against the Bridge Bill.

> They believe I am able to do them little good, whereas the sole end they aim at tis not he who brings most in his truest love but brings most in his purse shall be accepted.

He added sarcastically 'Sir Baptist's good deeds are to ensue'. Sir Baptist Hicks, later Viscount Campden, was a very wealthy London silk merchant. 'His great bounty' to Tewkesbury was acknowledged with some surprise, even so, by the town clerk. He and members of his family sat for Tewkesbury throughout the 17th century. Tracy never did secure election by Tewkesbury, though he found a seat elsewhere in the county.

In some ways the grant of parliamentary representation had disadvantages, because it brought Tewkesbury into the crossfire between king and parliament which continued for the rest of the 17th century. All the parliamentary boroughs became instruments in the hands of kings determined to control who was elected to Westminster. For a while, and especially during the Civil War, national politics assumed an enormous importance in this small west-country town.

The Civil War

The Civil War between Charles I and his parliament, which began in 1642, had a much more extended and debilitating effect on Tewkesbury than the more famous battle of the Wars of the Roses. For three years Tewkesbury was the scene of attack and counter-attack, together with occupation by a succession of armies, none of which we may suppose was very disciplined, though the Roundheads or Parliamentarians had a better reputation in this respect than the Cavaliers.

The disastrous quarrel between the king and parliament which led to civil war had its roots in the lack of mutual understanding from the beginning of Charles' reign in 1625, or even as far back as 1603 when James I arrived from Scotland. The conflicts and arguments were most clearly witnessed in London, where parliament met; it is perhaps surprising to find how much Tewkesbury inhabitants were aware of and reacted to the developing crisis. No doubt because Tewkesbury returned two members to Westminster, the concerns of parliaments generally were better known and understood than in the average English small town, bearing in mind the lack of newspapers or modern means of communication.

All the major themes of the Civil War can be found in two Tewkesbury record books. In the first minute book there are notes concerning many of the administrative problems faced by the council up to 1651. The record book of the large Geast Charity, however, as well as accounts, contains a most unusual yearly summary of what are called 'notable occurrences'. Generally the writer of these yearly comments thought comets and earthquakes particularly worthy of record, together with great frosts, droughts, late snow storms, floods, and, less often, exceptionally good harvests or the progress of foreign wars. But during the Civil War, as also during the French Revolution over a century later, political events were in the front of his mind. The Geast chronicler provides a marvellously succinct and immediate account of events year by year.

One of the roots of disagreement between Charles I and parliament was Roman Catholicism. Parliament represented directly the country gentlemen and the better-off inhabitants of the enfranchised towns. The great majority were vividly anti-Catholic. As early as 1623 the Tewkesbury chronicler noted in the charity book the collapse of an upper room in London where a crowd had gathered to hear a Jesuit preach. The event was seen as a sign of divine displeasure. Yet Charles I's Queen was Roman Catholic and so were a number of those at court. Tewkesbury council resolved in 1639 that no Roman Catholics were to hold office in the town.

Furthermore, the Church of England, under the direction of William Laud, Archbishop of Canterbury since 1633, seemed to be moving back towards Roman Catholic practices. The Puritans, who gained their name from their desire for simplicity and purity in the Church, were increasingly at variance with Laud's and Charles I's policies. Tewkesbury council had had something of a Puritan bias since at least the end of Elizabeth's reign. They had paid for a minister, for example, to preach twice every Sunday. Puritans thought the established church was very remiss in this respect. From the beginning of the century, also, the council had frowned upon festivities being organised in the church. In 1600 enterprising churchwardens had organised plays on three successive days in Whitsun week to be performed in the abbey. The object was to raise money for one item in the general programme of restoration work on the church which was being undertaken. Obviously refreshments were served, as the churchwardens paid for two butts of beer, 'cookery', and for waiters and cups. When they next proposed a 'church ale' or fete to be held in the abbey, the council refused permission unless 'accustomed abuses' were reformed, which effectively stopped the church ale for ever. All over the country in the early 17th century the traditional church ales were being suppressed through the influence of Puritan ideas.

Another general Puritan idea was that Sunday should be spent in religious devotions. The ordinances made by the council in 1609 contain several which attempted to enforce proper observance of the Sabbath. Drinking and gambling at the time of divine service were not allowed, and constables and churchwardens were asked to search the taverns. Butchers could not sell meat at this time. Malt was not be to dried on Sundays at all. These regulations incidentally make clear that many did not go to church. Even amongst the council, church attendance was not the invariable rule. The ordinances of 1639 plaintively suggested that it would be 'most decent and comely for principal burgesses to accompany the bailiffs to church'. Nonetheless a large number of townsfolk, as well as the council, took on Puritan ideas: 450 signed the Protestation or covenant of 1641 to defend the Protestant religion, perhaps half of the adult male inhabitants of the town. Mr. John Geree, Minister of Tewkesbury from 1628 to 1645 and described as a moderate or 'church puritan', may have had considerable influence in this.

The crown's financial policies were also generally unpopular. Although money was needed for running the government, after 1629 Charles I refused to summon parliament. In 1634 the king and his ministers decided to collect Ship Money without parliamentary sanction. The order to Tewkesbury was copied into the minute book. Traditionally the tax was paid by the ports, by supplying either ships or money when foreign dangers threatened. In 1636, Ship Money was demanded from the whole country. The amount of grumbling this provoked gave John Hampden the courage to refuse to pay. Before taking Hampden to court, the king sent a statement of his case to certain judges for their comments. Both the king's case and the judges' reply were also written out in full in Tewkesbury's minute book, which shows how closely the council was watching events in London. In 1638, £60 was required from the town for Ship Money; 243 people paid sums ranging from one shilling (5p) to more than one pound. The tax thus reached nearly two-thirds of all households.

After 11 years without a parliament, a rebellion in Scotland forced Charles reluctantly to summon a parliament in April 1640. He needed money and general consent to an army to put down the Scots. But after only three weeks he dismissed parliament again because the members were so critical of all his policies. The chronicler in the Geast book noted 'wettest summer ever known'; also 'the Scots came with an army of 30,000 foot and 3,000 horse and took Newcastle'. Talk of war was inevitably in the air

29. The Old Baptist Chapel was one of the first such meeting houses in the country, in use from about 1650. Nonconformity was very strong in Tewkesbury; 200 years later Mary Yorke said the town 'swarms with dissenters'.

30. The northern end of the *Royal Hop Pole Hotel* is 15th-century, with a 14th-century hall behind. A plaque records Dickens's reference to it in *Pickwick Papers*.

from the time of the Scots' invasion; the town clerk listed the 47 trained soldiers Tewkesbury could mobilise if necessary, and also the town's stock of arms.

The Scots' invasion led Charles I to summon his second parliament of the year.

3 November 1640. Memo. This parliament sprang from the broken splinter of a former parliament which began the 13th April last and ended the 5th May following and nothing done. Then the king and nobles met at York in September following, about the invasion of the Scottish army and there resolved on this parliament.

The Tewkesbury clerk wrote this summary under the heading 'This unhappy parliament', showing that his sympathies were generally with the king. Later, someone felt differently and attempted to blot out the first part of the word 'unhappy'.

The election of October 1640 was hotly contested, and revealed a deep split in opinion in the town. Since the earlier election of March 1640, when members favourable to Charles I had been returned, opinion had hardened, and a party had emerged that was hostile to the king. It was perhaps as a result of some desperate electioneering that in September and October 1640 there was a rush by a very unusual number of men to be admitted as freemen, no less than 28, in contrast with the six admitted earlier in the year. Most of the 28 were entitled to the freedom by apprenticeship, and up to this time they had clearly not bothered to register. Freemen were certainly allowed to vote, and it looks as if a royalist was trying to rally potential supporters while countering a much more adventurous campaign by the opposition, who were appealing to all the town's inhabitants. There was no standard parliamentary franchise, and the charter giving Tewkesbury representation was ambiguous, not defining who could vote but referring to 'bailiffs, burgesses and commonalty'. The bailiffs were responsible for the conduct of the elections. By this time they were so opposed in political opinion that they could no longer act together. One bailiff interpreted commonalty to mean freemen, and counted only their votes. He declared two supporters of Charles I elected. The other bailiff took commonalty to mean all the inhabitants, and returned two supporters of parliament's cause. The Geast chronicler noted laconically 'great differences about our burgesses'.

The result was that no-one was allowed to sit for Tewkesbury, and a fresh election was ordered. The royalist bailiff, however, was summoned to Westminster, and for a while imprisoned. At the next election he tried for a compromise. He returned one royalist and one moderate parliamentarian, Edward Stephens, who had been chosen by all the inhabitants in the first election. Later Stephens was to refuse to have anything to do with the trial and execution of Charles I. The other bailiff agreed in the election of Stephens, but also returned Sir Robert Cooke of Highnam, a parliamentarian who had been the inhabitants' choice before. Cooke was later to lead a regiment for parliament, briefly to command Tewkesbury and to die in Gloucester during the royalist siege. Eventually, in 1643, parliament accepted the inhabitants' choices, but by this time royalist members had departed from Westminster to be with the king, and the Civil War had started. In the next few years, whenever a by-election was expected in Tewkesbury, as after the death of Cooke and the imprisonment of Stephens, there was the same rush to become freemen. Events in Tewkesbury seem to support the general contention that at least some of the impetus behind the parliamentarian party was provided by the lower ranks of urban populations, as Clarendon commented at the time. While these disputes over Tewkesbury elections were taking place, there was increasingly bitter argument between Charles I and his parliament at Westminster. Events were closely watched in Tewkesbury. Under a heading 'Great Men Questioned' the town clerk wrote down the names of Charles I's four chief ministers who were being impeached by the House of Commons for high treason, and of the judges and bishops attacked for condoning Charles' non-parliamentary taxes. The 'barbarous murder' of Protestants by Roman Catholics in Ireland in October 1641 was recorded, too, an event which did much to increase tension nationally.

In August 1642 King Charles symbolically raised his standard at Nottingham, and appealed for an army to come and join him. The Geast chronicler tersely noted 'Civil war in England between the king and the parliament'. He continued:

> 23 October 1642 a battle near Kineton in county Warwick, where the king was in the field with duke Rupert his nephew and the Earl of Essex was general for the parliament, and many hundred were slain on both sides, the place called Edgehill.

This was the first major battle of the war, some thirty miles from Tewkesbury and ten miles south-west of Stratford. The next year the Geast chronicler lamented:

> The civil war between king and parliament still continueth and threatneth the ruin of the kingdom.

By this time Tewkesbury had experienced what civil war really meant. A small force of 200 foot soldiers and dragoons had occupied the town a month before Edgehill in September 1642, the first of many bands of soldiers in the next few years. These were parliamentarians, despite the royalist bailiff. 'Very forward and active for the parliament' was how the Geast chronicler summed up this period. Such resolution was short-lived. Tewkesbury now found itself in a most unenviable situation, threatened by both sides. To the north, Worcester was quickly abandoned by a parliamentary army under Essex and occupied instead by a royalist army under Sir William Russell. To the south, Gloucester was staunchly parliamentarian. Tewkesbury daily expected attack from Russell's army and saw itself as a battleground between the two sides. The town council was panic-stricken. A message was sent to Gloucester saying the town was unable to withstand a royalist attack. It was agreed that such military forces as there were in Tewkesbury should go to Gloucester, and be concentrated there. As a result, without any fighting, the council accepted in February 1643 the peace terms offered by Sir William Russell. It cost the town £500 to balance the £500 already contributed to parliament, and the provisioning of the garrison. It also meant the town from then on lacked any partisan force or spirit, and was obliged to contribute to whichever side was temporarily in possession. Faced with the reality of civil war, it now seemed that the town 'desired an everlasting neutrality', as one contemporary said, and may have suffered more as a result.

Between February 1643 when the royalists occupied the town and June 1644 when the parliamentarians won it for the last time, the town was occupied by turns and often in quick succession by armies of both sides. It changed hands four times in two months in the spring of 1643, and on occasions the soldiers fought in the streets. Tewkesbury's experiences in the Civil War were not unusual, and were repeated in other places throughout England. Towns were valuable and indeed essential to the armies because they alone could provide accommodation and food for the numbers involved. Largely because of their need for provisions, armies were relatively small, and often avoided each other; it was no use arriving in a town immediately after the opposing side had commandeered all the supplies. Tewkesbury was not only a centre for the agricultural produce of the Vale of Evesham, but was also important strategically. It commanded the bridge over the Avon and also two ferries over the Severn. The latter were particularly useful to the king, who wanted to be able to mobilise his supporters in South Wales. The royalists made a bridge of boats to cross the Severn at this point. The next bridge over the Severn was some miles upstream at Upton.

Tewkesbury was not defended by walls, though the rivers provided some natural defences. There were, however, some 'works' or 'bulwarks', associated with the bridges. Their exact location is unknown. Probably these were earth banks, perhaps strengthened with wooden fences. They were quickly destroyed in April 1643 by a departing parliamentarian governor, so as not to give their advantage to an incoming royalist force, and as quickly rebuilt. When the royalist commander, Sir William Vavasour, entered the town in October 1643 with 700 men, he devised a rota of work to put the defences back into readiness. The men of Barton Street worked on Mondays, the High Street men on Tuesdays, Wednesdays and Thursdays, and Church Street men on Fridays and Saturdays. Despite not being Puritan Sabbatarians, there was no work on Sundays. Every morning one of the constables had to present to the overseer of the works the names of those summoned for the next day. When the parliamentarians took the town for the last time, they also took over and continued the rota of work on the bulwarks.

As well as the misery of occupation by soldiers, and the requisitioning of food and supplies, towns suffered during the Civil War from previously undreamt-of levels of taxation. In every area there were supporters of both sides so that, once a place was captured, known sympathisers with the opposite side could be made to pay heavily for their misplaced loyalty. More generally, both king and parliament, when in control, collected taxes from the townsfolk. Parliament's weekly assessment was far more severe than Charles I's Ship Money. In one year, August 1644 to July 1645, it cost £4,640 to maintain the garrison in the northern half of Gloucestershire; Tewkesbury town's share was £280. The town had had to find £60 for Ship Money. Parliament's attempts to pay for its armies, and prevent them plundering, was in contrast to the king's management, and provided one factor in the steady military superiority of parliament. Scales of pay and maintenance were carefully specified and as carefully copied into the record book by the Tewkesbury clerk. When £100 was lent to some parliamentary soldiers, it was duly repaid a month or so later.

Tewkesbury's first experience of an actual battle in the town was in April 1643, two months after the surrender to Sir William Russell and consequent royalist occupation. Gloucester's parliamentary commander decided to try to capture Tewkesbury. A two-pronged attack was mounted. One force advanced up the River Severn, first destroyed the royalists' bridge of boats, and then approached across the Ham, though the Mill Avon still barred their way. The other force advanced along Lower Lode Lane, clambered over the bulwarks and lowered the drawbridge over the Swilgate. Some of the royalists fled northwards, some were captured. The royalists quickly regrouped and faced the pursuing parliamentarians at Ripple, a few miles north of Tewkesbury. A running battle was fought, finishing at the Mythe, the last part in a 'strait passage' which seems to have been below the Tute. Some of the soldiers were drowned in the Severn. Although the battle was militarily inconclusive, Tewkesbury was again in parliamentary hands.

After this experience, Tewkesbury attempted to save both the town and the neighbourhood from the dreadful effects of the fighting. In August 1643 the royalists made a major military effort to capture the important parliamentary stronghold of Gloucester. The king required Tewkesbury to provide all the 'spades, mattocks and shovells' it could to help make his camp. The siege lasted for a month. Tewkesbury took an understandable if not very courageous stance. A deputation was sent begging Gloucester to yield and so save the whole neighbourhood the privations of occupation by contending armies. Gloucester did not yield, as the parliamentary general, the Earl of Essex, arrived and the king abandoned the siege. Tewkesbury's fears were not unrealistic; provisions were requisitioned by Essex's men from the whole neighbourhood, and Essex then marched into Tewkesbury, staying five days. He collected one-twentieth of the value of any royalists' property to help defray Gloucester's costs. His troops were scattered about the neighbourhood, and the shortage of provisions was acute. No doubt to Tewkesbury's relief, a swift night march to Cirencester and the capture of a royalist food convoy saved the army from severe hunger, and Tewkesbury from further military occupation for about a month.

There was more fighting in Tewkesbury early in 1644, when Prince Rupert, the king's nephew, was in the town. Some parliamentarian soldiers found the drawbridge down and no guards. They marched into the town, but the royalists successfully defended it and drove them out. There was considerable damage, including the cutting down of the two drawbridges. Shortly afterwards, however, another parliamentarian force arrived; this time the royalists fled, leaving behind a number of their weapons.

For Tewkesbury this was the end of the fighting, though not of all military occupation. For a while the king himself was at Bredon, only four miles away, keeping Tewkesbury in a state of continual alarm but, when some more musketeers arrived in the town, he gave up any plans to attack. Gradually the king lost control of more of the country, and finally admitted military defeat early in 1646. There was enough confidence in Tewkesbury for the town to acquire two new silver maces, which were the bailiffs' symbols of office. A series of royalist risings in 1647 and 1648 brought more soldiers to be quartered in Tewkesbury. They were spread round the town and neighbourhood according to an apparently simple but inconvenient scheme based on each area's quota of taxes. The Park, with only three houses, quartered 16 men; Tewkesbury town, with its hundreds of houses, quartered 50 men. 'The villages were much discontented'.

The royalist rising of 1647 and 1648 convinced the parliamentarian leaders that Charles I should be punished. He was tried by an *ad hoc* court and executed. The Geast chronicler described the event with characteristic brevity:

> Memo. this year viz. the 30th day of January 1649 King Charles was beheaded upon a scaffold erected over against the banqueting house at Whitehall.

More troops were quartered in Tewkesbury in 1651, when the Scots invaded England on behalf of the young son of Charles I, whom they had proclaimed as King Charles II. The Scots were defeated only a few miles to the north, at Worcester, after which Charles escaped to exile again.

It was usual to apply to a new monarch for a renewal of the town charter, and seemed necessary after the change of regime in January 1649. The opportunity was taken to propose alterations to the existing charter, for example by reducing the size of the council. It was suggested that the town clerk rather than the chamberlain (or treasurer)

31. & 32. Lilley's Alley had been 'a scene of dilapidation and decay' until Thomas Collins restored it in 1894, so creating a pleasant short cut from Church Street to the cricket field. It contains some typical 16th-century timber-framing, with a first- floor jetty, showing the early development of the alley.

should be the recorder 'for sometimes the chamberlain cannot write his own name, which is ridiculous'. Negotiations for this charter were continuing when Cromwell altered the constitution by assuming the title of Lord Protector.

For Tewkesbury, Lord Protector was much like king. Indeed the bells of the abbey were rung to celebrate the event, and Cromwell was proclaimed at Gloucester on 21 December 1653 and at Tewkesbury on Christmas Eve. The order requiring the proclamation was written out in the minute book – it explains it was necessary 'to the end none may have cause to pretend ignorance in this behalf', a good reminder of the poor communications of the time. Negotiations for a charter began again, but this time were foiled by the death of Oliver Cromwell. From this date no new freemen were recorded until 1662, perhaps because the town clerk had been removed for suspected royalism; there is also a gap in the council minutes. Later it appeared that some of the sheets of the 1610 charter had actually been lost.

Confusion in town government was increased by the uncertainty of the parliamentarian regime. Typically, Tewkesbury council contained royalist sympathisers. Both the bailiffs were accused of being royalists in 1649, and in 1655 nine councillors and the town clerk were removed from office by the officious and dictatorial major-general of the area. For a short while the whole country was divided into regions with a military major-general in charge of each – a telling indication of the insecurity of Cromwell's regime. Yet some areas of administration continued without interruption. The Geast charity money was collected and distributed, the churchwardens continued to provide for the church's upkeep. Registers of baptisms, marriages and burials continued to be kept, though with the difference that from 1653 all registration was made a civil rather than a religious matter. Folk from surrounding areas had to come into Tewkesbury and have their banns of marriage published in the market place, after which the marriage was performed by a justice of the peace.

Although there were royalist sympathisers in Tewkesbury, the town had a Puritan majority. In the elections of 1654 and 1656 Tewkesbury supported sound Cromwellian candidates, though by 1659, when restoration was in the air, there was a prudent compromise of one royalist and one parliamentarian. The church ministers may have been influential. A 'godly preacher' succeeded John Geree in 1645, and won Puritan approval, and he was succeeded in 1650 by a more extreme man, Thomas Burroughs, who was labelled a republican. The Puritanism of the clergy was rewarded when the small income of the living was augmented; parliament did try at this time to reorganise the funds of the church to create more equality of income amongst parish clergy. Perhaps it was Burroughs' influence that persuaded the bailiffs to take down the High Cross; the stone came in useful for mending the Long Bridge, and all crosses were suspect to the Puritans as idolatrous. Was it at the same time that all the heads were knocked off the figures round the Beauchamp Chantry chapel? Similar actions elsewhere in the country were common.

Puritan ideals informed many of the bailiffs' actions. They set a charitable example by paying for bread to be placed in the church every Sunday for the poor. The war had exacerbated the problem of poverty. People drifted into Tewkesbury, as into other towns, hoping for work because the life of the villages was disrupted. As in other towns, too, materials were provided for the poor to work with, probably wool and yarn for spinning and weaving. The chancel of the abbey was repaired, and another pulpit installed there to help people hear 'when the minister hath a low voice'. The influence of Puritanism would have become very pervasive if the new charter had been obtained, because the bailiffs proposed that they should have power to send 'loud' people to the house of correction; 'loud' meant offensive – the bailiffs would have had great scope to punish all sorts of human frailties. Fortunately for some Tewkesbury inhabitants the new charter was not obtained.

Oliver Cromwell died in 1658. The local chronicler could not forbear to point out the hand of providence:

> This year 3 September the Lord Protector who upon the same day of the month in the years 1650

and 1651 had two eminent victories, the one at Dunbar, the other at Worcester, yet Death conquered him who had been pre-eminent in Arms. *Sic transit gloria mundi.*

The events of the next 20 months were closely observed and recorded by the Geast chronicler. Cromwell's son Richard was proclaimed Lord Protector 'but continued not long in that capacity'.

> 22 April to 7 May it seemed to be an Interregnum. The Protector's power came to be clouded.

The continuing attempt to gain a charter was thus foiled for the third time. After some jockeying amongst politicians in London

> 13 October the parliament kept out of their house by the Army (now comes another Interregnum).

General Monk resolved the crisis by arriving from Scotland with his well-disciplined army, and arranging new elections for a parliament.

> The parliament meet the 25th April 1660. Sir Henry Capell and Mr. Dowdeswell our Burgesses. They vote the king's Restoration, who accordingly came upon the 29th May 1660, in great triumph and Joy to the people through the City of London.

If many welcomed the restoration of Charles II, the town council must have been more uncertain, knowing how many of them had supported parliament and Cromwell in the past 20 years. They prudently started a new minute book with a welcome to Charles II:

> We the bailiffs of the borough of Tewkesbury and others of the common council and inhabitants of the same do with most humble and hearty thankfulness lay hold upon his Majesty's free and general pardon . . . and are and will continue his Majesty's loyal and obedient subjects.

None of Tewkesbury's politicians were punished very severely; the royalist councillors excluded in 1655 were reinstated, and a year or so later 13 of the parliamentarian councillors were excluded in turn, as 'expedient for the public safety', amongst them once again the town clerk. Town government continued, though Tewkesbury was still without a current charter. After considerable effort by one of the members of parliament, Richard Dowdeswell, a replacement of the lost charter of 1610 was obtained in 1672.

Restoration Politics

Puritanism was too deep-rooted to disappear at the Restoration. In Tewkesbury it was said in 1676 that three-quarters of the inhabitants had not returned to allegiance to the Church of England. They were encouraged in their nonconformity by another very independent minister, whom the council struggled to remove. After 1678 more conventional ministers were appointed, and it was possible to have the surplice worn again in church services; the old one had been symbolically torn up by a Tewkesbury glover in 1641.

There were more difficulties in store for all borough corporations in the last years of Charles II's reign and in James II's short reign because of the election of members of parliament. Charles II found many members too assertive and critical, particularly of his policy of fixing the succession to the throne on his Roman Catholic brother, James. Sir Henry Capel, who sat for Tewkesbury from 1660 until 1690, was an example. His father had been beheaded in 1649 for loyalty to Charles I and himself had been knighted by Charles II. Nonetheless Capell was opposed to the succession of James to the throne, and joined the band of 'exclusionists' led by Anthony Ashley Cooper, from 1672 Earl of Shaftesbury, and a former member for Tewkesbury. The exclusionists tried unsuccessfully to pass a bill through parliament to prevent James from succeeding to the throne. They were given the nickname 'Whigs' – a political label which long outlived the exclusion crisis. The supporters of James' right to succeed were dubbed 'Tories'.

The only way the king could hope to prevent his critics reaching Westminster was by close supervision of borough elections. The franchise in each borough was governed by the provisions in its charter. Hence Charles started to call in borough charters and issue new ones giving councillors alone the right to vote in parliamentary elections and the king authority to appoint councillors. Charles II died in 1685, and was peacefully succeeded by his brother James, who continued the attack on the borough charters. When the greatest borough in the country, the City of London, was forced to yield, obviously Tewkesbury could not resist. A new charter was issued in 1686, naming the 12 members of the council who were expected to be reliable. One of the council was now mayor, instead of the traditional leadership by two bailiffs. Yet, although only councillors now voted, the king failed to alter the representatives for Tewkesbury in parliament, who continued to be Whigs.

James II was ousted from the throne and from England after only three years, with the help of the Protestant William of Orange, and his wife Mary, James II's daughter. Although the mayor and council were apparently in office, the procedures for the new charter were not completed. The lawyer in London who was handling the business wrote to Tewkesbury on 11 December 1688 breathless with excitement about

> the stupendous and surprising news of last night's revolution . . . about 2 o'clock the king went away privately down the river . . . but that which is as strange is, to see the peace and tranquility that hitherto continues in this great city.

Tewkesbury opinion was divided on this bloodless or 'Glorious' revolution. The election of 1689 was apparently a 'long, severe contest'. Something like three hundred and fifty voted, so that the arrangements of James II's charter had obviously been ignored. The voters, it later appeared, were probably the inhabitants who owned houses with frontages on the three main streets. 'Inhabitants' never meant all the population of the town. In the end, the same two members were returned to parliament. As Whigs, they were in favour of the new Protestant king and queen.

After William and Mary became king and queen, it is not clear what happened in Tewkesbury. A mayor continued to serve until 1692, but there are no council records between 1689 and 1698 when it was said there had been no town government 'for divers years last past'. There were still elections in Tewkesbury, in 1690, 1692 and 1695. At this last date it was alleged that one candidate threatened to turn out of their houses anyone who voted for his opponent, though all three candidates were Whigs.

In 1698 William III issued a new charter which restored the traditional government of the town, of bailiffs, burgesses and commonalty. Seven guilds were reconstituted as part of the revival of ancient customs and 'provided their flags to attend upon Mr. Bailiffs'. Tewkesbury was governed under this charter for nearly three hundred years. The new charter still left unclear the question of who voted in parliamentary elections, a question which did not cease to have importance in the next century, particularly at the time when the French Revolution was upsetting many political norms. But for most of the next century Tewkesbury politics seem to have followed a peaceful and stable course. Bennett, indeed, considered there were so few 'public occurrences' in Tewkesbury in the 18th century that there was no real history to be written. This is to ignore the social and economic developments which have very much influenced modern Tewkesbury. Before examining these, however, the occupations and living conditions of the inhabitants during the century and a quarter of the borough's establishment will be described.

Above the carriage-way of the *Swan Hotel*.

Chapter 5

Work and Home: 1550-1700

One of Tewkesbury's special characteristics is the number of timber-framed buildings surviving from the mid-16th and 17th centuries. All over England at this time more substantial and therefore durable houses were being built, but in few towns are there so many still standing today. More, indeed, survive in Tewkesbury than is at first obvious, because frequently the basic timber frame has been given a new front at some later date, and so hides its antiquity from a casual view. After the disruption of the Civil War, building continued in the later 17th century with as much vigour as earlier.

By 1600 there could have been little street frontage left undeveloped. The original wide burgage plots had been split up and the larger houses, too, were being subdivided. One answer to the shortage of land was the accumulation of buildings one behind the other along the plots, a development which obviously occurred frequently. The irregularities of buildings and of boundaries which resulted have led to the jumbled but picturesque landscape of the town today.

The crowded conditions in which many of the inhabitants lived were inevitably unhealthy; there was no piped sewage disposal nor piped water. The livestock in the twice-weekly markets added to the problem. Plague was a recurrent hazard. The council paid attention to the problems of public health, and tried to enforce certain standards. Public order, too, was a concern of the council, especially as the number of poor people in the town grew at the time of the Civil War.

Tewkesbury's economic base continued to be mainly agricultural marketing and the provision of manufactured goods to the surrounding area. The population grew from between 1,500 and 2,000 in the mid-16th century to about 2,500 in the later 17th century. Many men were without a skill and so particularly subject to fluctuating employment, though overall the town became one of the most prosperous in Gloucestershire, overtaking Cirencester as the second town in the county.

Quite a lot of information about daily life can be drawn from the council record books. As well as major decisions concerning new public buildings or the repair of roads, bridges and the quay, the clerk also recorded comments on such matters as exceptional harvests and consequent high or low prices of food, and on outbreaks of plague. There are also several taxation lists. Another source of information which becomes more common towards the end of the 17th century is inventories. These are lists of householders' possessions made in connection with proving wills. Two or more local men of repute made the inventory room by room as they walked round the house, and these lists give us some knowledge of the life inside Tewkesbury's timber-framed houses. Inventories have survived mainly from 1660 and have been examined particularly for the years 1660-85.

Social Structure and Occupations
In the late 16th century, when Tewkesbury became a borough, its economy was

typical of small market towns throughout the country, with many craftsmen running small businesses and a few larger merchants. There was also a population of labourers, widows and poor folk whose numbers are difficult to estimate.

William Harrison, living in the peaceful security of a small Essex village rectory, wrote a *Description of England* in 1577, in which he divided the whole population into four categories. His analysis can be applied to the information about Tewkesbury drawn from the first freemen's register of 1575. At the apex of society were the noblemen and gentlemen. A gentleman was recognised by his style – he could 'live without manual labour, and thereto is able and will bear the port, charge and countenance of a gentleman' – in other words, provided he did not work with his hands, and that he dressed and lived like a gentleman, society accorded him this status. In Tewkesbury, only one gentleman was recorded as a freeman in 1575, though others certainly lived in the town, and sometimes gentlemen served as bailiffs and on the council. Secondly, Harrison placed the town merchants and burgesses, the class which obviously played the major political part in any borough. The 259 freemen of Tewkesbury, with their households of family, servants and apprentices, probably made up two-thirds of the town's population in the Elizabethan period. (In 1563 there were said to be 396 households.) Unusually, the freemen were a large proportion of Tewkesbury's inhabitants, showing it to be an 'open' town, not tightly controlled by its manorial lord. Thirdly, Harrison placed the rural yeomen (or prosperous farmers), and finally 'the fourth sort'. This last group was defined as having 'neither voice nor authority in the commonwealth, but are to be ruled and not to rule others'. Harrison said they were artificers and labourers. Although making up a third of the population of Tewkesbury, we rarely catch a glimpse of them in the standard records. They were beginning to crowd into the alleys and courts behind the main streets; to the council they were a 'rabble' which was sometimes threatening, as in 1673 when they prevented members reaching the town hall and the meeting had to be postponed.

Among the first freemen of 1575 there were eight mercers or merchants. Though few in number, the merchants were very important, linking the economy of the town with a much wider market than it would otherwise have served. The merchants bought and sold the cloth which was both made and finished in Tewkesbury. The most important merchant family in later 16th-century Tewkesbury had the unusual name of Geast. Giles Geast was a notable benefactor, who died in 1558, the year of Queen Elizabeth I's accession to the throne. In his will he described himself as a mercer, but he was also a clothier, who organised the actual production of cloth. His will referred to two big houses containing looms; tenants in some of his other smaller houses were clothworkers: a sherman (who sheared the cloth to finish off the nap evenly) and a weaver, and probably there were others. He had the authority by royal warrant to check that cloths made in Tewkesbury were of proper quality, and then to fix a seal to them to prove that they had been inspected and that the tax had been paid.

Giles Geast had benefited from the break-up of the Abbey estate, purchasing at least 11 of the Abbey cottages which backed onto the monastery wall. In his will he gave these and 11 other houses to a trust for the benefit of the poor. One of the trustees named in the will was John Geast, also a merchant, who died in 1561. The first trustees started the record book which was used for 300 years and in which a chronicle of Tewkesbury history was written in the 17th and 18th centuries. At the time his will was made, Giles

Geast was living near the Cross in Tewkesbury. His home might have been part of today's Cross House. Structurally this building seems to consist of three timber-framed units, and Giles Geast's will refers to the house in which he was living and two adjoining houses, all three left to his wife; also, the lane at the side of Cross House was once known as Geast Lane. The rest of his property was distributed among his four children. Giles Geast owned a total of 48 houses in Tewkesbury.

In 1575 three Geasts were freemen, two of them called Thomas. One Thomas, a merchant, was the first junior bailiff under the Elizabethan charter, and the other was a draper. In 1608 John Geast, mercer, headed the list of able-bodied men in Tewkesbury, and in 1648 his eldest son, another John, succeeded his father as a freeman, but after this there seems to be no other record of the family in the town.

The occupations of the first freemen tell us something about Tewkesbury's economy in 1575 and indicate a town of some individuality. Occupations are recorded for just over four-fifths of the 259 freemen. Of those not specified, some were perhaps gentlemen, unwilling to put down their status as though it were a trade; some were perhaps transient inhabitants, not known to the clerk, like the brothers John and Griffith, listed both as Price and Apprice.

Maltmakers, bakers, butchers and one fishmonger formed an important group supplying the townsfolk. Malting was a distinctive feature of the town, contributing significantly to its prosperity; at this date a specialism in textiles or leatherworking was more usual. There were 25 maltsters and only the shoemakers were more numerous. Barley for malting would have been grown on farms around Tewkesbury and some of the malt was used locally, in maltsters' own inns, and by households who brewed their own beer. Much of the malt was shipped from the quay to Bristol or to South Wales, and perhaps from Bristol it went to Ireland – seven freemen coopers supplied the barrels for this trade. Each maltster's business was probably quite small, and there are few traces of maltings today, though a small, partly timber-framed building dating probably to the 16th century can be seen on one side of the Old Baptist Chapel Court.

A third of the freemen whose occupations are known worked in the different branches of the textile trade. If we add the men engaged in leatherworking, mainly shoemaking, the proportion employed in providing clothing rises to half. A miscellany of trades and crafts supplied other requirements. There was a barber freeman, four carpenters, a slater, a millwright, a saddler, a painter, three smiths, a bowmaker and an arrowmaker. New freemen admitted during the reign of Elizabeth included bottlemakers, parchment-makers, an apothecary and a salter. The freemen were the employers; at this time their workshops were expanding down the long thin plots behind the smarter frontages of the main streets. Their apprentices and workmen are not known.

Some thirty years after the date when the first Tewkesbury freemen were admitted under the Elizabethan charter, there is a muster list of men and their occupations which covers the whole of Gloucestershire. Muster lists give the names of able-bodied men aged between 16 and 60 who could be called on for military service. Occupations were not normally recorded, but in this case they were, giving a more extensive indication of the trades and crafts in the town than the freemen's register and allowing a comparison to be made between Tewkesbury and its two rivals, Gloucester and Cirencester. The survival of this information is due to the special interest and 'delight' in his county's history taken by John Smith, steward of Berkeley Castle; it is preserved amongst his 24 volumes of papers, and has been printed as *Men and Armour for 1608*.

The list names 490 men in Gloucester, 455 in Tewkesbury and 349 in Cirencester. Cheltenham was comparatively small, with 164 men. At the beginning of James I's reign, therefore, Tewkesbury was the second largest town in Gloucestershire. In all three towns there were significant numbers employed in the textile and leather trades, and in food processing and retailing, generally confirming the typicality of the picture drawn from the Tewkesbury freemen's register.

Tewkesbury was less important in the weaving of cloth than in the various finishing processes, like shearing and dying. For this reason there was a merchant in the town, who had the right to seal cloth there, as Giles Geast had earlier, and a number of townsfolk were obviously manufacturing dye from woad. The 1609 by-laws forbade anyone to 'make, season or break any woad' if it caused annoyance to their neighbours. It was a smelly plant, as Celia Fiennes observed. She talked of woad cultivation round Toddington: 'the smell of the woad is so strong and offensive you can scarce bear it at the Mill: I could not force my horse near it'. The leaves were ground into paste which was then dried. There was also a large number of tailors in Tewkesbury making use of the finished fabric.

Tewkesbury's character as a port is also clear from the muster list, as 23 mariners and four trowmen were employed in the river transport. A mariner was not necessarily a simple sailor, as one mariner in 1608 was amongst the small number of wealthier citizens who had to pay the national tax called the subsidy. The road, too, was important. Tewkesbury had many innkeepers, tapsters, tipplers and vintners who catered for travellers as well as for the local inhabitants.

One striking aspect of Tewkesbury in 1608 is the large number of labourers, 83 in all, many more than in either of the other two main Gloucestershire towns. This needs explanation. The description 'labourer' was perhaps used more sparingly elsewhere, or perhaps Tewkesbury's prosperity attracted unskilled men looking for working opportunities. On the other hand, as a town without a strong resident lord, it may have been easy for poor folk to find a lodging in the alleys and courts.

New Trades

Judging from the freemen's register, the economic structure of the town did not alter very much in the 17th century. The food and leather trades remained the most important numerically. The main change was in the smaller numbers concerned with clothmaking which reflected a real decline in the trade. On the other hand, quite early in the 17th century, stocking manufacture was carried on in Tewkesbury, probably drawing upon unemployed but skilled textile workers, and this trade had become important to the town by 1700.

Queen Elizabeth I started the fashion for knitted stockings instead of cloth hose. Hose were breeches and stockings all sewn together. Production of knitted stockings was facilitated by William Lee's invention of a stocking frame or knitting machine, first made effective for wool and by 1599 for silk. Old-style hose disappeared and the word itself became simply an alternative to stockings. The new hosiers organised all the stages of manufacture in a similar way to the clothiers; they purchased the raw materials and often owned the frames on which the knitters worked.

The first hosier to become a freeman in Tewkesbury was John Sewell from Bisley in Gloucestershire, admitted in 1619. By 1634 William Crafte, hosier, was working in the town. His apprentice, Thomas Atkinson, was one of three Tewkesbury hosiers who issued tokens in the mid-17th century, the only hosiers known to have done so in the county. Tokens served locally instead of money; because of the unusual demand for pay for the soldiers, there was a great shortage of coin during and immediately after the Civil War. More tokens are known from Tewkesbury than from Cirencester or even Gloucester, reflecting the town's frequent military changes of fortune. Later in the century, several more hosiers became freemen, and stockings were shipped from Tewkesbury quay down the Severn to Bristol, and thence to Ireland and America. At this time, the stockings were made of wool worsted, grown and spun locally; a century later, when the trade was at its height, cotton was used.

During the 17th century some other new occupations of interest appear in Tewkesbury, though unlike the hosiery trade they did not involve many people. For example, two gunsmiths became freemen in 1647 and 1682; in 1608 an arrowmaker had still been working in the town. A bricklayer was admitted as a freemen in 1647, just at the time when brick was becoming a more usual building material, though still for chimneys rather than walls of houses; the brickworks at the Mythe existed by 1634. A 'brick chamber over the kitchen' in a Tewkesbury inventory of 1675 probably dates fairly closely the introduction of brick buildings in the town.

From 1636 there was also a retailer of tobacco in Tewkesbury. Tobacco was imported into England very early in the 17th century, and by 1619 it was being widely grown in north-east Gloucestershire. The government prohibited cultivation in England in order to protect the new Virginia trade, but once introduced it proved difficult to stamp out. Thomas Crumpe, a freeman, was given sole right to retail tobacco in Tewkesbury in 1636. His monopoly was not popular, especially when he tried to enforce it and prosecuted other dealers in the town. It was claimed that Virginian tobacco was 'basely and unwholesomely compounded' with the local product and with 'worse things', but even so local tobacco was popular because cheaper. Even the constable of the town bought it. By the end of the century, however, tobacco cultivation had died out in Gloucestershire, and tobacconists handled the American product alone.

Both the malt and the stocking trade of the town obviously depended on Tewkesbury's position as a port on the Severn. Until 1638 the quay served the whole vale of Evesham, as the Avon was not navigable above Tewkesbury haven. In that year, despite the opposition of towns along the Severn above Tewkesbury, William Sandys of Fladbury succeeded in making the Avon navigable as far as Evesham; a lock or 'double sluice' was constructed to link the Old Avon and the Mill Avon, thus enabling boats to pass the weir above King John's Bridge. This was a quite serious blow to Tewkesbury's trade: the council estimated in 1649 that they were losing £200 a year as a result. In compensation, when there were discussions about a new charter, Tewkesbury asked for the right to collect tolls from boats passing under their Avon bridge, like Gloucester at Over bridge. By 1672 the Avon was navigable as far as Stratford-upon-Avon, and boats of 30 tons could reach the quay there, near the present-day Memorial Theatre. The boats were hauled up the Avon by men, not by horses. Improvements to river navigations preceded the construction of canals, and showed the increasing pace of commerce in the mid-17th century.

Plague and the Poor

One of the underlying themes of life in this period for both rich and poor was the plague. It had been a recurrent danger ever since the first great outbreak in 1348-9, the Black Death, when probably a third of the population of the whole country died. Plague inspired understandable fear: there was no knowledge of how disease was carried, though gradually it was recognised that cleanliness was some protection. Tewkesbury experienced several attacks up to the mid-17th century, one very severe. Yet always the population was replenished, usually from those rural communities fortunate enough to escape a particular outbreak. The converse was also sometimes the case. In 1609 plague was in the neighbouring rural hamlets of Southwick, Tredington and Fiddington, but Tewkesbury was unaffected.

The town council tried to contain the disease. In 1578 and 1579 a policy of isolating the households where it appeared seemed successful; in six weeks in 1578, 30 people died, and when plague returned the following year another 10 died but no more. The clerk wrote 'by the diligence of the bailiffs shutting up the suspected houses God stayed the plague'. They were not successful next time. Plague raged in London in 1591, and in November 1592 it appeared in Barton Street, Tewkesbury, affecting one or two houses. Next April, 1593, an epidemic started. It lasted all summer and winter, only ceasing in April of the following year. The clerk recorded that 560 people died – a third of the town's population. For Tewkesbury the disaster was on the scale of the Black Death, and the burial registers were abandoned. The oldest burial register which survives dates from 1595.

It was no longer a case of shutting up individual houses – the whole of Tewkesbury was isolated. Inhabitants were barred from visiting other market towns, and but for money and provisions sent from neighbouring areas the death toll must have been worse. The justices of the peace required the whole county to contribute money to the town's relief. No markets or fairs were held until May 1594. By this time Gloucester was experiencing an epidemic. Only four years later plague returned again to Tewkesbury, killing 40 people. The 1590s were, indeed, a very bad time throughout the country.

Yet plague began to die out after 1600. The town clerk was aware of it in other towns, and in 1603-4 and 1624-5 wrote down the numbers of deaths suffered in Oxford and London. When plague reached Tewkesbury in 1624, the council combatted the disease with some success. Inhabitants were enjoined to keep their houses clean and to wash the streets with water twice a day. Victims were isolated in temporary houses built in the Oldbury. Children were forbidden to play in the streets 'in troupes' or to be out at all unless going to school – a rare reference to children, who must have been numerous. Strangers were not allowed on the streets and townsmen were not to provide lodging. Only 20 people died on this occasion, and it also seems to have been the last plague in the town. The efforts of the council to improve the cleanliness of the streets possibly contributed to its decline, but after the epidemic in London in 1665 plague gradually died out everywhere, retreating eastwards across Europe. The next epidemics in Tewkesbury were sore throats and fevers in 1729 and cholera in 1832.

Another theme in people's lives in this period was the fear of harvest-failure. The lives of the poor were always precarious; in bad times they became desperate, unable to pay the high prices consequent on a shortage of grain. Unrest amongst hungry folk strained the minimal machinery available for keeping the peace. As in other towns, the

Tewkesbury council attempted to regulate food supplies. In the first council by-laws, maltmaking was prohibited between the last day of May and the first day of September, the critical period when the old harvest was used up and the new harvest was not yet in, so that barley had to be used as well as wheat to make bread flour. In bad years the malt prohibition was extended, and offenders were fined. Freemen were also forbidden to hoard grain but were to bring their stock to market.

There were two particularly difficult periods in the late 16th century, in 1585-6 and 1596-7. In 1586 it was reported to the Privy Council that the poor 'weep and cry for corn openly in the markets, not able to buy above a peck or half a peck at once'. Not surprisingly, when they could see food being carried away from them, there was sometimes violence. A corn barge on the Severn, it was said, was attacked and rifled by men 'driven to feed their children with cats, dogs and the roots of nettles'. It was presumably to curb unrest that the council ordered the curfew bell to be rung at 8 p.m. in summertime as well as in winter, thus keeping folk off the streets at night. The 1590s were still worse, as the crisis was deepened by the outbreaks of plague. The Corporation of Gloucester went so far as to fix a chain across the river Severn to prevent ships from carrying corn past the town, but both Tewkesbury and Bristol complained about the interruption of trade and Gloucester was obliged to remove the chain.

Poverty was apparently increasing in the late 16th and early 17th centuries, and Tewkesbury was by no means unique in its efforts to control the problem. 'Nothing doth more tend to the ruin of the town or any other place than the increase of the poor', the council lamented. 'They bring great peril of fire and infection of the plague'. In 1623 the council noted that 'the poor of the town have lately greatly increased', and in 1630 it was said they numbered more than five hundred, or at least a third of the population. The poor were those whose earnings were often insufficient to maintain a family, and they needed occasional or regular help if they were to be clothed, fed and housed; they were never in a position to pay the town's taxes. Several Elizabethan Acts of Parliament required each parish to care for its own poor, and Tewkesbury churchwardens and overseers must have distributed relief both in money and in some of the practical necessities of life, as was customary, but no record remains of this work. The town had received a series of charitable bequests, most notably that by Giles Geast, and there was the very ancient charitable dole given to the 'Founder's Thirteen Almsmen' or 'Queen Mary's Almsmen', but these were relatively small amounts in relation to the numbers needing relief. The main burden therefore fell on the rate payers but the 'better sort' were no longer making their homes in the town, it was claimed in 1623.

The answer seemed to be to prevent poor from settling in the town. As early as 1577 there was a 'Beadle of Beggars', whose job was to move such folk on. He was ineffective because too many inhabitants were willing to give shelter to poor men and their families. Inhabitants were forbidden to take lodgers without the bailiffs' permission. Despite this, the council stated in 1623 that two or even three families were crowding into one room. It was decided that planning consent should be obtained from the bailiffs in future, as 'stables, barns, beast houses and pigsties' were being converted to habitations; occupants were dissolute and disorderly, and, it was suspected, had to pilfer and steal in order to pay their rents. The experience in the freezing winter of 1607, when 'no one could keep his trees and hedges from being cut by the poorer sort', was probably not unusual. To help in the apprehension of malefactors, townsmen were bidden in 1639 to keep ready a 'black bill, club or other weapon' in their shop, entry or alley, by day and night. Another stratagem to limit the population of poor was to require newcomers to find two sponsors who would guarantee to meet the cost of relief should it become needful. It was proposed to include a clause to this effect in the charter when it was being reconsidered in 1649.

Charles I and his government were held responsible for the economic difficulties of the time, for instance in the cloth trade, which certainly contributed to the growing problem of poverty and helped create the climate of disaffection before the Civil War. Events thereafter obviously exacerbated Tewkesbury's problems, 'a very great number of poor having crept into the town since the beginning of the war'. However, at the very end of the 17th century, the same complaints and remedies were being repeated.

The Streets

The streets in Elizabethan and Stuart times were not, as today, highways bordered by houses and shops, but were simply open spaces, used for all manner of different purposes, commercial and otherwise. On market days, they were filled with animals and traders. We know how the streets were used from the first by-laws of 1575, which regulated where the different markets were to be placed. Cattle, oxen and kine occupied all the upper end of High Street, between the *Black Bear* and Quay Lane, and sheep filled Church Street. The corn market was in the lower part of High Street, between Quay Lane and the Cross. Traders' horses were banned from this area; a prescribed scale of charges prevented innkeepers exploiting the need for stabling. New positions for hatters and cappers were now at the end of Barton Street, and next to them were coopers and Welsh traders. Tanners, iron men and ropers were allocated more space, and could trade from Barton Street through to Church Street. The positions of other markets, like country produce and butter, were not altered, and so not described, but the Buttermarket at the north end of the town and the Cross and Boothall in the centre obviously accommodated traders with smaller perishable goods for sale. Down the centres of the streets there were gutters which stall holders were ordered to keep free. Once a year, on St Bartholomew's Day, there was also a horse market in Lilleycroft, the area beyond King John's Bridge and the Stanchard Pit.

Animals obviously made the streets very dirty, but council regulations of the early 17th century were made to prevent Tewkesbury's inhabitants adding to the problem. Rubbish was not to be left in the streets. Butchers and fishmongers particularly were forbidden to throw out offensive waste. Pigs and sows were not to wander in the streets nor were dead dogs to be ignored. Householders were to use the ancient public refuse dump at the 'Pudding House' on the Avon, and rubbish was not to pile up in backyards. The council tried to encourage higher standards in other ways. Householders were required to maintain the paving in front of their houses, and clean their section of gutter and roadway. Builders and coopers alone were excepted from the ban on leaving materials on the pavements, and carts were not to be left in the streets at night. Because of a particularly notorious murder case which had recently gone to the Star Chamber Court in London, efforts were made to light the streets. Lanterns or candles were to burn between nightfall and 8 p.m. 'except in the time of the moon shining', through the dark months of November, December and January. After 8 p.m., of course, inhabitants were not supposed to be out on the streets at all. These by-laws were still

33. The Old Hat Shop was probably rebuilt in 1664 by Bartholomew Read, glover; the side alley was intensively developed by this date.

34. The Nodding Gables was the one picturesque property, according to North, which many did not want to see disappear; the key indicates an ironmonger's. It was adjacent to the former *White Hart*, now part of the *Swan*.

considered relevant at the end of the 17th century and were re-enacted when the new charter was obtained.

Many goods were displayed for sale on racks in front of the houses, even including foodstuffs. Several butchers were amongst those fined at the end of the 17th century for having their racks too far out in the street, or 'hanging too low, being thereby dangerous to people going along the streets'. Some tradesmen and shopkeepers built permanent stalls in the street in front of their houses. There were also shops in the front part of some of the houses, with living accommodation above. The decorative, wide bay windows which characterise a number of Tewkesbury's old houses were designed to light these principal rooms. An example is the old Hat Shop in Church Street; the bay windows on the first floor still contain the original glass, and the doorway below is dated 1664. Downstairs, on the street frontage, there was a glover's shop in 1685, equipped with chests of small drawers stocked with pairs of ready-made gloves. Another shop, which may have been in High Street, contained six dozen pairs of shoes – a small stock compared with today. It is rare, however, to penetrate into a 17th-century shop: inventories sometimes mention a counter or weights and scales, but usually leave us ignorant of the goods offered for sale.

High Street remained in the 17th century, as it had been in Leland's time, 'the chiefest street'. The relative wealth of the inhabitants of the three streets can be gauged from taxation lists. There were nearly as many taxpayers in High Street as in Church Street and Barton Street together, and also more paying at higher rates. The lower part of High Street, between the Cross and the *Swan*, contained more taxpayers than farther up, which is reflected today in the concentration of elaborate timber-framed houses on very narrow plots in this section of the street.

The tax lists give no indication of the population behind the main streets, in the alleys and courts. Customarily a front door onto the street made a person liable for rates and until the 18th century this was also a qualification for voting in parliamentary elections. The council had tried in 1649 to forbid the sub-letting of tenements unless they had doors opening on the street, in part because such inhabitants did not contribute to the town's revenue, though they might well draw relief because of poverty; it was also suggested that there should be no more than three families under one roof. About a third of the town's households did not pay rates.

The alleys, which are so characteristic of Tewkesbury, had started to develop before the mid-16th century. They occur in the 1540 survey of monastic property, and some of the surviving alleys contain 16th-century buildings, such as the Old Baptist Chapel. Double Alley, at the north end of High Street, notorious for the poverty and raucousness of its inhabitants in more recent times, was full of medieval buildings which were demolished and replaced by a new shopping development; as the name implies, the houses faced each other across a narrow passage way. The alleys were partly a response to the shortage of building land around the main streets, but partly they represent a method of making a small income for the property owner. Provided he could arrange access, rear buildings or part of his own house could be let out.

Bartholomew Read's will, made in 1681, provides an unusual insight into an alley off Church Street. The house fronting the street was lived in by the owner, his wife, and probably their four children. It consisted of a shop, two chambers, a cockloft and a cellar and was the most modern part of the property; Bartholomew Read had rebuilt

Facades in the High Street.

it in style in 1664, as we learn from the carved doorway at the side of the house. The
family also made use of the ground floor of the hall behind, which was part of an older
house on the site. The rest of this building and the series of structures which extended
down the plot were occupied by eight separate tenants. Two had more than one room,
the others occupied single tenements. At the rear of the plot there was a stable, also
let, a pigsty, limepit and court, and on the other side of Poulton's Lane a garden
reaching to the Avon and a workshop. At his death, the property was divided by
Bartholomew Read into three separate lots.

All the inhabitants of the alley had to share the one well and pump, and were
guaranteed access through the alley to the street. Wills, proved in 1743 and 1744, refer
to 'Mr. Read's alley' and confirm the continuance of the tenurial divisions of the
property. Today, though closed, the alley is named Bank Alley, referring to the bank
which at one time occupied the adjoining property (the word is carved over the front,
though somewhat obscured by a modern shop facade). The lane separating garden from
alley still exists, and a door at the rear of the Church Street plot made the necessary
communication.

There was some concentration of occupations in particular streets. In 1608 tailors were grouped in Church Street and maltsters in High Street, where there were some larger businesses located convenient to river and quay. A horsedrawn malt-mill in Quay Street, off High Street, in 1540 showed a substantial scale of business at that date, and a High Street maltster's inventory had the highest value in personal possessions of any in the period 1660 to 1685. Most of the mariners were in the same area. Some less common trades could be found in High Street, like pewterers, a stationer, cutlers and the only fishmonger. The more usual trades were scattered through all three streets: most numerous were carpenters, shoemakers, coopers, glovers and innkeepers.

The workshop of a skilled carpenter or joiner in Barton Street is described in the inventory of Thomas Pritchett, who died in 1678. Two joiners from a little farther along Barton Street listed and valued his tools, which in their number and variety show that several men or perhaps apprentices were employed. There were three vice benches, 61 curved ('bowen') planes and a number of other planes, 80 small cutting tools, 19 saws, 11 augers, five mallets, a lathe, gauges, compasses and squares, and in lesser quantities many other tools which could be found in a skilled carpenter's shop today. Amongst the items being made were beds, one a four-poster with a tester or wooden canopy, a round table, a livery cupboard (with a wooden grill to allow air to circulate like the example to be seen in the Little Museum), a screen and nine stools. In an upstairs room there were further items: a cradle, close stools, a mahogany table and a selection of ready-made coffins.

In each of Tewkesbury's three main streets there was one major inn: the *Swan* in High Street, the inn now called the *Royal Hop Pole Hotel* in Church Street and the *Star and Garter* in Barton Street. The *Star and Garter* could still be described as one of the three principal inns in the late 18th century, and the remains of a wooden gallery in the courtyard show it had been important in Tudor times, but it is no longer an inn today. An inventory of the possessions of Thomas Crumpe, made in 1664, almost certainly relates to the *Star and Garter*. It describes seven public rooms, various service rooms and a warehouse equipped with scales, where visiting salesmen possibly stored their wares. Several of the rooms had names, as was not uncommon at this period. Were there emblems painted on the doors to help illiterate travellers find their proper lodgings? Downstairs, the Spread Eagle contained a table and bench. Upstairs, the White Hart and the Crown chambers were the principal bedrooms, with four-poster beds and testers, cushions, and in the White Hart chamber leather chairs and 10 pictures. There were five other bedrooms, two parlours and a hall. One room was used for the gambling game of 'shuffleboard' or shove ha'penny. A cellar contained numerous empty barrels and 13 hogsheads of beer. Five pigs and four flitches of bacon contributed to feeding the guests.

Surprisingly Thomas Crumpe was not described as an innholder but as a carrier. It might be imagined that a carrier was a relatively poor man, making a living by delivering goods with his horse and cart. Thomas Crumpe's inventory shows that he was a carrier on a much larger scale: he had nine wagons and horses and five tons of hay to feed them. He was probably the same man as received the king's patent in 1636 to retail tobacco in Tewkesbury.

The inventory of Robert Lane, made in 1676, relates to an inn in Church Street, to be identified with another of the three principal inns, and now the northern part of the

Royal Hop Pole Hotel. Here there were 11 rooms altogether, and part of the building was three storeys high, including a 'room over the entry', which corresponds to the older part of the *Royal Hop Pole Hotel* today. The rooms did not apparently have names, and none were as grand as at the *Star and Garter*. Two other innholders' inventories, both made in 1685, describe rather smaller establishments; in one there was a 'shovel-board' room. Only one of these innkeepers had a store of hops to flavour his beer.

The Houses: Appearance, Design and Furnishing

In the three principal streets there are approximately a hundred timber-framed buildings from the 16th and 17th centuries, and this is counting only once structures which today are subdivided. These buildings can rarely be dated precisely, especially as certain styles of timber-framing persisted throughout the period. Features like the wide, flattened Tudor arch of some doorways can help in dating. There are two good examples close together in High Street: No. 12 (The Old Fleece, 1519) and No. 15 (The Ancient Grudge café) which has lively gilded dragons carved over the arch. Sometimes quite drastic alterations have been carried out in later years: for example, completely removing the front and replacing it with a new timber-framed structure or, more often, with brick. Less drastically, the front has often been covered with a brick or stucco facing; there are at least thirty timber-framed buildings hidden behind brick facades. Other alterations have included inserting floors to make two rooms where formerly there was only one; adding large bay windows which sometimes seem to be almost toppling the structure into the street; and adding further storeys and gables on top of the original structure. The Abbey Cottages are particularly noteworthy because the street frontage has been restored nearly to its original appearance.

Certain stylistic features of the timber-framing are common, particularly close-studding, in which upright timbers are placed very close together. This seems to have been the fashionable appearance of a Tewkesbury house of the 16th and 17th centuries. There is very little decorative timber-work such as may be found in some western counties. The Ancient Grudge in High Street is unique in the town in its flamboyant herring-bone studding. This is a very early example of a new front, built about 1500, on a structure some fifty years older; the bay windows in the first and second storeys were added in the 19th century. Close-studding was expensive, and the side panels of the houses were often constructed more economically of wide-spaced timbers.

Characteristic of many 16th- and 17th-century Tewkesbury houses is the jetty or overhang, sometimes to two storeys, each projecting farther than the last. The jetties are usually only on the front elevation. A few houses occupying corner sites, like the *Black Bear* at the top of High Street, No. 66 Church Street, on the corner of St Mary's Lane, and Nos. 1 and 2 Mill Bank, opposite the Abbey Mill, have jetties on both street frontages. To make the floor joists project on two sides, at right-angles to each other, posed the builder a technical problem, solved by using a diagonal 'dragon beam' into which the two sets of joists were jointed. At the corner of the building the dragon beam was supported with an ostentatious corner post, called a 'teazle post', which could be carved and moulded. This suggests that the jetty was as much a feature of fashionable prestige as it was useful, though it did have two effects: it helped to stiffen the floor joists and to keep rainwater away from the ground-floor frontage. Only one Tewkesbury house is known to have a jetty at the rear, No. 88 and 88a Church Street. As there were

35. The underbuilding of a jetty is very clear in this structure of c.1500 in Church Street; there are remains of intricate traceried windows on the first floor. Mrs Craik is reputed to have stayed in the right-hand house when she visited Tewkesbury.

36. Another timber-framed house in Barton Street has been completely encased in a new front.

generally no back lanes and the houses were already close together, owners saved the trouble of jettying both front and back. Tewkesbury examples of jetties extend in time from the 15th-century Abbey Cottages to the *Bell* of 1696.

With the general adoption of brick for house construction, and of gutters to take the rainwater from the roof,the jetty was unnecessary and also embarrassing evidence of the old-fashioned nature of the house. As a result, many were obscured, either by building completely new fronts or by underbuilding the ground floors to bring them flush with the first floors. Tell-tale signs of former jetties can often be seen. Good examples are at the House of the Nodding Gables in High Street (restored by the Halifax Building Society), and the *Berkeley Arms* and *Royal Hop Pole Hotel* in Church Street. In each of these cases the end joist and jetty support can be seen in the side wall. A drastic alteration which removed the posts underneath the jetty necessitated an

37. Over the door of the *Bell Hotel* is the date 1696 and the initials IK, perhaps those of Jacob Kingsbury, tailor and freeman of Tewkesbury.

38. *Tudor House Hotel* contains buildings of several different periods. The brick front was covered with imitation timber-framing in 1897. The gateway leads to an older building, once an open hall.

alternative means of support and cast iron columns were sometimes employed, as in the House of the Nodding Gables.

There is interesting written evidence from the late 17th century concerning the construction of new fronts onto Tewkesbury's old houses. Such fronts were necessarily built into the street. These encroachments, like the stalls in front of some houses, gave opportunity to the council to raise money by fining the householder concerned, for example for 'building the frame of his house farther out than he ought', or for 'setting the whole frame of his house too far out into the street beyond the old foundations'. These all seem to show that timber-framing was still being used. Other fines were for 'setting out the front of his house two feet further than formerly' or 'building the wall of his house out beyond the old front'. New fronts often disguised parts of a larger and older house which had been subdivided.

The fashion for brick fronts and for gutters with decorative rainwater heads is neatly epitomised in the *Tudor House Hotel* in High Street. The rainwater heads are dated 1701. The building is well-known because for a short while it was a noted Dissenters' Academy, which provided higher education for a number of men who were prevented from going to Oxford or Cambridge because they were not members of the Church of England. The house was still a school in the 19th century; a small girls' boarding school was recorded there in the 1841 and 1881 censuses. The *Tudor House Hotel* does not look as if it is brick-fronted; in late Victorian times mock timber-framing was applied. The former *Star and Garter Inn* in Barton Street, which has been restored and converted, has a brick building on the street with rainwater heads dated 1715. Brick fronts, or for that matter sides and backs too, were built around older structures all through the 18th and 19th centuries. Looking at the roof line will often reveal that this has happened.

Old-fashioned timber-framing could be obscured with stucco or plaster. Cross House was pargetted in 1693 and the date incorporated in the design. The plaster was stripped off again in a Victorian restoration. Clarence House (140 High Street) was expensively coated, presumably at the same time as the rather top-heavy fourth storey was added. Many timber-framed houses are covered with stucco as a weather-proofing measure, but some were intended from the first to be treated in this way.

A number of Tewkesbury's timber-framed houses have been altered by the addition of an extra storey or by converting lofts. Clarence House and the Wheatsheaf in High Street are examples of an extra storey added to the structure. The House of the Nodding Gables was also raised one storey, but the twin gables were not soundly constructed; subsequently they tipped forward so much that they were in danger of collapse.

House Plans

Surviving buildings from the Tudor period suggest that at this date the larger houses were often arranged in an L shape: one range fronting the street was of two or more storeys, and often contained shop or workshop; behind, at right-angles to the street, was the main living room, called the 'hall', with other domestic and industrial accommodation. An alternative arrangement was to have the hall opening onto the street and a two-storey cross wing at the side stretching down the plot; this arrangement may have been favoured by those wanting a purely domestic residence.

A house on the first plan seems to be described in one of the very few inventories surviving from the Tudor period, made on the death in 1587 of Thomas Underhill, a

39. Tradition states that the Duke of Clarence stayed in Clarence House, which is 15th-century, though the top storey was altered in the 17th century and it has a Victorian shop front.

40. The early Victorian front of Auriol House records a date found inside. The padlock on the nearer house proclaims Haywards' ironmonger's business, established 1820.

prosperous baker and freeman. The two- or three-storey part of the house fronting the street contained bedrooms with a cockloft used for storage. Also in the front there was a shop and tavern, where there were five cheese vats and four gallons of butter. At this period a tavern was usually in a cellar, and was reached by stairs from the street, as is implied in a by-law of 1609 which required 'sufficient doors, gate or grate' to be set at the head of the stairs by cellar- or tavern-keepers. Stretching down the plot, in addition to the hall, was a servant's room, kitchen, parlour and a 'new room' over the parlour, malthouse, flour store, bakehouse and slaughterhouse. Beyond these there was a yard, stable and garden.

This property may possibly be identified with the house in High Street now called the Wheatsheaf. Carved into the typical flat arch of a Tudor archway at the front of the

Wheatsheaf are the initials IV, which could be John Underhill's initials. John Underhill had been apprenticed to Thomas Underhill, his uncle, whose inventory has been described, and he inherited the baker's business. He became a freeman in 1588, and was junior bailiff of Tewkesbury in 1614. The Wheatsheaf was built about 1500, but has been given an elaborate new front associated with the carved doorway. It is recorded as a public house in the mid-18th century and behind the adjoining property there is a bakehouse. Opposite the Wheatsheaf is the Ancient Grudge, with the initials RB over the fireplace. It is an interesting coincidence that Richard Bradford was twice bailiff of Tewkesbury between 1610 and 1616, and with John Underhill was a signatory to the sale of the Severn Ham to William Ferrers. Was there a little rivalry between the two men?

Smaller houses contained simply a hall and side passageway, with one room or chamber over the passageway and over part of the hall. This design utilised all possible space while leaving a part of the hall open to the roof, which was necessary because there was no chimney. The smoke from the fire on the open hearth found its way out through the roof but must often have filled the hall. The upstairs room was reached by a ladder. The Abbey Cottages were built on this plan; extensions were sometimes to accommodate a staircase. The modern usage of the word 'hall' has derived from the medieval and post-medieval arrangement whereby the entrance to the house was into the main room which in turn gave access to the other rooms.

By 1600 brick chimneys were becoming common and were being inserted into existing houses. William Harrison, writing in 1577, said that the improvement had taken place within his lifetime. The addition of chimneys to the Abbey Cottages can be clearly seen from the Abbey precincts. At the Ancient Grudge, the stone Tudor-arched fireplace, which contains RB's initials, was built at the time the chimney was inserted. The inventory of John Arpen, a bottlemaker, who died in 1622, contains an unusual reference to 'his inglenook' which contained two benches.

Chimneys must have been usual in Tewkesbury by the beginning of the 17th century. In a town crammed with timber buildings, new by-laws were particularly designed to minimise the danger of fire: householders were required not to set fire deliberately to their chimneys to clean them; thatch was not to be used near any chimney or oast, nor straw laid in front of houses; chimneys were not even to be built near stables and barns. Such regulations were not uncommon in towns; however, Tewkesbury was fortunate in escaping a major fire.

Once a chimney had been built, an upstairs floor could be inserted into the open hall, even if there was not much headroom either upstairs or downstairs. The upstairs rooms were also ceiled, so that the roof timbers, soot-blackened from the fire on the open hearth, were hidden in the loft. The shop called Petal in High Street clearly shows today the dimensions of the former hall. The floor joists when inserted were jettied; in later times the posts supporting the floor and jetty were removed and a new front constructed. In Nos. 15-16 Church Street, the upstairs rooms have never been ceiled.

The visitor has a good example of a 16th-century hall house in the Old Baptist Chapel, where neither chimney nor floor has been inserted into the open hall. When first used as a chapel, probably in the 1650s (the burial ground is dated 1655), the pulpit was built in the hall with a gallery on either side where there had been an upstairs room. About 1720 the roof was altered; the tie beams were removed and the present barrel-shaped plaster ceiling was constructed. Although elegant, it was structurally a mistake, and iron rods had to be inserted to hold the roof together.

A larger timber-framed house, reconstructed in the mid-17th century, can also be visited at the Museum in Barton Street. Its plan of a central hallway with rooms containing fireplaces on either side, though unusual, seems to derive from the same design as the Old Baptist Chapel. The railings in front of the house are a unique survival of what was once a common feature of Tewkesbury town houses. A number of householders were fined for having 'pales' in the street in 1698, which kept drays at a minimum distance.

The brick chimney made it easier to provide fireplaces in upstairs rooms, and large houses obviously had more chimneys than small ones. Consequently in 1662 parliament agreed to a tax which made the occupier pay two shillings 'for every fire-hearth and stove'. The tax had the advantage of being easy to assess and of making the rich pay more. It was difficult to conceal a chimney, and indeed the tax-collectors were known as 'chimney men'. Householders who did not pay local church and poor rates, or whose possessions, house or land were of very small value, were exempt.

The Hearth Tax list for Tewkesbury for 1671 shows 460 separate households. Very nearly half were assessed at one hearth only. A third of the households were excused payment. Less than a third, or 129 houses, had three or more hearths. The largest house had 12 hearths; there were no mansions in Tewkesbury. The Hearth Tax lists more households than the town's rates of the Civil War period, but it does not seem to include the occupants of Bartholomew Read's alley. Read himself is listed, assessed for two hearths, which were in his two principal chambers. Did the occupants of the tenements in the alley not have fires? One of the tenements contained a furnace, belonging to Bartholomew Read, perhaps a closed stove of some sort; similar arrangements may have existed in other small tenements. It seems likely that tenants in the alleys were not counted as proper 'households' and so were omitted from the Hearth Tax.

Twenty-four inventories survive for Tewkesbury inhabitants who died between 1660 and 1685. Some of these can be collated with the Hearth Tax list. The size of houses described in the inventories ranges from the two rooms of Robert Mopp, labourer, with one hearth, to the 16 rooms of the *Star and Garter* inn in Barton Street with five hearths. The inn in Church Street had 11 rooms and six hearths, and these two inns were the largest houses detailed in the inventories. The most comfortable houses were not those with most rooms but with most hearths, like the 10 rooms and 10 hearths of William Wakeman, gentleman, on the Mythe, or the six rooms and six hearths of John Higgens, freeman and maltster, in High Street. The house of John Higgens, who died in 1662, represents the standard of the more comfortable Tewkesbury inhabitant. Downstairs were the kitchen, parlour and hall, and upstairs a great chamber over the hall, a green chamber (all the furnishings in the room were green) and a chamber over the kitchen. The description seems to reflect a house like the Old Baptist Chapel in design; a similar house was occupied by a Major Nanfan, with four hearths. This was probably a fairly common design of house in 17th-century Tewkesbury.

Furnishings

The interiors of Tewkesbury's 17th-century houses would seem to us very bare indeed, and those of a century earlier still more sparse. Yet, during Elizabeth's reign, William Harrison had noted definite changes in standards of comfort. Pillows, he said, had been substituted for good, round wooden logs, and pewter for wooden plates. Thomas Underhill's inventory illustrates the standard of one of Tewkesbury's more prosperous inhabitants in the Elizabethan period. There were no carpets, very few soft furnishings of any kind except on the beds, no window-curtains or upholstered chairs – indeed, very few chairs of any sort. Benches and forms were the usual seats. Trestle tables, coffers and chests, and a few cupboards were the main items of furniture. There were beds in nearly all the rooms, one a four-poster with a wooden canopy or tester; at least there were pillows on every bed.

A hundred years later, the better-off had more material possessions. Jointed furniture instead of simple chunks of wood is commonly listed in the inventories, and there are more chairs, tables and cupboards. Cushions often softened the wooden seats, and occasionally there are window-curtains mentioned, as in Widow Clarke's new brick room over the kitchen. Window-curtains were only then being introduced. The inn in Church Street had both curtains and carpets from Kidderminster. The better standard of living is illustrated in the furnishings of John Higgens' house. He had a clock, a map in one bedroom, numbers of tables and chairs, pots and pans, and plenty of linen and soft furnishings. With his stock of malt, he had the highest value in personal possessions of those whose inventories have survived from this period. Even so, his wealth did not compare with that of some of Gloucestershire's clothiers, nor with the general level of personal estate in the county town itself. Major Nanfan, who had the status of gentleman, had his pistols and carbine, holsters, buffcoat and sword as evidence of his occupation. He also had plenty of furniture and a horse and saddles. William Wakeman's gentlemanly status was defined by his rapier, and he had books in his study, a pair of virginals, and a carved cabinet. Unusually, his house contained a dining-room.

For poorer folk there was little difference in the standard of furnishings from the 16th to the 18th century, as there were few possessions of any sort in their houses. Items of linen and tableware and cooking vessels were so precious they were specially bequeathed in wills, and best and second-best carefully allocated. Clothes, too, were bequeathed in wills.

The two-roomed house on the Millbank owned by Robert Mopp contained a minimum of comfort at the time of his death in 1663. His appraisers described 'the lower room being his hall and kitchen' and 'the chamber above where he died'. In the downstairs room there was a table and three stools, some pots, a pair of bellows to blow up the fire; upstairs a bed, two pairs of sheets, a piece of hempen cloth enough to make two shirts, a stone jug and pail, a lantern, two wooden coffers and a trunk. His best suit of clothes, of two coats, a doublet and pair, hose and best waistcoat, he willed to his younger brother.

Social Relationships

Some of the ways in which family problems were met are found in this sample of wills and inventories. When Thomas Crumpe died, for example, he made a condition of the inheritance that the eldest son should care for his mother and the younger children. Sometimes the widow had part of the family house reserved to her use. Thomas Underhill gave his nephew a joint share in his house and business so long as his wife was alive, but specified that she should have the parlour and nearer part of the garden to herself. Some such arrangement perhaps underlies the situation of a widow who had considerable resources in linen and jewellery all packed away in boxes. Her stylish furniture (a pair of virginals, books, silk and turkey-work cushions) was all evidence that she was not poor. Yet, despite owning other houses in Tewkesbury, she was living in two rooms which she did not own. In this respect, inventories may mislead, especially as they do not cover rooms and items specifically willed, like Thomas Underhill's parlour.

By no means all of those making wills owned their own homes, though they might have owned property elsewhere in the town. The income from such property was a form of insurance or pension. Thomas Crumpe did not own the inn in Barton Street but did own the house next door which was rented out. None of the innkeepers in fact owned his premises; even at this date it seems inns were owned by larger businessmen, like the village inn at Oxenton owned by the maltster John Higgens in 1662 and the *New Inn* in Tewkesbury owned by the chandler John Jeynes in 1706. Probably the more splendid timber-framed houses were owner-occupied, like Bartholomew Read's, and he too owned tenements elsewhere. Most of the poorer inhabitants rented their homes; the labourer Robert Mopp was unusual in owning his small Millbank cottage.

The social relationships of the town are interestingly illuminated by the comparison of Hearth Tax and wills and inventories. Together they point to the reality of Harrison's divisions of society. The political community comprised those liable to pay taxes, who made wills, acted for each other as trustees and appraisers and who served as officers of the town. These men belonged in the upper three classes of society as defined by Harrison. The names of those excused from payment of the Hearth Tax do not occur in these contexts. They were the fourth sort who 'had no voice' in the commonwealth. In effect it was a two-class society, and continued so to be into the 19th century. The significance of the change in political attitudes implied in widening the parliamentary franchise is seen more vividly when placed against the division of society in Tudor and Stuart times. Tewkesbury participated quite strongly in the movement for political change in the late 18th and early 19th centuries, which was in turn partly the result of changes in economic organisation. These developments in the town's life will be examined in the next chapter.

Chapter 6

Travellers and Turnpikes: 1700-1840

Defoe's account of his travels in Gloucestershire was published in 1724. Gloucester he described as 'an ancient middling city' and Tewkesbury as 'a large and very populous town situate upon the River Avon'. He noted also that Tewkesbury 'is famous for a great manufacture of stockings, as are also, the towns of Pershore and Evesham, or Esham; on the same river'. His enthusiasm was more stirred by the 'fruitful and plentiful country' of the Vale of Evesham, and by the trade of the River Avon:

> The navigation of this River Avon is an exceeding advantage to all this part of the country, and also to the commerce of the city of Bristol. For by this river they drive a very great trade for sugar, oil, wine, tobacco, iron, lead, and in a word, all heavy goods which are carried by water almost as far as Warwick; and in return the corn and especially the cheese, is brought back from Gloucestershire and Warwickshire, to Bristol.

The most attractive features of the countryside around Tewkesbury as Defoe described it were the orchards, commented on also by a number of other travellers:

> From Tewkesbury we went north 12 miles, to Worcester, all the way still on the bank of the Severn; and here we had the pleasing sight of the hedge-rows, being filled with apple trees and pear trees, and the fruit so common, that any passenger as they travel the road may gather and eat what they please; and here, as well as in Gloucestershire, you meet with cider in the public-houses sold as beer and ale is in other parts of England, and as cheap.

Defoe's *Tour through the whole island of Great Britain* was not the first traveller's gazetteer, but it marks the increasing interest in this genre of writing. In the same year as Defoe's account was published, the first Turnpike Act was passed for the improvement of the roads radiating from Tewkesbury. A number of author-travellers passed through Tewkesbury in the next 100 years, a period which was the golden age of the stage-coach. George III was a famous visitor, coming several times in 1788, while he was staying in Cheltenham. Dickens brought Mr. Pickwick on his fictional travels to dine at the *Royal Hop Pole Hotel*, though by 1836-7, when *Pickwick Papers* was published, the age of the stage-coach was nearly finished, ended by the railway.

As well as published accounts of journeys, the 18th century was also the first for a number of notable county histories. Atkins' history of Gloucestershire was published in 1712, and in 1781 Rudder expanded the work, drawing on information supplied by 'the gentlemen in every parish' in answer to a questionnaire. The first guidebook and brief history of Tewkesbury appeared in 1790, through the enterprise of a local printer, W.Dyde, who was rewarded with the freedom of the town. Before this date there was a church guide, though it was described as 'meagre'. Bennett's *History of Tewkesbury* (1830) owed quite a lot to Dyde. Directories are a further addition to the published material available from the late 18th century; they often contained short histories as well as lists of major tradesmen and the gentry of each place.

With the 19th century, Tewkesbury entered a different world, industrial and full of bustling collectors of statistics, in which its position as one of the foremost towns in

Gloucestershire was steadily eroded. Although Cobbett, who also came here on his travels, could still say in 1826 that Tewkesbury was 'a good substantial town', he saw it just as its prosperity was about to decline. Its most prosperous time was before 1820, when framework knitting employed the poor, and the inns and markets provided for, as well as reflected, the prosperity of the commercial classes.

The population of Tewkesbury was twice counted by local officials during the 18th century: in 1723 it was 2,866 and in 1791 it had increased to 3,768. The first national census in 1801 returned 4,199, an underestimate because the inhabitants of the Mythe were counted with Twyning. The census marks the 19th century right from its start as a century of statistics; consequently, much more systematic information is available. The town records also became increasingly voluminous from the later 18th century, not just through the accident of survival but because of the greater amount of formal organisation which was developing. For example, civic enterprise was redefined through private Acts of Parliament creating bodies such as Paving Commissioners, though to the 20th-century reader of the minutes it seems regrettable that enterprise resulted in demolition of some of the town's historic buildings.

An unusual source of information about 19th-century Tewkesbury also exists in the notebooks of the auctioneering firm of Moore and Sons. John Moore, the 20th-century author, was a descendant of this Tewkesbury auctioneering family, and he too entered the family firm in 1923. In *Portrait of Elmbury* he described the premises, 46 High Street, whose window until recently had engraved on it 'Moore and Sons, Established 1751, Auction and Estate Offices':

> The walls of this office – and indeed of every room in the building – were lined with books: books in red morocco bindings, several thousand of them, which contained the 'Particulars of Sale' of every property that had passed through the firm's hands – almost every dwelling-house, in fact, every farm, smallholding, shop, pub, orchard and meadow within six miles of Elmbury.

The notebooks, which start in 1800, have been deposited in Gloucester Record Office. They contain many details of the goods and chattels of Tewkesbury inhabitants.

Letters written by Mary Yorke from Forthampton Court between 1762 and 1823 are a lively addition to the sources of information for this period. Mary Yorke was a keen and able correspondent; during her life she wrote over a thousand letters to the Marchioness de Grey and her two daughters. A selection of those concerning the Tewkesbury area appeared in a series of newspaper articles in the *Tewkesbury Register* in 1950-2 but, apart from this, are unpublished. Forthampton Court was her own house, left her by her father. Her husband, one of the sons of the 1st Earl of Hardwicke, became Bishop of Ely. They came to Forthampton for holidays, and then when she was widowed she lived there permanently until her death in 1823. Her letters give immediate and characterful descriptions of some local affairs.

George III in Tewkesbury

George III's visit to Tewkesbury in July 1788 is known both from the brief mention in Fanny Burney's diary and from the account in Dyde's guidebook of 1790. Bennett published some extracts from Fanny Burney's diary in his *Yearly Register and Magazine* for 1842; he also drew information from local journals. The king had decided to spend some time in Cheltenham drinking the waters, in the hope of finding a cure for the illness which finally incapacitated him and led, for the last eight years of his life, to his son acting as Regent. From Cheltenham the royal party visited Tewkesbury. The king rode on horseback, the ladies in carriages. The townsfolk greeted him enthusiastically; the Geast Charity chronicle recorded how 'people of the lower class expressed their joy by loud acclamations'. The *Gentleman's Magazine* recorded that they dressed themselves in their Sunday suits. The royal party visited the Tute and the abbey. A second visit was made when the king was on his way to Croome to be entertained by Lord Coventry, who was High Steward of Tewkesbury. This time a triumphal arch of flowers and evergreens was erected over High Street near the *Swan*. On four other occasions the king came through Tewkesbury, and impressed all with his amiability.

41. A good view of the Tute is obtained from the Mythe Bridge; the name is derived from the Old English word for a 'look-out'. After George III's visit, it was often called 'Royal Hill'. The approach is from the Worcester road.

42. The bridge was opened in 1826. It is a good example of Telford's ironwork.

Mary Yorke's accounts of the visits are more personal. Two letters give the details; in one, we have a glimpse of George and his queen struggling enthusiastically up the Mythe Tute. There is also a typical story of the king's interest in farming; he was called 'Farmer George' and his model farm at Windsor encouraged new ideas in farming practice.

18 July 1788

When my Friends used to receive Letters from this sequestered Spot, they could flatter themselves with the hopes of hearing nothing more than that we were well, had a Good Journey, found the Hay nearly got in, or perhaps half-drowned, and that the Apple Trees bore a promising appearance; but now, situated as we are in the Neighbourhood of Royalty, and under the Eye as it were of majesty, the news from Forthampton may have a St James Air with it – As for instance Yesterday the King, Queen and Princesses arrived at Tewkesbury about one o'clock his Majesty on Horse back, the Queen and Princesses in two Coaches. They proceeded slowly up the *Town* (which fortunately now is in great order, being just new paved and lighted by the Act) and viewed the Church etc.; *fame* said they were to dine at Forthampton Court today but fame is a Liar.

14 August 1788

Our very *great* Neighbour leaves us on Saturday; his condescension and affability have endeared him to all Ranks in this neighbourhood. The Papers so faithfully detail all and indeed more than all relating to him of any consequence, that nothing is left for me to tell you unless you will accept of some trifling rural anecdotes that are probably local . . . the King was so charmed with the view from the red cliff that he would make the Queen etc. come and see it. They both fell on their hands scrambling up, but Steps were cut for their return. When at the Top his Majesty said 'The Bishop of Ely has a House some where here, show it to me'. The Trees that shade us from view were pointed out, but as he could not see the House he only added 'Where? What? What?' and so we have escaped without further honour.

The farming story was given to Mary Yorke by one of her tenants. The king went to see sheep and purchase a horse. The horse, he said, was

too Dear for *him*, it might do for some Lords and Dukes – the Sheep were too large, he wanted little Sheep. . . .

On riding off after this Conversation he seemed rather at a loss about the Road. The Farmer kindly said 'Shall one of my Fellows show your Majesty the way?'

The king gave a guinea to the Butcher's Boy who 'kept off the Mob with an oaken stick'; to the man 'that keeps the Gate to the drive down to our house from the Turnpike road', who had presented the queen with a posy of flowers, a similar reward was given, 'which in the joy of his heart he brought immediately to our House to show, being a nice, new Guinea'.

Cheltenham's rise as a fashionable spa town owed much to George III's stay there, and for a while Tewkesbury thought it could perhaps emulate its successful neighbour. Similar mineral water flowed out of the ground a mile out of the town on the south side of the Ashchurch road. Hopefully, Richard Smithsend, the owner of the land, built a house called Walton Spa. Dyde's guidebook in 1790 contained extracts from the technical description of the waters by a doctor from Worcester, published three years before.

The venture did not prosper, though Bennett said in 1830 that the pump in the house yard was 'much frequented' and Walton Spa was included on the first Ordnance Survey map. In 1837 a new 'pump house' was built on the north side of the turnpike road. Lewis's *Topographical Dictionary* of 1842 mentioned the waters, but no great surge of visitors came. Some Cheltenham businessmen ensured this by buying out their potential rival. The spa building was demolished in 1961 and houses built on the site.

Turnpikes

Travellers complained as much about the state of the roads as about the weather in 18th-century England, yet from early in the century there had been quite energetic attempts to improve the condition of the main roads. In Gloucestershire the road from the county town to the top of Birdlip was the first to be covered by a private Act of Parliament, passed in 1698, which set up a Trust to organise repairs, the cost being defrayed from tolls paid by road users. This was only the third such Turnpike Act in the country. The turnpike itself was a barrier set with spikes which prevented travellers avoiding the toll-collector. Then in 1726 there was quite a flurry of activity in Gloucestershire, with Turnpike Trust Acts covering a number of the main roads from Gloucester, Tewkesbury and Cheltenham, and, a year later, the roads in the Bristol area.

For the next hundred years, a great number of roads were improved and repaired by the Turnpike Trusts. To some of the humbler road users the tolls were most unwelcome and gates were destroyed and toll-collectors attacked; in 1734 some men were hanged at Gloucester for destroying turnpikes near Tewkesbury. The protests were unavailing. The Turnpike Acts gave the Trusts powers over roads passing through several parishes, thus suspending normal parish responsibilities, and also gave the Trusts larger financial resources than parishes were permitted to raise by local rates. They were thus a useful mechanism to match the increasing scale of travel.

The battle to secure an Act to turnpike the roads round Tewkesbury had started in 1721. The initial impetus came from those wishing to improve the road to the top of Stanway Hill, which was 'the great road to London'. The petition said that the roads 'are so very bad in Winter-time, that they are almost impassable, and enough to stifle Man and Horse; and that Waggons cannot travel through the said roads in the Sumertime'. It was quite often alleged that horses could drown in the mud of the roads.

The attempt to secure an Act in 1721 failed, but in 1726 a second and successful attempt was made, despite some local opposition. Richard Dowdeswell of Forthampton, a Member of Parliament for Tewkesbury, was afraid turnpike tolls would make travellers less willing to pay the toll on his ferry at the Lower Lode. He perhaps knew that a new route between Gloucester and Tewkesbury was planned, which would result in the disuse of the Lower Way which brought travellers past his ferry. Other opposition came from users of the Bredon to Tewkesbury road, which they said was already 'a good hard way'. They accused Tewkesbury of trying to pass on the financial burden of roads which benefited the town. In practice the Bill had wide support, and as well as Tewkesbury council a number of peers and gentry were named as Trustees.

It is interesting to note how many elm trees were markers in the Act's descriptions of roads to be turnpiked: for example, Isabel's elm in Ashchurch, Oxenton elm, Woolstone elm and Piffs elm. Elms were notable landmarks in the countryside; Isaac Taylor's map of Gloucestershire published in 1777 shows a number. An elm in Southwick, when it was blown down in 1780, was recorded in the Geast Charity book, and was stated to be 90 feet high; it had been named the 'Tulip Tree'. Although the trees have disappeared, the names often survive. For example, Isabel's elm is marked today by a house called 'The Elms' at a crossroads in Ashchurch, and Piff's Elm is named on a public house at a road junction near Coombe Hill.

The first Tewkesbury Turnpike Trust was probably responsible for some alterations in the routes of the ancient ways to Tewkesbury, though no record of its work exists, and the story has to be pieced together. Part of the road northwards, for example, seems to have been re-routed up Mythe Hill, where a cutting was made, instead of passing round the Tute close to the Severn. When Ogilby published his pioneering set of road maps in 1675, which covers the whole country, he described the road north towards Worcester as keeping close to the Severn; this route must have been affected by the crumbling of the Tute's red marl cliff, as the footpath is today. The disused section of road was closed in 1825, though the council preserved the 'right of footway'. From the top of Mythe Hill, the new road passed down Paget's Lane and resumed its course near the Severn. In 1756 it was said by a witness to the committee considering a new Tewkesbury Turnpike Bill that a lane over Shuthonger Common was only used when the lower road was flooded; this lane was in turn turnpiked and later straightened to give the modern road line.

The road from Tewkesbury to Gloucester was also altered by the first Turnpike Trust. Ogilby showed a route through Tredington and Deerhurst Walton. As far as Tredington, the road followed closely the line of the Swilgate, as the other road followed the Severn. It was a natural route linking the dependent chapelry at Tredington with the mother church at Tewkesbury, and part is the parish boundary between the two places. Taylor's map of 1777 showed a new route to the west. Traces of the old road close to the Swilgate were still evident in 1825 on the large-scale map of Tewkesbury drawn by Croome, and a footpath marks its course on the 1982 Ordnance Survey (1:25,000 sheet SO 83/93).

The Ogilby map suggests that even before 1675 the alternative Lower Way from Tewkesbury to Gloucester, close to the Severn, was not the most usual route. Though it was included in the first Tewkesbury Turnpike Act, and in subsequent Acts until 1818, it never attracted much of the Trustees' attention. It was described as 'a bridleway only' and 'generally overflowed' in 1756, but still provides a pleasant riverside walk to Deerhurst.

The first Tewkesbury Act expired in 1747 after 21 years, the usual term for Turnpike Trusts, leaving the roads round Tewkesbury in a far from satisfactory state. The town's two Members of Parliament were elected in 1754 on the strength of their offers to donate very large sums to road improvement, a precedent some of their successors were also required to follow. In 1756 a new Tewkesbury Turnpike Trust was set up, and the very next day gates were erected across the roads. From this time, the Trust was not allowed to lapse until its final end in 1872, and a number of Acts of Parliament were consequently passed to continue and to extend its powers. Each Act increased the number of roads to be turnpiked; the Tewkesbury Trust also interlocked with the Cheltenham and Gloucester Trusts, so that by the early 19th century the area had a considerable network of turnpike roads. Not all have survived, but many form the basis of the present road system. One which has become disused, for example, went from Tewkesbury to Gotherington and then over Cleeve Common to Whittington, and was turnpiked in 1794.

The second Trust improved the bridges on the roads into Tewkesbury, which were obviously not appropriate to the increasing quality of the roads. In 1757 the Swilgate bridge carrying the Gloucester road, the Carrant bridge carrying the Bredon road, and

Salendine's Bridge carrying the Ashchurch road were all raised and widened, together with Salendine's Causeway. King John's Bridge was not repaired until 1810.

A new section of the Gloucester road was authorised in the 1794 Act, by-passing Deerhurst Walton and following a more direct line from the Hoo Lane to Walton Hill. Another section of the modern road was constructed in the early 19th century, cutting diagonally through the Gaston field, where once the Battle of Tewkesbury had been fought, and so removing two right-angled bends on the approach to Tewkesbury. As a result, the modern road runs to the east instead of to the west of Gupshill House, which presents its back to today's traveller. The original carved tudor entrance is on the west side of the house. A second edition of Taylor's map, published in 1800, does not show this new road, but a printed version, two inches to the mile, of the first Ordnance Survey (surveyed in 1811-17) shows both the new and the old roads. By the time Croome made his map in 1825, the old road had largely been absorbed into the surrounding fields, though traces are still to be found at the back of Gupshill and in footpaths.

In the 19th century the Turnpike Trust was active in further widening and straightening the roads around Tewkesbury, and also in reducing gradients on the two hills north and south of the town by cuttings. On the Mythe Hill this involved making a second and more substantial cutting. The old roadway, where subsequently a Roman Catholic church was built (now converted to a house), was closed in 1827 and a new footpath to the Tute was opened. The earth from the Mythe cutting was used to raise the causeway to King John's Bridge. It was substantial even before this, as an account of an accident given in the *Gloucester Journal* reveals:

14 March 1774

> Edward Vickers, who distributes this Paper, through Worcester and Bromsgrove, on his return on Thursday was by the violence of the wind blown horse and all from the high causeway, between Tewkesbury and the Mythe, into the flood; his horse swam with him for a quarter of an hour, and just as the poor beast was exhausted, a boat most providentially came and saved both the man and his horse. Our thanks are particularly due on this occasion to William Buckle, Esq. of the Mythe, for his great humanity to the poor man.

Widening the bridges on the approach roads to Tewkesbury had to be tackled again, to modernise them in step with the continuing road improvement. King John's Bridge was only 12 feet at its narrowest; it was widened in 1836 to 21 feet with iron brackets and plates cast at Coalbrookdale.

Bennett boasted in 1830 that the roads in the area were 'unrivalled', and he attributed their quality to the use of local pebbles mixed with Bristol stone, which was carried up the Severn to Tewkesbury quay. By this date, the traffic was no longer mainly animals and farm produce coming to market, quay or mill, but post-coaches and mail-coaches passing through the town. In 1760, three times as much money was collected in tolls at the Barton Street gate as at any other of the gates, showing why the original impetus to turnpiking had concerned this road; in 1829 the largest revenue was collected on the road north from Mythe Hill, and nearly as much on the Gloucester and Cheltenham road to the south.

Modern road-widening has obliterated many of the characteristic markers of the turnpike roads, the toll-houses and the milestones. All the roads into Tewkesbury were turnpiked and gated; on the Worcester road there was a gate near the *Black Bear* at the top of High Street closing-off King John's Bridge, in addition to one on Mythe Hill. Three toll-houses may still be seen but all are early 19th century. One is on the approach road to the Telford bridge over the Severn; one is in Barton Street by the junction with Chance Street; one is opposite the former hospital and workhouse on Holm Hill, but the earlier house was at the junction of the Lower Lode and Gloucester roads, collecting tolls from both. A carrier of letters lived in the old toll-house in 1841. It stood in an area of Tewkesbury known as the Hermitage, perpetuating one of the boundary marks in the first charter of 1575. Today, the Hermitage is a pleasantly landscaped area on the Gloucester side of the Lower Lode Lane. A few milestones may be seen: two are on the Worcester road, and another is close to Tewkesbury along the Ashchurch road. There is a particularly fine milestone in Bredon near the tithe barn.

The efforts of the Turnpike Trustees did not concern the minor roads, which remained their local parish's responsibility, but their example made the state of the minor roads unacceptable. In 1792 a 'road club' was formed in the Tewkesbury area, with the purpose of instructing the parish surveyors and compelling the parishes to mend their roads. It must have had some effect. Bennett reported as very surprising the fact that some fifty years earlier farmers in the neighbourhood of Bishops Cleeve and Gotherington had had to bring corn to Tewkesbury market on the backs of pack-horses – 'their roads being wholly impassable with waggons or carts'. The experience of road engineering was a useful precursor to the much more extensive civil engineering of the railways, which in the 1840s suddenly destroyed much of the posting business. The Turnpike Trusts had made a revolution in road transport, though on nothing like the scale that the use of tar and construction of motorways has produced in the 20th century.

Stages and Posting Houses

As a result of the improvements by the Turnpike Trusts, journey times were considerably reduced. Carriers between Tewkesbury, Oxford and London could advertise in 1777, perhaps somewhat optimistically, their 'flying waggons'. 'The flying Stage Waggon will not be so long on the Road by two days as the old Stage Waggon'. Setting off from the *Maidenhead Inn* in Tewkesbury early every Monday morning, the wagon arrived in London on Thursday morning. Coaches could go much faster and accomplished the journey to London in a day. It was no longer necessary for advertisements to carry a warning, after the destinations and journey times had been stated: 'Performed, with good, able Horses (if God permit)', as John Restell, of Tewkesbury's *Pack Horse Inn*, had declared in 1745. The amount of travel greatly increased throughout the country during the 18th century, encouraging the government in 1779 to impose a tax on post-horses and carriages.

By the early 19th century it was possible to discuss alternative routes for the journey from Oxford to Forthampton, for which Mary Yorke seems usually to have allowed more than a day:

> From Oxford you come to Witney (10 miles) to the inn called *Staples Hall*, kept by Coburn; from Witney to the *King's Head*, Northleach (16 miles). These are both good inns. From Northleach to Cheltenham (12 miles), where there are two inns. I usually go to the *Plough*. From Cheltenham to the *Swan*, Tewkesbury (10 miles). But the best way will be to take the horses from that place to Forthampton Court (2 miles), and when I know nearly your time of being there, I will send my carriage to meet you at the waterside, that you may not be delayed by waiting for your own to be brought over. If you dislike crossing the river, you must then go round by Gloucester (7 miles) but the drive is not unpretty.
>
> There is another road from Oxford which I like better, through Stow-in-the-Wold. The roads are

43. The toll-house, of unusual design, is believed to be contemporary with the Mythe Bridge.

44. After the bridge was opened, the Upper Lode ferry was disused; the *Dowdeswell Arms* or ferry-house was left isolated when the lock was built and the Severn diverted to a new channel. The old river course is still visible in the foreground of this photograph.

less rough, and it is more dressed with gentlemen's seats near Chipping Norton. The stages are as follows: Oxford, to the *White Hart*, Chipping Norton, a good inn (18 miles); from Chipping Norton to the *Unicorn*, a neat inn with good rooms, Stow (8 miles), where the horses will take you on to Forthampton (21 miles). This road Lady Somers recommended to me and says it is two miles shorter. The only objection is the length of the last stage, 20 miles to Tewkesbury.

She went on to discuss alternatives from Witney, saying that a route through Burford might be preferred 'in order to divide the number of miles more equally'.

In summer Mary Yorke wrote of travelling to Forthampton 'in one continued cloud of dust' but on another occasion she makes the reader feel the desolate wetness of her journey from Oxford, undertaken when she was 76 years old. The meadows round Oxford were flooded: 'As we arose a little from this scene and up into the Cotswolds, the poor sheep on the hills appeared unable to support the weight of their own fleeces, so loaded as they were with water. It continued to rain incessantly the whole day'. She did not like the look of the inn at Northleach so continued on in the rain to Cheltenham. There she decided not to go via Gloucester and stay the night but 'desiring to get home, I courageously resolved to cross the Severn at my own ferry, the mildness of the air making me less afraid of suffering than the sharp north-east winds of the week before would have done'. Her ferry was the Lower Lode at Tewkesbury. Her father had bought Forthampton Court and its ferry from the Dowdeswell family who had owned it at the time the first Tewkesbury Turnpike Act was passed.

From Tewkesbury in the early 19th century coaches, wagons and carts travelled to London and to all the more important west country towns. Gell and Bradshaw's *Directory* of 1820 provided a timetable. Three times a week a London coach stopped in the town, and also one from Shrewsbury. Coaches linking Birmingham, Malvern and Worcester to Gloucester, Bath and Bristol went through every day. There was also a daily service to Cheltenham, which was an indication of that town's growing importance; ten years earlier there had been no connection, ten years later there were ten coaches a day.

Mail-coaches changed horses in Tewkesbury, and a light mail-cart arrived at 11 in the morning from Cheltenham, bringing letters from Oxford and London. From Worcester the post arrived at 11 at night. The Gloucester and Bristol mail-coaches clattered into the town at two in the morning. By 1830, altogether more than thirty coaches passed through Tewkesbury every day. Their names conjure up images of this period before railway and motor car supplanted the colourful but élite horse-drawn services: the *Sovereign*, the *Telegraph*, the *Duke of Wellington*, *Hero*, *Traveller*, *Mercury*, *Hibernia*.

Wagons and carts also linked Tewkesbury with London and with Birmingham, Bristol, Worcester, Cheltenham, Stow, Evesham, Pershore, Gloucester and with nearby Kemerton. The particular service to Kemerton was perhaps the result of a business connection: one of the hosiery manufacturers lived there.

The two major posting houses in the 19th century were the *Swan* and the *Hop Pole*. By this date the *Star and Garter* was no longer in business; by 1805 its once busy carriageway led to the Baptist chapel erected in its grounds. Post-houses were where travellers regularly broke their journeys, and hired a fresh set of horses and often the carriage, too, to take them on the next stage. In 1812 when the landlord of the *Swan* changed, there were five new post-chaises and 23 horses in the stables. At the *Hop Pole* in 1816 there were four chaises, one coach and 10 horses. There was a difference in the character of the trade at these two inns. The *Hop Pole* was the regular stop for the London coach and for most of the Bath coaches. It was mainly an eating place although it had seven bedrooms. The *Swan's* business was with the mail-coaches and it was Tewkesbury's main hotel with 15 bedrooms in 1812. George III had taken breakfast there with Lord Harrington in 1788. Mary Yorke always used the *Swan*, but regretted that the windows had no shutters.

The comforts available for guests at the *Swan* were a marked advance on those in the inns described in the 17th-century inventories. The *Swan* was rebuilt in brick about 1730; it was not as large then as now because another small inn called the *White Hart*, next door, was sold with the *Swan* in 1807 and was subsequently incorporated. Even so, there were 25 rooms as well as numerous outbuildings. All 15 guests' bedrooms had four-poster beds, floor carpet or bedside rugs, chairs (some described as easy chairs), wash-stands, dressing-tables, stoves, and locks on the doors. There were two dining-rooms and two bars, a parlour and a 'travellers' room' which was furnished like a café today, with numerous tables and chairs. Draughts, dice and cards were amongst the guests' means of whiling time away. Some guests had a private room for the evening; the travellers' room was a general sitting-room, as is illustrated in Mr. Pickwick's stay in Bristol:

> 'Shall I order a private room, sir?' inquired Sam, when they reached the *Bush*.
> 'Why, no, Sam', replied Mr. Pickwick; 'as I dined in the coffee room, and shall go to bed soon, it is hardly worth while. See who there is in the travellers' room, Sam'.
> Mr. Weller departed on his errand, and presently returned to say, that there was only a gentleman with one eye; and that he and the landlord were drinking a bowl of bishop together.
> 'I will join them', said Mr. Pickwick.

The *Swan* had enormous quantities of cutlery, china and earthenware (250 table plates and 110 white china plates, for example), egg-cups, vegetable dishes, teapots, salad bowls and glasses including jelly and custard glasses. There were large quantities of linen, too. It seems quite modern to find glass-cloths, roller towels and table-cloths amongst the stock. No wonder there were lots of ironing-boards in all the service rooms. Visitors dined well: in the bar there were fruit baskets, jars of sweetmeats and jars of pickles; in the cellar, more than fifty gallons of sherry and quantities of madeira, port, claret, gin, rum, brandy, French, shrub (a mixture of fruit juice and rum) and various cordials like peppermint, cinnamon and raspberry. In the yard there were two sets of pigeon-holes complete with pigeons.

The fictional Mr. Pickwick stopped at the *Hop Pole* on his journey from Bristol to Birmingham, a distance of 106½ miles as Mr. Pickwick reckoned. Bob Sawyer was anxious to eat after only 19 miles had been accomplished and consequently lunch was taken at the *Bell* at Berkeley Heath at 11 o'clock; here the 'case-bottle' was replenished with a substitute for milk punch, to be drunk while travelling.

> At the *Hop Pole* at Tewkesbury, they stopped to dine; upon which occasion there was more bottled ale, with some more Madeira, and some Port besides; and here the case-bottle was replenished for the fourth time. Under the influence of these combined stimulants, Mr. Pickwick and Mr. Ben Allen fell fast asleep for thirty miles, while Bob and Mr. Weller sang duets in the dickey.

The party could have dined off rabbit pie. In 1816 there were 26 white rabbits in the yard, and in the cellar at the *Hop Pole* a stock of 1,000 gallons of beer, and cider and spirits, too, in smaller quantities.

Travellers calling at the *Bell* at that date found the liquor was not of a high standard (the ale was 'very bad' and the sherry only 'supposed sherry'), but in the bar and Large Parlour there was a tempting array of foodstuffs: Knowles essence, Anchovy essence, nutmeg, jars with sweetmeats, jelly, pickled cabbage, pickled cucumber, pickled onions, pickled walnuts, bottles of gooseberries and blancmanges. In the garden and bowling green, for which the *Bell* was famous, they could take their ease on the garden seats, play with the stock of 49 bowls, and drink ale, cider or porter from the bowling green cellar. The townsfolk of Tewkesbury also spent summer evenings thus pleasantly engaged.

Severn and Avon

Communication with Tewkesbury by water continued to be important at this period. On the Avon, disputes over the rates of toll led to a regulating Act of Parliament in 1751. Cargoes of wine and cider and other 'merchants' goods' paid at the heaviest rate, followed by all types of agricultural produce; cheaper rates were fixed for iron, brick, stone, lime, wood and coal. In 1800 and after, trows went regularly from Tewkesbury to Evesham and Stratford.

The Severn remained a free river and agreement to improve the navigation was not secured until 1842. In 1800 'market boats' were arranged to take shoppers and traders to Gloucester and Worcester, and to bring them to Tewkesbury. When Lady de Grey left after a visit to Mary Yorke, 'she went in a barge from Forthampton to Tewkesbury, with very extraordinary companions, market women with baskets full of cackling ducks, other women and men and children, and – to complete the chorus – a jackass!' By 1820 links with London could be made by water, using a trow which went on Fridays to Worcester, where a connection with Pickford's canal boats was made. The trow was an almost flat-bottomed sailing barge of up to as much as 80 tons displacement, which carried an enormous sail on an 80-foot mast. It could only pass the shallows of the Upper Lode and reach Bristol when a spring tide or flood water was flowing. The Upper Lode lock was not built until 1858.

On rare occasions the Severn was frozen: for example in 1740, when at the Lower Lode pack-horses crossed on the ice for some weeks, and at the Upper Lode the ice was broken to allow a boat to pass. Several wagons loaded with coal were drawn over the Severn and a sheep was roasted on the ice of the Mill Avon above the Quay bridge. There was some very cold weather in January 1814, when Mary Yorke wrote from Forthampton describing her outings:

> I do not shut myself up, but walk or drive every Day – and on Thursday last was tempted by some of my Neighbours to cross the Severn on *Foot*. It has been for some time compleatly Frozen, and I understand is become the fashionable Promenade for the Tewkesbury Ladies (and by the by of the Forthampton ones likewise). The Day was fine and the Scene gay and cheerfull in the *Dutch Style* to which I thought an Old Woman with her Jack-Ass and Paniers contributed not a little. The Severn being so much within its Banks makes it warmer and more sheltered than the *Road* which is too cold to tempt me to another excursion of the same kind . . .

At the other extreme, in circumstances of exceptional drought, it was possible for the Severn to be forded at the Lower Lode, as in August 1835.

The river Severn was a barrier as well as a means of communication. Until the 19th century there was no bridge between Gloucester and Upton-on-Severn 20 miles upstream. There were two ancient crossing points at Tewkesbury but both were relatively minor: one took travellers to Forthampton Court, the other to Pull Court;

thence journeys could be continued to Ledbury. The two Tewkesbury ferries were not as hazardous as those crossing the mouth of the Severn below Gloucester, but they nonetheless had their perils. One of Mary Yorke's letters describes a near-fatal accident in January (?1817):

> I dressed my Haunch [of venison] of Twelfth Day and invited my Neighbours to it; but instead of being a Day of rejoicing it nearly proved to some of my Party – a Day of *Mourning*. Poor Mr. Broome went that morning to Tewkesbury; at that time the Severn had flooded the Ham, and he was obliged to *Boat* all the way to the Town from my Ferry. On his return the Wind rose and the Waves run high; himself and some other Gentlemen got into the usual Ferry Boat with three men to Navigate, but when got half over, they discovered that the Master was in Liquor and confused – yet so obstinate that he would *Guide*. They were carried above Mr. Dowdeswell's Ferry, and just at the passing of the junction of the Avon and the Severn where the water is very deep, the Waves dashed them against a Tree! All agree this must have sunk the Boat but for a providential circumstance. It was a Willow Tree, and the Branches hung down and received the Shock, the Stream at the same time carrying them on till they got to a Bank near the Bee hive where they were landed.

The 'Beehive' was a thatched summer-house about half a mile from Forthampton Court on Cork's Hill, built by Mary Yorke's husband:

> It commands an extensive and beautiful prospect, and a good view of Tewkesbury, which is about a mile distant . . . The Severn winds sweetly through the valley, and a number of small vessels are continually passing, and are a very great addition to the beauty of the scene. A view down the Vale of Evesham completes the landscape.

So wrote a visitor to Forthampton Court, Mrs. Mary Morgan, in 1791. Dyde used the view from the Beehive as the frontispiece to his guide, and the hill above the Upper Lode provides the walker still with a wide view of Tewkesbury.

Naturally there was discussion about the possibility of a bridge, but the expense and difficulty of the project deterred action. It was canvassed in 1816 and again in 1818, perhaps stimulated by the knowledge of achievements a little farther north. In Shropshire, Thomas Telford had bridged the Severn at Montford as early as 1792, and in 1815, after a number of years of canal, road and bridge building in Scotland and abroad, Telford had been appointed to improve the road from London to Holyhead, whence communication to Ireland was made. Also, a number of iron bridges had recently been built, the most ambitious up to this time being Telford's bridge at Craigellachie in Scotland, built in 1815, which made bridging the Severn at Tewkesbury look more feasible.

Telford was not initially involved in the Tewkesbury bridge scheme. Another notable engineer, John Rennie, first gave advice. Mary Yorke sets the scene:

> 5 August 1818
>
> A little controversy where the Bridge is to be erected upon my Estate will do no harm – *I* say it shall be at my Ferry – the Tewkesbury [People] wish to place it a little below my Bee hive, nearer Mr. Dowdeswell's Ferry. Lord Somers and Mr. Smirk come to the next meeting tomorrow Fortnight, and I hope will be on my side – for I dont intend to *give way*. Your Ladyship shall hear the result. I am to be paid for my Ferry, and the Lands the Turnpike Road is to go through. If it was to go over at the spot the Tewkesbury People wish it to do – they must raise a high Causeway across the Meadow called the Ham, which would cost them £4,900!

John Rennie came from London to consider the site, and his opinion was a compromise between the two possibilities discussed by Mary Yorke. He thought an arched causeway over the Ham should be built, the Severn to be bridged halfway between the sites of the two ferries; a new connecting bridge over the Mill Avon would carry the road out at the south end of Church Street where traces of the old abbey wall exist next to the houses of Gloucester Row. Despite his opinion, for the moment the proposal died. It had some interesting features: for example, providing a by-pass to King John's Bridge, and, if the main weight of traffic were from the south, a by-pass to the town itself. Bennett was of the opinion that it would have been a less expensive project than the bridge finally embarked upon in 1823.

Mary Yorke wrote later in 1818:

> Nothing more is said about the bridge at present, but my neighbour, General Dowdeswell, a very reserved man, who keeps no sort of company, is alarmed at the thought of a bridge between himself and his constituents at Tewkesbury. If it were built, they might be coming to see him at any hour and in all sorts of ways – horse, foot or chaise – and drunk or sober. In short, he hears of it with terror!

The Tewkesbury Severn Bridge and Roads Turnpike Trust was set up by Act of Parliament in 1823, and work started in June. Mary Yorke's family watched the ceremony of laying the foundation stone from the opposite bank. The engineer and architect was George Moneypenny, who selected the site near Mythe Hill where the bridge is today. Local supporters subscribed £18,600, the two Tewkesbury members of parliament contributing £1,000 each. General Dowdeswell of Pull Court, the brother of the M.P., whose Upper Lode ferry was bought out for £1,650, contributed £500 despite his earlier terror at the prospect of a bridge.

The Trustees quickly lost faith in Moneypenny, suspecting that the foundations of the bridge were inadequate. In December 1823, Thomas Telford was appointed. Although engaged in his most daring project, the suspension bridge over the Menai Straits (1818-26), Telford came to Tewkesbury. He inspected the site chosen by Moneypenny, found it 'judiciously selected', and within three months submitted a new design for a bridge with one cast-iron span of 170 feet in place of the previous scheme for three arches. It cost the Trustees damages for their rejection of Moneypenny, despite Telford's criticism of the feasibility of building two piers in the river. The selected site still involved building an embankment, this time across the meadows on the west side of the Severn to link the bridge with the turnpike road, instead of Rennie's route across the Ham.

Although Telford said his single-span structure could be built for the same price as the original design, it soon became evident that the costs of the scheme had been very much underestimated, possibly through Telford taking over some of the original engineer's work. In 1825 a further £16,000 was required, and a new Act of Parliament was necessary; meantime, Thomas Taylor, Esq., of the Mythe advanced the whole amount on the promise that his debt would have 'priority of claim' over the first subscribers. Unhappily, as Bennett hinted, the tolls did not prove adequate to pay even the interest, and other Turnpike Trusts refused to subsidise the bridge by amalgamating with it. In 1850 arrears had to be written off and the rate of interest reduced to enable the Trustees to begin to pay back the second loan. It ceased to be a toll-bridge in 1891 and was transferred to Gloucestershire and Worcestershire County Councils jointly. Out of the £35,000 which the bridge and all associated road-works cost, £5,500 was spent on procuring Acts of Parliament. The ironwork, cast by William Hazledine of Shropshire with whom Telford had worked for many years, cost £4,540. Moneypenny received £750 and Telford £250. While the Mythe bridge was under construction,

Telford advised against the construction of a bridge to replace the Haw ferry a little lower down the river, intended to carry a new road from Cheltenham to Hereford; the bridge was built and opened in 1825, but not the new road. Telford also designed Over Bridge at Gloucester, completed the same year. Mythe Bridge was opened in 1826.

Mythe Bridge can be seen particularly well from the former highway which skirts the Tute or from the Tute itself. Telford himself wrote a description of the bridge in 1828 for Bennett's *History of Tewkesbury*. The ironwork consists of six main cast-iron ribs

The Mythe Bridge.

which support the 'lozenge pillars' carrying the road. Telford used this design again in Galton Bridge at Smethwick in 1829. The masonry abutments at each side are a special feature of the Mythe design:

> The masonry is carried up solid to three feet above the level of the springing of the great arch; at this height is introduced a series of open arches, in place of having solid masonry. I was led to this from having observed, in all the other cast-iron bridges, constructed under my direction, that the great mass of solid masonry in the wings did not accord well with the openness of the iron-work; these arches are also of use when the floods rise more than three feet above the springing; and as this is the first instance in which this mode has been adopted, as well as some other improvements, I reckon this the handsomest bridge which has been built under my direction.

Coming at the end of his notable civil engineering career, in which he had earned from Southey the names 'Colossus of Roads' and 'pontifex maximus', and then aged over seventy, this is a remarkable judgement. A modern biographer echoes his view of the Mythe bridge, suggesting it stands with Bonar (1812) (no longer existing) and Craigellachie (1815) in Scotland as the example of his mastery of cast-iron construction. With the abbey, it is Tewkesbury's special inheritance.

Paving the Town

The town was 'in great order, being just new paved and lighted by the Act', Mary Yorke said in her letter describing George III's visit to Tewkesbury. The Act for 'paving, repairing, cleaning, lighting and watching the streets, lanes, ways, passages and places within the town of Tewkesbury' was passed in 1786; 18 months of energetic work followed before George III's visit.

The preamble to the Act said that Tewkesbury was a 'large and populous market town on the great road from Holyhead, Chester, Shrewsbury and Worcester to Gloucester, Bath, Bristol etc.'. One of the contexts to the Act was the great improvements made to the roads around Tewkesbury by the Turnpike Trust, while the roads in the town itself continued to deteriorate under the pressure of heavy-laden wagons and flying coaches. The preamble also spoke of the need to regulate the traffic. A general Act of Parliament in 1753 had attempted to limit the weight carried and to control the width of wagon wheels, since it was generally agreed that wider wheels did less damage to the road. Tewkesbury council had been ineffective in enforcing restrictions, and in despair had even attempted to forbid local hauliers employing wheeled vehicles at all, which apparently were replacing the older dray sledges. The Paving Act contained clauses requiring wheels or runners to be flat, with no protruding nails, rivets or stubs. There were also clauses 'limiting the weight to be drawn on wagons and other carriages within the said town of Tewkesbury and the precincts thereof'. A copy of these clauses was immediately despatched to the owner of the Birmingham to Bristol broad-wheel stage wagon. There was authority, too, to set up a weighing machine.

A further motive for the Paving Act was a desire amongst the townsmen to modernise Tewkesbury. They wished to pave, clean and light the streets, widen Church Street, and remove all sorts of obstructions. In the concern for the cleanliness and appearance of the streets, Tewkesbury was one amongst a number of modernising towns at this date, but well ahead of the nationwide campaign in the 19th century.

The initiative to improve and modernise the town did not come from the council, though they agreed to support the scheme. The bailiffs had been asked by a number of 'Principal Housekeepers' to convene a public meeting to consider applying for a private Act of Parliament. The meeting, held at the Tolsey in July 1785, was 'numerous and very respectable', and had determined unanimously to proceed. A committee was formed, which kept in close touch with the council through its chairman who was the town clerk. The council instructed him to safeguard its rights. In the Act, 64 commissioners were named to implement it; all the town dignitaries were included, as well as a large number of other inhabitants.

The Act certainly gave the commissioners more specific powers than the council had, but the main reason for setting up this special body was probably to delegate work to a group of keen townsmen while retaining to the council its overall authority and status. Twenty-five men initially took part in the Pavement Commission meetings, of whom only five were councillors. In widening the circle of those administering the town's

45. The first two houses in Barton Street replaced the 'half-burgage near the Toll Booth' given to the town in 1562 by Margaret Hicks.

46. After the demolition of Tolsey and Boothall, a new town hall was built. The Corn Exchange facade in front is one of the town's few 19th-century stone buildings. Next to it is a modern copy of Tudor style.

affairs, the Pavement Commission could include dissenters; they were excluded from offices of all sorts by 17th-century legislation which required subscription to the Church of England. The oath which the Paving Act required was not so restrictive, and there was also provision for Quakers to affirm, rather than swear. Four men took advantage of this. There was a property qualification for commissioners – an income of £30 a year or personal estate of £600 – so the circle was still tightly circumscribed.

The Paving Commission set to work immediately. The three principal streets were to be re-surfaced and the pavements re-laid. The footpaths had last been paved 50 years before. The question of drainage was considered:

> A deep and muddy gutter formerly ran down the centre of each street, and lesser ones, from the several lanes and alleys, united with it; these were considered so dangerous, that poor persons regularly stationed themselves at the several entrances into the town, and obtained a livelihood by leading the horses of travellers from one end to the other.

The commission resolved very early on to camber the streets, or make them 'rounded or barrelled'. It must have involved covering over the central drain; iron gratings were ordered from a local ironmonger, Mrs. Mary Webb and Co. Gutters or culverts at the side of the pavements were not introduced until 1826.

Orders were quickly issued to improve the cleanliness of the streets. There are reflections of 17th-century council ordinances in the orders forbidding inhabitants to throw rubbish into the streets, into the rivers or onto the river banks; butchers, it seemed, still offended by displaying meat in the open and by slaughtering in the public ways. The commission ordered several 'noisome and offensive' pigsties to be removed from the side streets and they rented a field in the Oldbury for depositing soil and dirt. Householders were obliged by the Act to clean the street in front of their houses on Saturdays – or to pay for the task to be done.

A very determined effort was made to remove all sorts of objects which protruded into the streets:

> Signs or other Emblems used to denote the Trade or Occupation or Calling of any person or persons, and all Sign posts and Sign Irons, Penthouses, Bow windows or projecting Windows, Shew Boards, Stalls Windows Shutters and Flaps, Porches, Shops, Sheds, Bulks and Gallowses, Blocks or pieces of Timber, Posts, Rails and all other Encroachments Projections Nuisances or Annoyances whatsoever

– all were required to be removed if they projected more than eight inches (20 cm) from the street frontage. The owner of the house on the corner of Church Street and St Mary's Lane, occupied by William Turner, schoolmaster, the father of the great landscape painter, had to take down the front and rebuild it to first-floor level, providing a rounded corner at the same time. Numerous attempts had to be made to secure compliance with this part of the Act. It must have provided some stimulus to the insertion of new, larger shop windows in the fronts of the houses – quite a number described as 'early Victorian' in style still exist – and to the re-fronting of the houses in brick which is common at this period.

Another requirement was for rainwater to be taken from the roofs into gutters and down-spouts, and thence into drains, rather than onto the pavements. The commissioners had to get legal support for their power to command house-owners to do the necessary work and to remove projecting roof tiles which shot the water into the street. When they met with refusals, they employed a man to do the work. The Paving Act gave the commission strong powers over property owners.

It was common practice to accept information about infringements of regulations or about nuisances from 'informers' or 'spies'. These members of the public could receive half the fine imposed on the offender. Generally the responsibility for checking that the commissioners' orders were carried out rested with the surveyor. John Millard was discharged from the office in 1792 'he having refused to make such Information against Nuisances as the Duty of his office requires'. The task could have been embarrassing in many ways.

The costs were borne partly by ratepayers generally – the Paving Commission had powers to collect rates – and partly by householders. The contractor was paid by each occupier as soon as the pavement in front of the house was laid; the maintenance of that section of pavement was a traditional obligation on occupiers of front houses. The local Members of Parliament contributed also with large donations.

A certain amount of difficulty was experienced over workmanship and materials. A London surveyor prepared the initial plan, which was regarded with great respect, but local contractors did not carry it out accurately, even though 'proper masons, paviours and workmen' were employed. 'The Office of Surveyor of the Streets and the Works . . . requires a person of Skill and Ability and one who from Experience is perfectly acquainted with the nature of that Business'. Handy Edgecombe, the joiner and carpenter who built the new town hall, was found an inadequate supervisor; his successor, an engineer from Bristol, was no more effective, 'refusing or neglecting to give proper directions to the workmen'. The stonemason from Worcester did not personally supervise his workmen either, and his presence had to be required in Tewkesbury. Complaint was made that not enough men were working to get the job done. Lamps had to be provided where the work was proceeding to prevent accidents at night. Twice, some of the work had to be redone: first 'a great part of the Foot Pavement which is now done is improperly laid and not agreeable to the plan' (October 1786) and then 'the workmanship in paving the said Streets hath been ill-done' (July 1787).

It was difficult to find the right materials. Welsh pebbles had to be rejected because too expensive. The commissioners searched widely for supplies, and also advertised. Some material was extracted from the local rivers; some was obtained from Stourport, and stone from Hanham near Bristol was also used. Some forty years later the road stone was considered too large, and it was taken up and sold to the Turnpike Trustees; at that time the camber, too, was reduced.

The most dramatic effect of all this activity was the widening of both ends of Church Street. At the south or abbey end of the street, five houses were compulsorily purchased and demolished, as authorised by the Act. The entrance to the town from the Gloucester direction was thus opened out, whereas previously the line of the Abbey Cottages used to continue on the farther side of the bell tower (where the National School now stands). At the north end of Church Street, the Tolsey and the Boothall were demolished. To 18th-century eyes, educated in the new technique of building in brick, these timber-framed buildings looked very old-fashioned and mean. They occupied the junction of the three streets and were 'so situated as to render the passage for carriages from Church Street into High Street very inconvenient, and sometimes dangerous'. The passage was, indeed, only 8 feet (2.4 metres), at the widest, and was even narrower on the Barton Street side.

These historic buildings had been under threat some fifteen years earlier, when discussions had started about building a new and more convenient town hall in their place. They were reprieved because the council purchased a site in High Street but did not have the money to continue the work. The Paving Commissioners asked for permission to demolish only the Boothall, now divided into two cottages, in order to facilitate the paving of the town. This was agreed in June 1787, on the assurance that the Tolsey would not be affected. September 1787: it was reported that the Tolsey was now unsafe. The materials salvaged fetched £60. Dyde observed with satisfaction that 'the space on which they stood now forms a noble opening and adds greatly to the beauty of the Streets'. He was equally convinced of the benefits of the Paving Act generally, saying that it 'has infused a spirit of improvement into the inhabitants which is constantly displaying itself more and more'.

Not everyone shared his optimism. The Geast chronicler noted somewhat grimly that, even after a flood in 1770 which had covered a great part of Church Street,

> such was the imprudence of the Major part of the Commissioners who were appointed by an Act of Parliament to make *Improvements* in the Streets . . . in the year 1787 they caused that part of the Church Street which was most subject to Inundation to be sunk about 20 inches lower – and made an underground water-course or Drain across the Street and down St Mary Lane – which will in all probability in any common Flood of long continuance fill many (if not all) the Cellars in that Neighbourhood, hurt the Foundations of Houses and be very detrimental to property if not to passengers.

Although there was another great flood in 1795, his fears do not seem to have been realised.

Once the main task was accomplished, interest in the commission began to wane and meetings had to be adjourned because of insufficient attendance. The main work was obviously done by the time George III arrived in Tewkesbury in July 1788. By 1790, eight of the original commissioners were dead. It was now a case of keeping the roads swept and repaired, and of making further minor improvements, like numbering all the houses that fronted the streets and erecting street name boards in 1790. Not until 1791 did the commission fulfil its obligation as indicated in the Act to light the town. In the six winter months, 81 oil-lamps were provided, 'the lamps to be lighted every Night except Nine nights before full and one Night after the change of the moon'. To people accustomed to travel at night by the light of a full moon, it seemed unnecessary to pay for lamps at these times.

In the 19th century there was a resurgence of activity. The town's roads were resurfaced and further improved in 1824. Then the commissioners decided, in 1827, to investigate the cost of installing gaslighting. A committee enquired into the experience of other west midland towns, Gloucester and Birmingham, Leamington and Warwick. Warwick they judged 'perhaps lit as well as any town in the kingdom'. The enquiries were encouraging; a contract was negotiated with William Hill of Worcester. It fell through at the last minute on the question of whether the land on which the gasometer would be erected should be re-rated to the poor's rate. William Hill declined to allow his business to make a contribution.

When the matter was raised again in 1832, a contract with William Morely Steers of Leeds was quickly finalised; a site for the gasometer at the top of the Oldbury was agreed and by 21 January 1833 'the greater part of the town was, for the first time, brilliantly illuminated'. Ninety-two gaslights replaced the 120 public oil-lamps. Bennett said everyone had 'reason to admire the excellent quality of the gas, the elegant forms of the columns and lamps, the beautiful and novel appearance of the bridge for suspending the gasometers, and the very neat and skilfull structure of all the buildings and apparatus'. Not all would share Bennett's enthusiasm for gasometers. In his opinion the new system was more expensive, but superior, providing protection for property, an improved appearance to the town, and convenience, in that order. Householders and shopkeepers followed suit, and introduced gaslighting indoors.

The Quay and Quay bridge had been specifically excluded from the Paving Act. The tolls provided the council's main revenue, and they obviously did not want to see this money disappear into the general road fund. When the bridge was inspected in 1806,

47. & 48. Quay Bridge over the Mill Avon, built in 1822, replaced an old sandstone structure. The pattern of the ironwork is similar to that of some bridges cast at Coalbrookdale. The arms of the town are displayed in the centre panel. Next to it is the former brewery of Blizard, Colman & Company, now part of Healings' Borough Mills.

it was found to be 'very ancient and decayed'. It had certainly been built some considerable time before 1592, when the stonework was repaired. Bennett deemed it still repairable but, in the vein of the modernisation occurring in the town, it was decided to apply for an Act and rebuild, at the same time constructing a new quay. Finance was not available until 1822, when the still-existing iron bridge was erected. The design incorporates a bold central feature with the arms of the town. The circles in the spandrels look stylistically somewhat like a Coalbrookdale design, for example a bridge of 1810 over the Kennet and Avon Canal; the arch on the south side of the Quay bridge is partly obscured by a later railway bridge. It ceased to be a toll-bridge in 1849.

Stocking-knitters' cottages in St Mary's Lane.

Chapter 7

People and Politics: 1700-1840

A 'spirit of improvement' was infused into Tewkesbury's inhabitants by the Paving Act, Dyde suggested in his guidebook of 1790, 'which is constantly dispaying itself more and more'. He perhaps had in mind the town's reorganisation of the care of the poor, accomplished in an Act of Parliament a few years after the Paving Act. He may also have been thinking of the second wave of rebuilding, transforming the 16th- and 17th-century timber buildings into the brick townscape of today. The spirit of improvement also sponsored the new town hall, touched the abbey church and its surroundings, and led the townsfolk to provide schooling for the children of the less well-off. In the enthusiasm for modernisation, one of Tewkesbury's oldest features disappeared: the Oldbury field, which had brought market gardens and allotments to the back doors of Barton Street and High Street.

All this enterprise was founded on an increasing affluence for at least a fortunate minority of the town's inhabitants. Their rising standard of living is evident particularly in the variety and quantity of furniture in their homes. Traditional trades and handicrafts, malting and corn-dealing, shoemaking and tailoring, and the entertainment of travellers, continued to create prosperity; but alongside, although not large, there was a growing 'middle class', placed socially between the proprietors of large traditional businesses and the labouring families. 'Capitalists, bankers, professional and other educated men', as the census described them, made up about seven per cent. of the occupied men of the town in 1831. They were not admitted to the traditional circle of the town council, however, until Parliament imposed a more open structure in 1835.

Surprisingly, Tewkesbury was counted by Mary Yorke in 1814, with Birmingham and Worcester, as one of 'the great manufacturing Towns in my Neighbourhood'. The claim rested on the development there of machine knitting of cotton stockings. The industry was welcomed because it employed the poor though it brought affluence to only a few. Much information about the hosiery trade was collected by Gravener Henson, who had himself been a framework knitter. He published a *History of the Framework Knitters* in 1831, and also supplied evidence to the House of Commons Select Committee in 1845. Local sources help to fill in the picture of the development of stocking knitting in Tewkesbury.

Trade directories – a few published in the 18th century, a regular stream in the 19th century – are an indication of the growing complexity of the country's economic life. The *Universal Directory* of about 1800 puts Tewkesbury's claims well: 'for trade, situation and neatness of streets and buildings, Tewkesbury may vie with most market towns in the kingdom'.

The Workhouse

After the Paving Act, the second major initiative towards improving the town was the creation of a new poor law administration by a private Act of Parliament passed in 1792. The care of the poor was a parish responsibility rather than a corporation one; the Act constituted all the householders of the town who occupied property rated at £10 or more as 'Guardians of the Poor'. The Guardians elected nine 'Directors' to carry out the actual work, three retiring each year. The attempt to spread the work amongst the citizens seems equitable, but many tried to avoid what Bennett termed 'troublesome and unpleasant duties', and preferred to pay a £20 fine rather than serve.

Part of the impetus behind the Act of Parliament was the intention to create an efficient workhouse. Although few records of the parish administration survive, it is clear that several times in the 18th century there had been experiments with a workhouse; a general enabling Act of 1722-3 had given parishes the necessary powers. Its purpose was to test how real the need for relief was; in 1724 Tewkesbury parishioners agreed that the poor were not to be given relief 'if they refuse the workhouse'. Several subsequent parish decisions related to the provision of a suitable building, making it uncertain whether one was, in fact, established before 1756. In that year, having decided that it was 'absolutely necessary', premises on Millbank were equipped and a contract made with Richard Allen, a glover, for its operation. Within a short time the parish was experimenting with supplying food direct instead of leaving the purchasing to Allen, and after 18 months the workhouse was abandoned as 'very burthensome and expensive'. All the goods were auctioned. Ten years later, it was again resolved to establish one; the former *Red Lion* in High Street was fulfilling this purpose in 1788.

The contract made with Richard Allen gives some insight into working and living conditions, which probably did not change very much in the next century. The diet contained little variety: broth for breakfast nearly every day, with milk porridge twice a week; meat for lunch on three days, peas porridge or rice pudding on non-meat days; bread and cheese for supper every day; no liquor, except beer for breakfast on Sunday. There was to be morning and evening prayers, grace before meals, and church on Sunday for those who could walk. Poor people able to work had to do so between seven a.m. and six p.m. with half an hour for breakfast and an hour for dinner. No cursing or swearing was allowed, and no-one was permitted to go out and beg. The children were to be taught to read and spell, and to know the catechism. Twice a week the children could stop at three p.m. and 'have the liberty of playing in the court and yard' for two hours.

The containment of expense was uppermost in the minds of overseers and directors of the poor at all periods. The workhouse was one of several stratagems which was tried to deter poor from seeking relief. One humiliating method was to make the poor wear a badge on the right shoulder of their 'upper garment'. In the mid-18th century, effort was put into enforcing this and into preventing likely poor folk from living in the town. Lodgers were required to have certificates which indicated that another parish acknowledged its legal obligation to provide relief if need arose. Those without certificates were removed out of the town. The policy was not enforceable; when a Royal Commission was investigating the Poor Laws in 1832, it was said to be impossible to ascertain how many in Tewkesbury did not legally belong.

The first directors elected under the 1792 Act immediately set about building a workhouse on a grander scale. Mary Yorke, visiting Tewkesbury Park in 1793, saw 'a very large quantity of *Bricks* at the Rivers edge, which we were informed were landed there in order to build (that Enemy to rural Taste) the Tewkesbury workhouse'. The building, later much extended, survives on Holm Hill. It was finished in 1796, at a cost of £7,000, and here the poor were taken for the next 150 years.

Bennett was highly critical of the conception of a 'house of industry'; an asylum perhaps, but as a means of extracting work from the 'idle and profligate' the workhouse was never very effective. It cost over £1,000 a year to run, while the earnings of the poor in 1814-15 amounted to £170 according to a statement of accounts which survives. An annual statement had to be printed and distributed to all ratepayers by the terms of the 1792 Act; it was held to be a useful device for limiting expense. There were on average 68 paupers in the house during the year 1814-15, employed in 'stocking-weaving, spinning, knitting and other Business'. In 1802-3 there had been 83 inmates, and in 1832 there were seventy-seven, including 16 children under the age of ten.

National legislation in 1834 promoted the workhouse as the way to control the number of poor, despite much evidence to the contrary. The Tewkesbury directors, for example, had suggested that relief to the poor in their own homes was cheaper than forcing them into the workhouse. The 1834 Poor Law Amendment Act required groups of urban and rural parishes to amalgamate into poor law unions. Tewkesbury was joined with 22 rural parishes round about, from Bredon and Twyning to Deerhurst and Chaceley, and the workhouse was enlarged to serve the more-than-doubled population. Despite the intentions of the legislators, it never accommodated more than a fraction of the poor of the area.

Poverty and Charity

For most of the poor in Tewkesbury, who lived in the alleys, it was possible to maintain independence except when trade was depressed, the harvest bad or the winter exceptionally cold; then the better-off dipped into their pockets to provide help.

The year 1795 was everywhere exceptionally difficult for the low-paid. Action was prompted in Tewkesbury by a riot on 24 June: 'A mob, mostly of women, rise and seize flour lying on Tewkesbury quay. The Riot Act read. Several of the rioters taken into custody and 5 sent to Gloucester castle'. In this way the Geast chronicler described the scene, which provided material for Mrs. Craik's novel *John Halifax, Gentleman*. The public-spirited subscribed to subsidise bread, giving at a reduced price a shilling loaf to every grown-up person and a sixpenny loaf to every child once a week, for about twelve weeks. This type of relief measure was common in parishes all over the south of England, so that a scale of benefit was frequently adopted in succeeding years, becoming known through the well-publicised Berkshire example as the 'Speenhamland scale'. Some Tewkesbury bakers unscrupulously exploited the poor, and were prosecuted for selling short-weight loaves.

The high prices of corn and bread continued over the next several years. The gentry tried to set a good example. At Hatfield House, Mary Yorke records, the housekeeper said 'his lordship and family all lived on very brown bread'. She adopted their practice of no pies or puddings, but instead 'fruit with rice raised and baked round it'. She found it very good, but was 'sorry to find that, except in my own family, hardly any of the brown bread is used hereabouts'.

At the turn of the century there was a second crisis in wheat prices. An Act of Parliament was passed prohibiting the making of fine white flour, which involved a great deal of sieving to remove the bran. The 'standard wheaten loaf' was to be made

49. The now derelict workhouse on Holm Hill was first built in 1796 and was extended to serve the Tewkesbury Union after 1835.

50. These maltings were erected in the Oldbury, close to and shortly after the first railway. They have recently been replaced with buildings which echo the old, even to the engine shed on the left.

and flour after milling was to weigh not less than 75 per cent. of the original weight of the wheat. It was supposed to contain more bran than millers customarily allowed. Making browner flour was a way of increasing the food supply.

Cold weather was another of the miseries of the poor. In Forthampton and the neighbouring parishes, the indefatigable correspondent from the Court wrote in 1814 that the poor 'are in great distress from the want of firing. There is no coal to be had till the Severn becomes navigable again'. The better-off again raised subscriptions; in Tewkesbury in 1830 the allowance was half-a-hundredweight of coal twice a week.

On other more cheerful occasions, the prosperous provided generously for the poor to celebrate – George III's jubilee, for example:

> The King's jubilee was fully celebrated in our neighbourhood. Worcester and Gloucester were very loyal. At Tewkesbury five oxen were killed, and one pound of beef distributed to each person in each poor family, distributed to the number of above 3,000, and drink was given in the same proportion. The members of Parliament gave one of the oxen and the town the others.

Bennett reported that potatoes and beer were distributed as well as the oxen while the respectable dined at the *Swan*. When peace was first declared in 1814, before Waterloo, every poor man was given a shilling and every poor woman sixpence. George IV's coronation earned them a pound of beef and a pint of ale (children under 14, half the quantity). A 'substantial entertainment' celebrated the passage of the 1832 Reform Act and school-children got a dinner of roast beef, plum pudding and beer to celebrate the Act of 1833 abolishing slavery in the British colonies. These charitable festivities must have helped to perpetuate the social relationships of superior and inferior, while setting them in an acceptable and non-rancorous mould.

If Mary Yorke's information about 3,000 people given George III's jubilee dinner is at all near the truth, then two-thirds of the townsfolk were objects of charity, and this fits with other indications of the relative proportions of prosperous and poor. In 1780, only a third of Tewkesbury's one thousand or so families were assessed for town rates, and even within the third there were a few noted as unable to pay because poor. The tradition of rating only those who were 'able' to pay continued into the 19th century. It was realistic; and saved much pointless clerical work. Yet it seems that a century earlier, two-thirds of the town's inhabitants had been able to pay; as the population increased, it was largely concentrated at the lower levels of income. In the period of acute depression after the Napoleonic Wars, regular relief was given to about one hundred families, and occasional relief to as many as three hundred. Another third of Tewkesbury's families struggled to maintain their independence without suffering the humiliation of applying to the directors for assistance.

Rebuilding and Refurbishment

There were sharp contrasts in 18th-century Tewkesbury between the poverty in the alleys and the prosperity of the front houses. To Dyde, it was clear that the town had been recently much improved, by the substitution of brick for timber-framing along the street frontages: 'The general style of building shows no inconsiderable degree of opulence. The houses are chiefly of brick; stone being a scarce material in this vicinity. Most of the old wooden habitations are now pulled down, and modern edifices erected in their room; but some specimens of the ancient mode of structure still remain'.

To the visitor today, the timber-framed specimens catch the eye; also more are seen now than in Dyde's time. In reality, some had not been demolished, but had had their timbers hidden by stucco which has since been removed; others had been given a brick front, a characteristic refurbishment in 18th-century towns. Even so, there are many brick houses built during the period when the four Hanoverian Georges ruled England (1714-1830). At the top of High Street, three large houses are good examples: Kingsbury House, Avonside and Hereford House. Another good example is 77 Church Street, unusually built sideways to the road.

The second great rebuilding had started before the Paving Act was passed – the *Swan* in High Street, for example, is early 18th century – but the Act certainly stimulated further building in the town. The Geast Charity's experience was probably not untypical. Two small houses near the Tolsey, 2-3 Barton Street, which had comprised a half-burgage given by Margaret Hicks in 1562, had to be refronted. Six years later the houses were considered beyond repair, probably because main timbers had been cut or removed. They were rebuilt in 1792, and the small stone under the eaves perhaps once recorded the date. Three more charity houses at the Bull Ring, described as dilapidated, were rebuilt in brick in 1813, forming the Crescent.

Much of the brick building shows some pride on the part of owner and builder. The houses were often decorated with carved stones at the head of the windows, though 18th-century style was generally restrained. So-called 'Venetian' windows were fashionable locally; the larger central window has a curved top, and is flanked on both sides by a smaller window. Quite small houses have this feature, like 6 and 50 High Street and 102 Church Street, while the *Swan* has an impressive one over the central carriageway.

A major improvement to the town, in Dyde's estimation, was the erection of a new town hall. The facade which is now an important feature of High Street is not the building erected in 1788 to replace the Tolsey but a new front of 1857. The town hall was built well back from the street; in front there was a cobbled area which was intended for a corn market. Dyde thought it was 'a noble opening and adds greatly to the beauty of the streets'. Fifty years later the ground floor was enclosed to provide a police station and cells. The open space was roofed and stone facade erected in 1857 for a corn exchange. Perhaps unfortunately, the porticoed building and its first-floor balcony were hidden from the street. The town hall had a court room downstairs and a banqueting or ball room upstairs. Now the building serves the Tewkesbury parish council. It can be visited, and contains some interesting prints and portraits.

'Improvement' touched the abbey, too. The repair of the ancient stonework had often been necessary; in 1724 there was the equivalent of a national appeal for funds, by means of a 'brief'. An organ was installed in 1737, now known as the 'Milton organ'; it had first been built in 1610 for Magdalen College, Oxford, and during the Protectorate was moved by Oliver Cromwell to Hampton Court. Fortunately this organ was retained when a more modern instrument was installed in the later 19th century and it is suggested that there are more pre-Restoration pipes here than in any other British organ. In the mid-18th century the churchyard was improved, with paving and two sets of iron gates, those near the church given by Lord Gage, and those adjoining the street by William Dowdeswell, both M.P.s for Tewkesbury.

George III spent some time looking at the abbey when he visited Tewkesbury in 1788. He was interested in architecture, and attentively surveyed the outside of the church; 'having likewise inspected the remains of its internal decorations, he could not

51.   The Crescent was rebuilt by the Geast Charity Feoffees in 1813. In front is the Bull Ring where, until the mid-18th century, country butchers set up their market stalls. The space has been enlarged since the demolition of Abbey Lawn House.

52.   The side of the 18th-century Hereford House shows the bent boundary line of High Street plots.

help expressing his regret, that so venerable a fabric should have been suffered to crumble into ruins for want of seasonable reparation'. Really substantial restoration was not undertaken for another 40 years, but some repairs and improvements were carried out shortly after his visit.

Most significant from the point of view of today's visitor, all the old pews were stripped out in 1796. The inside of the abbey would have seemed to the modern eye more like a theatre than a church. Fanny Burney, travelling with George III, wrote in her diary:

> The pews of this cathedral seem the most unsafe, strange and irregular that were ever constructed; They are mounted up, story after story, without any order; now large, now small, now projecting out wide, now almost indented in back, nearly to the very roof of the building. They look as if, ready made, they had been thrown up, and stuck wherever they could, entirely by chance.

New pews and new paving were installed, costing £2,000. The local M.P.s headed the subscription lists. The carpenter did not hesitate to make the stonework fit his pews, rather than the other way round, and the pillars were quite severely damaged. At this date, and for another 70 years, pews were still the churchwardens' main source of income; there was much jockeying among the better-off about their place in church and payment secured the same seat for a year. Allocations of pews were carefully recorded.

A small hint of the change in living standards from the early 19th century to today may be seen in the decision of the churchwardens *not* to warm or 'stove' the church. By 1827, at least one stove had been installed and solid fuel stoves were still in use until recently; they are now converted to burn gas. About this time a party went to Worcester to gain ideas about how to render the inside of the church; the decision to use stone-coloured distemper did not please later restorers.

New Schools

The religious revival, stimulated by John Wesley's life and work, was one reason for the surge of interest in education in the early 19th century. The simple fact of a growing population contributed, because it meant existing schools were inadequate, but most important was the realisation that poor children were growing up without religious beliefs or Christian morals.

The Nonconformists led the way in Tewkesbury. The British and Foreign School Society had been founded in 1808 by Joseph Lancaster. He came to Tewkesbury in October 1812 to talk to a large audience at the *Swan* about his system of education, which made the older children 'monitors' to teach the younger ones. Fund-raising had already started; the defeated Whig candidate in the parliamentary election that year headed the subscription list. In 1813 a school was built at the end of Barton Street; it was one of the earliest in the country and one of the few in Gloucestershire. In 1838 it was educating 142 boys and 54 girls. Equipment for lessons consisted of slates, Bibles, spelling boards and other lesson boards. Boards were hard-wearing substitutes for books.

The Church of England hastened to meet this challenge. A Committee for the National School Society in Tewkesbury was formed in 1812 to provide for 'the education of the Poor in the Principles of the Established Church'. The system of the Reverend Dr. Bell was adopted which, like Lancaster's, employed children as monitors. By 1813 a school was established in the north transept of the abbey. Instruction was chiefly from the Bible and prayer book. Girls were allowed to take in plain needlework at prices fixed by the governors; the work in Tewkesbury at that date was mainly seaming stockings .

Mary Yorke took an interest in the school. She wrote in 1816: 'I must observe how much I was pleased with the pains taken to make the girls work well, perhaps one of the most material parts of their education, being the most likely to draw them from that pernicious Tewkesbury straw-manufactory'. Rather than stockings, it was plaiting straw to make hats that she regarded as the usual Tewkesbury employment for young girls. There is a hint of the feminist in her comment. The governors of the school, reporting in 1818, noted that it was very successful in keeping the children from idle habits and from playing and gambling in the streets as they had done formerly. The National School took over the endowments of a charity or blue coat school which had provided primary education for some Tewkesbury children from the early 18th century.

A stone building of modest pretensions was provided for the National School in 1817 at the southern end of the Abbey Cottages in Church Street. It is on the site of the old bell tower, which had served since the late 16th century as the town gaol. The tower had several large cracks in it, and once a new borough gaol had been built in 1816 it was demolished. The National School Committee purchased both site and materials, and collected subscriptions, including handsome donations from the town's two M.P.s. In the *Gentleman's Magazine* for 1818 the school was described enthusiastically: 'an elegant stone structure, which rivals any similar edifice in any provincial town of the kingdom'. Looking at it today, it is difficult to imagine that it was supposed to accommodate 300 children, moreover on the ground floor only – a second storey was added in 1843 in order to separate the 200 boys downstairs from the 150 girls who were sent upstairs. In practice many children who were nominally enrolled did not attend very regularly; in 1818 there were 119 boys and 78 girls, grouped into five classes and of all ages from five upwards, though there were no girls in the top two classes. In 1838 there were only 76 boys and 104 girls.

These two schools made a contribution to the education of the town's children, but the parliamentary report of 1818 nonetheless concluded that 'the poor have not sufficient means of education and are desirous to possess them'. By 1838 only 300 attended the day schools, whereas nearly 1,000 were enrolled in the town's Sunday schools, of whom a small proportion attended day school as well. The Sunday schools were taught in the churches of each of the four main denominations in the town. The first Church of England Sunday school had been started in 1788, following the example of Robert Raikes of Gloucester; a minimal amount of education could be taught on such a part-time basis, but the aim was to teach children to read, not to write. All the children of school age, however, received at least this amount of education by the early 19th century. In the mid-18th century only a third of the women married in the abbey could sign their name in the marriage register; by the 1830s the proportion had slightly increased to 40 per cent. Two-thirds of the men could write their name at both dates.

For the children of the better-off inhabitants, there was probably a number of small schools charging a weekly sum for lessons in the three Rs. Usually run by women, these dame-schools rarely leave any record, but there were three schoolmistresses who signed a petition in 1778. These little schools did not disappear until after 1870. A very few of the pupils went on to the grammar school. It was taught, as it had been from 'time beyond living memory', in the room attached to the north transept of the church. It had never provided secondary education for very many. The vicar in 1714 'visited the Grammar school; only nine boys and not profiting much'. It did not improve as time went by; in 1818 there were four scholars, in 1828 only one. It was suggested then that the inhabitants showed a reluctance typical of a town 'chiefly engaged in trade'; in 1835 the 'improper severity of the master' deterred parents. The schoolmaster's job was something of a sinecure, but at the same time he took fee-paying pupils, 20 in 1838, and taught writing, arithmetic and English literature.

Another response to the need to teach religious principles was seen in Tewkesbury. The abbey, it was thought, was remote and awe-inspiring, and so the churchwardens and principal inhabitants decided to build a church which would seem more accessible. Trinity church was completed in 1837. Although it was designed by the son of a Tewkesbury Baptist minister, it was not on the modest scale of a Baptist chapel, but echoed in brick the impressive west front of the abbey. A new road had recently been opened between High Street and the Oldbury, and the church was sited to take advantage of this and be visible from High Street. It is certainly the largest public building of the period in Tewkesbury.

Enclosure of the Oldbury

Trinity church is one of many buildings erected at this time on what had once been the Oldbury field. For centuries the field had been part of the town, and all burgesses shared common rights there. It was divided into long narrow strips, each about half an acre, but some larger and some smaller. Many of the strips were used for market gardening. John Jaynes, for example, had a holding of two- and-a-quarter acres, and from his stock sold in 1810 it seems the staples of Tewkesbury's dining-tables were cabbages, gooseberries and currants. Seven hundred gooseberry and currant bushes were sold, and 350 nut, crab and damson trees. Most of the ridges, or lands, were planted with cabbages and savoys, but he was also growing broccoli, celery, parsnips, carrots and turnips; he had 20 pounds of onion seed and lettuce, mustard and cress, and parsley seed, too.

In 1808, at the same time as obtaining an Act for the demolition and rebuilding of the Quay bridge, Tewkesbury town council asked for an Act to enclose the Oldbury. It was probably the need for building land which led to the decision. Once the burgesses' common rights had been extinguished, owners could develop their land. A considerable alteration in the appearance of the town resulted. Unfortunately, there was no development plan, so that the building was piecemeal – houses, warehouses, a school, a hospital, almshouses, industrial premises and the church were all built somewhat haphazardly, with results still visible today. The market gardens gradually disappeared.

Trades and Professions

Only the more prosperous townsmen could contribute to the substantial cost of each private Act of Parliament. Sixty-six people in 1780 occupied houses rated at £10 or above, which marked them out as the upper group, qualified to vote for the Directors of the Poor; 70 people paid rates for their 'stock-in-trade'. The conventional assessment was £80-worth of stock – such as malt, liquor, leather, timber or shop goods. A handful had stock valued at two, three or four times this amount, and one at seven times. The

53. Elaborate brick facades in Barton Street front older structures; one has 'Venetian' windows. The house with the mansard roof is known as the Mustard House, and has recently been restored.

54. Trinity church was built in the Oldbury in 1837 to serve the expanding population but did not have its own separate parish.

Swan, the Upper Lode ferry and the corn mills were conspicuously higher-rated than any other businesses. The numbers of the prosperous had not therefore increased since the 17th century: in the Hearth Tax there had been 129 households with three or more hearths, which had indicated a good standard of living; but the select upper group who sustained the initiatives for improvements in the town were enjoying a very substantial increase in prosperity.

The rising standard of living of these men occurred before Victoria came to the throne in 1837, and is witnessed in the auctioneers' notebooks. The contents of their houses were quite recognisably like today, and far removed from the spartan interiors of earlier periods. Dining-rooms, with mahogany tables, sideboards and upholstered chairs, were now quite common. Window curtains were universal, and often there were Venetian and roller blinds, too. Even quite small houses had floor carpets in bedrooms and living-rooms. A few had a sofa or easy chairs, and a number of houses contained bookcases, bureaux and smaller items like hat stands, longcase clocks, barometers, trolleys and side tables. A wine merchant had a 'cabinet pianoforte'. There were quantities of china, earthenware, pots and pans, canisters, glassware, pictures, cutlery, trays, cruets and so on.

The occupiers of the front houses who enjoyed these comforts were traditional tradesmen, like the baker, candlestick maker, shoemaker and grocer, or they belonged to the new middle class, like the chemist and wine merchant. The subscribers to the Mythe bridge fund were a typical cross-section of Tewkesbury's better-off inhabitants. More than fifty contributed £100 each. No-one in Tewkesbury was comparable in wealth with the town's two members of parliament, who could each subscribe £1,000 – they came from a quite different order of society. The only comparable subscribers from the town were firms of bankers.

The 1831 census provides the most complete general summary of the occupations of Tewkesbury's inhabitants in this period. It counted men aged 20 and over; women were not dealt with except as domestic servants. Neither Tewkesbury nor Cirencester was large enough to be included in the full analysis of occupations which was provided for Gloucester and Cheltenham. As would be expected in a market town, over a third of the men were in the retail and handicraft sector. This made Tewkesbury less of a shopping centre than Cirencester, where the proportion was half. Men in the professions or 'middle class' were a relatively small group, seven per cent. in Tewkesbury and eight per cent. in Cirencester. Manufacturing was Tewkesbury's particular characteristic, in which nearly a quarter of the men were engaged, mainly in cotton but a few in lace making; in Cirencester, and even in Gloucester, manufacturing was insignificant. This description meant something different from the traditional handicrafts; it implied an element of mechanisation, even though still carried on in the home rather than in a factory. There was also a large number of 'general labourers' in Tewkesbury, a fifth of all working men – unskilled, casually employed and very vulnerable to fluctuations in trade. This had similarly been a characteristic of the town two centuries earlier.

Directories, which started to be published in the late 18th century, provide more detail about the economy. Gell and Bradshaw's directory of 'professions, trades etc.' of 1820 was particularly full. It contained an alphabetical list of selected inhabitants and, if not gentry, indicated their occupations. For Tewkesbury it named 288 men and 37 women, and registered occupations for one hundred and seventy-four. Some of the women were genteel and had no stated occupation, but some ran businesses. Most of the men were probably the principals of small businesses. Though the directory lists only a small fraction of the occupied population (the 1821 census showed there were 865 families engaged in 'trade, manufactures or handicrafts' alone), it is helpful in describing how Tewkesbury earned its living.

The most striking characteristic of the town in 1820 is the continuing predominance of the processing and selling of food and drink, in which a quarter of all those listed (81) were involved. There were 17 maltsters, and 27 innkeepers and victuallers, as well as corn factors, bakers, grocers and butchers. A dozen to two dozen businesses were in each of the traditional areas of clothing, leather and metal working, building and carpentry. Amongst the traditional occupations, malting had formerly led to considerable prosperity, but it seems to have declined in numbers during the 18th century. Twenty-five maltmakers were freemen in 1575; there were 42 malt houses rated in 1780, but only 17 maltsters were named in 1820. Maltsters were often also either corn factors or bakers, and in 1820 two combined corn and coal with malt. This was a natural combination, as outgoing cargoes on ship or wagon were corn, and return journeys were made loaded with coal. One maltster was also the postmaster. The *British Universal Directory* of 1800 commented that 'the town carries on a considerable trade in malt', and this and the 'cotton-manufactory' were the two economic characteristics of Tewkesbury which it noted. By 1830, the malt trade was said by Bennett to be of much less importance.

As would be expected in a list of this sort, the proportion of middle class men is exaggerated, but they did form a growing element in English town life. Even in a small town like Tewkesbury, there was a surprising number: for example, there were as many attorneys as shoemakers. Also listed were two bankers, six doctors, four schoolteachers, three printers, two surveyors, tax collectors, accountants and insurance agents, a policeman and a postmaster. There was an auctioneer, John Moore, at this time in Church Street. William Moore in High Street was a wine and spirit merchant, one among five such, another indication of a new, more sophisticated type of business in the 19th-century town. Three wine merchants were on the council in 1835.

Shopkeeping, too, was increasing, as shops ceased to be primarily places where goods were made and sold, and became modern-style retailers. There were 19 shops apparently of this type. Shopping in Tewkesbury in 1820 would seem more like today than it was like the town 100 years earlier, with a hardware and toy shop, three china, glass and earthenware shops, five ironmongers and gunsmiths, three chemists,

55. This early Victorian terrace for middle-class Tewkesburians was built in the Oldbury, near the turnpike gate and on the site of the pound.

three booksellers and printers, two clock- and watchmakers, and nine general shops. Pigott's directory in 1822 summed it up: 'the shops are well supplied with every article for domestic uses'.

Many of the shops were in practice general stores, stocking a variety of goods which reveal surprisingly modern features. The auctioneer's notebooks show the large assortment of spices which could be bought in Tewkesbury: cumin, allspice, nutmeg, caraway, black pepper, cinnamon, coriander and cardomon seeds, mustard, aniseed and fenugreek. England's world-wide trade network is very apparent: rice, vermicelli and macaroni, congo tea, cocoa and chocolate, chicory, liquorice, lump and brown sugar, and treacle could all be purchased in Tewkesbury in the early 19th century. There were odd mixtures of goods. A baker's shop in Church Street sold baskets, coloured thread, brushes, pickled pork and herrings, and pocket knives. As well as making bread, this baker also made and sold pattens. Pattens were shoe-sized wooden platforms on iron frames to which outdoor shoes were strapped to raise them above the mire – a reminder of the amount of dirt in the streets despite the efforts of the Paving Commission. Another miscellany of goods was stocked by a candle-maker in High Street: pins, blacking, gunpowder, scouring paper, soap, tobacco and snuff were sold alongside spices, sugar, tea, and, of course, candles.

A chemist's shop in Barton Street stocked a great variety of patent medicines, like Goulard's extract, Dalby's carminative and Daffy's Elixir; the names alone might seem to have curative properties! Cough lozenges were available in many flavours. It is interesting to see that tooth-brushes and tooth-powder could be bought here; the chemist had tooth-drawing equipment also. Two gallons of best castor oil, a hundredweight of Epsom salts, 12 pounds of magnesia and 14 pounds of senna suggest one common form of medication. All round the shop were small drawers, each labelled and containing an array not only of chemicals but also of foodstuffs. This chemist also sold best Havana cigars. The variety in the bakers', candlestick makers' and chemists' shops is in no way even hinted at in the simple indications of trades in the directories.

The textile interests of the town are represented in the directory by 14 hosiers and 12 other related textile businesses, but these figures give no indication of the importance of stocking knitting to the economy of the town. There were over three hundred men in the industry in 1831, as well as many women and children workers.

Tewkesbury Manufacture

Tewkesbury has some claim to be one of the early industrial cotton towns. Atkins wrote of Tewkesbury in 1712, 'the chief trade of this town is knitting of stockings, and working of cotton, and other woollen manufactures'. Bailey's *British Directory* in 1760 simply said 'Manufactory, cotton etc.', and in 1766 an Act of Parliament regulating the quality of cotton stockings was called the Tewkesbury Act. The mechanisation of cotton spinning by Arkwright soon after the date of the Tewkesbury Act made the town's share in the industry less and less important.

The first mention of cotton manufacture in Tewkesbury's records is in 1707, when Kenelm Bubb, a manufacturer of 'knit cotton works' was licensed as a hawker and pedlar. Atkins' statement suggests that cotton working was quite important at this date, as it was also in Gloucester, where Celia Fiennes noted, 'they follow knitting, stockings, gloves, waistcoats and petticoats and sleeves all of cotton'. The cotton was hand-knitted, and a number of products was made besides stockings. It was customary for knitters to buy the raw cotton wool from the hosiers, and get it spun before they could start work on it. The finished products were then sold back to the hosiers, who exploited the knitters by not allowing the price of the finished article to reflect the cost of the spun cotton. During a cotton famine in 1745 the price of raw cotton doubled, but in Tewkesbury 'those that bought the poor people's work gave rather less for it than they used to do when the cotton was cheaper'.

In the early part of the 18th century, stockings of silk may also have been manufactured

56. The cottages in St Mary's Lane are associated with stocking-knitting, though the large first-floor windows are the main evidence. Two of the cottages were restored by the Landmark Trust in 1971.

in Tewkesbury, using the stocking frame. By the mid-17th century the frame had spread through Leicestershire and Nottinghamshire and a great number of finer-gauge frames for silk were being used in London. Gravener Henson said that some fifty or so frames were moved from London to Tewkesbury about 1714. If so, they were probably silk frames; two silk weavers had become freemen in 1686 and 1699.

The knitting frame was not successfully adapted to cotton until 1730, in Nottingham, using spun cotton imported from India. It was introduced into Tewkesbury about the 1740s. Nottingham hosiers complained about Tewkesbury's hosiers undercutting their market, using an inferior yarn. The basis for Tewkesbury's success was locally-spun yarn, produced throughout Worcestershire, Gloucestershire and Somerset. The spinners had been able to adapt their skill with short-staple, fine Cotswold and Spanish wool to cotton, the staple being the length of the hair or fibre. Cotton was spun in Tewkesbury, too. Mary Yorke wrote in 1769, 'in general the girls here understand nothing but spinning'. The women in Nottinghamshire, used to long-staple wool, could not apparently handle the cotton, so hosiers there used expensive Indian yarn, which consisted of three or more threads twisted together. Some hosiers mixed Indian and homespun threads; in Tewkesbury they used two homespun treads only, suggesting that local spinners were not as skilful as their Indian counterparts. The stockings were 25 per cent. cheaper, though it was claimed they lasted only half as long. The difference in yarn was not apparent in the finished product, so the Nottingham hosiers secured an Act of Parliament in 1766, the Tewkesbury Act, requiring hosiery made of three or more threads to be marked. It did not prevent the Tewkesbury hosiery being made, and fraudulent marking of two-thread hosiery was apparently not covered. Henson considered it was an 'absurd act' showing that 'neither the parliament nor the hosiers understood the subject'.

The Act was in any event a dead letter. Competition from Tewkesbury was merely added to competition from India and from France. This formed the background to Arkwright's search in Nottingham for a sponsor for a cotton-spinning machine. Patented in 1769, Arkwright's water frame revolutionised the production of English cotton yarn, and ensured that the knitting and weaving industry should be sited farther north.

John Dickman, who died in 1767, is the only Tewkesbury stocking framework-knitter for whom an inventory survives, but his business may not be untypical at this period. It was small and Dickman was not a freeman. He had a modest five-roomed house: shop, workroom and kitchen downstairs, two bedrooms upstairs, and a cellar. In the workroom he had four frames, valued at £10 each. In the shop he had £70-worth of stock, mainly dozens of pairs of assorted sizes and styles of cotton hose, for men and women, maids and boys. He also sold several varieties of caps, socks and mitts. He owed money to the cotton merchant and to the whitener, making it likely that the goods he sold were manufactured on his four frames.

Frames were quite expensive items; an entrepreneur owned a number and either employed the men to work them or rented them out. Framework-knitting seems to have started with small investments by businessmen. One of the early frame-owners was a cordwainer; two hosiers served their apprenticeship with him, though his own son was a cordwainer. Another of the first hosiers was a tobacconist and bookseller. A boat-builder who died in 1785 had two frames, and in the early 19th century 12 frames in Sparkes Alley were rented out to provide a small pension for a widow. When five frames were sold in 1804 for Mr. John Adams, they were 'occupied' by three different men. It was probably unusual for a knitter to own his own frame; indeed it was said in 1779, 'a master will not employ a man who has a frame of his own'.

The frames themselves, as Bennett said, were 'exceedingly ingenious and complex'. An 18th-century frame looked superficially somewhat like Arkwright's water frame, with four solid posts supporting the mechanism at a height convenient for a worker to sit at. In the 19th century the frame was made of iron. Each frame was adapted to a particular thickness of thread; finer-gauge frames were more expensive, and the knitters earned higher wages on them. As mechanical cotton spinning improved, Tewkesbury's frames for thicker count yarns became obsolete. The material produced was 12 to 16 inches wide, but again frames producing wider cloth were developed in Nottingham, and Tewkesbury hosiers failed to invest sufficiently in new machinery to save the town's trade.

The material knitted on the stocking frame was not at all like modern stockingette, as might be supposed. A small sample of 'Kemerton' fabric exists in a letter of the early 19th century; it is a very fine, thin plaid and looks like a modern woven cotton. In effect, the stocking frame was the first mechanisation of cotton cloth production. The material was used for many items of clothing besides stockings, like shirts and caps, until the development of the power loom.

There were about 650 frames in Tewkesbury by 1782, and in the whole country about 20,000 mainly in Nottinghamshire, Derbyshire and Leicestershire. Thirty years later the number in Tewkesbury was said to be 800, but by this date there were 30,000 in the country, and numbers continued to increase elsewhere, though not in Tewkesbury. The industry provided employment for more than knitters – for example, seamers, framesmiths and needlemakers. Altogether up to 800 were employed in the hosiery business in 1782, controlled by 15 to 20 hosiers; in 1830 Bennett estimated that 1,500 were employed. Many were women and children.

Expansion in the industry did not bring prosperity. The framework knitters petitioned Parliament in 1778, asking for regulation of wages, because they said they were 'incapable of providing the common necessaries of life'. They petitioned again the next year, and the first witness was John Long from Tewkesbury. Worse hardship followed the end of the Napoleonic blockade in 1812, and the renewal of French competition. One hosier from Tewkesbury reduced wages and was sent a letter threatening his life if he did not raise them again. Once peace was made, all trades were affected by post-war depression. Mary Yorke wrote of 'the dreadful consequences and affliction that so many families are thrown into'. More than 300 families were given poor relief in December 1816, just over half connected with the hosiery trade. There were many cases of assault and stealing heard at the Quarter Sessions; one man had stolen potatoes from the Oldbury field, and another was transported for stealing three pairs of shoes.

The stocking makers who were receiving better wages created a benefit fund for their fellows; the parish meeting praised the scheme as 'exemplary and honourable'. It was admitted in 1819 that the stocking maker earned 'much below what is necessary for his proper and comfortable subsistence'; anyone who 'labours incessantly through the day ought to be enabled to gain a sufficient maintenance'. On the other hand there was sympathy with the hosier, who could not be expected to 'ruin himself with high wages and unlimited employment'. The 'peacable and orderly behaviour of the suffering' was commended, and the Directors of the Poor were requested to be generous in their relief, without reducing aid because of the stocking makers' fund.

It is clear that stocking making was now in decline in Tewkesbury. There was a temporary improvement in 1825; the stocking makers went on strike briefly in support of a demand for higher wages, possibly encouraged by the prospect of alternative employment in the new cotton lace factory opened in the town. In the generally difficult period of the early 1840s, unemployment was again high. In 1844 there were more frames idle than were in use in the town. For the Tewkesbury framework knitters it was certainly not the result of the application of mechanical power to the frames, because this was not successfully accomplished until the following decade. A fall-off in demand for particular types of stocking may be relevant; it was suggested that the Napoleonic Wars had accustomed people to a plainer fabric and Tewkesbury's frames were probably out of date. Another factor was the quantity of yarn produced cheaply in the cotton mills in the north. Continuing technical innovation and low transport costs by this date favoured the northern hosiery producers.

The Decline of the Council

During all the activity to improve the town at the end of the 18th and beginning of the 19th centuries, the council rarely played an initiating role, though it was generally supportive. Gradually the council seems to have become more isolated, a ceremonial élite, concerned mainly with its own perpetuation. The erosion of the economic base of town government had begun before 1700, in the decline in the number of freemen. The disruption of the Civil War and the succeeding difficulties over the charter had undoubtedly weakened the council's ability to insist on newcomers buying their right to trade in the town. Whereas in 1575 there had been 259 freemen sworn in after the granting of the charter, in 1685, when a similar event occurred, there were only 86, and amongst their number were six lords. The freemen were no longer the whole body of working men in business in the town, but were an élite of merchants and larger business men. The attempt to revive the trade guilds in 1699 was for ceremonial purposes and was short-lived.

Nonetheless, until the later 18th century the freemen were still generally representative of the economic life of the town. In 1685 just over half were craftsmen and merchants, and a third were connected with the food and drink trades; there were only two professional men. Between 1751 and 1780 craftsmen still predominated amongst new freemen, though gentlemen and professional men were increasing in number, and made up one in five of those admitted. After 1780, nearly all new freemen were described in the register as 'gentlemen'. A third of the town's more important citizens, listed in the *British Universal Directory* of 1800, were not freemen.

Apprenticeship, too, was declining in economic importance. A good proportion of freemen in the mid-18th century had qualified by serving a seven-year apprenticeship, but the newer industries or retailing businesses did not, or perhaps could not use the formal apprenticeship system. It was customary in the leather trades, particularly amongst cordwainers (skilled shoemakers), but very uncommon in, for example, the hosiery trade. Of the 15 to 20 hosiers mentioned by John Long in 1782, only a handful were freemen who took apprentices. A few of those with capital and the prospect of setting up in business themselves seemed to have learned their trade in this way.

57. Before enclosure, Chance Street was a narrow pathway to the Oldbury field and marked the end of Barton Street and of the town.

58. The stocking factory off Chance Street, now converted for housing, has a notable range of large windows. It was sold as a 'silk' factory in 1867 with the seven cottages in front.

The status of freeman of the town had become of more honorary than practical use, especially as the freemen did not elect the council. In theory, new council members were drawn from this body; in practice, the existing members nominated whom they wished, and swore them in as freemen and assistant burgesses simultaneously. Consequently the council acquired the political complexion of the longer-serving members. In this way the links with the work of the town grew more tenuous. In 1784 three maltsters were on the council, a mercer and a tanner; in 1800 two mercers, a tanner, two bakers, a grocer and the innkeeper of the *Swan*. Increasingly in the 19th century the new professional class entered the council – doctors, solicitors, bankers and clerics. In 1834 James Bennett, the bookseller, printer and author of the *History of Tewkesbury*, was made a member. When the council was abolished by Act of Parliament in 1835 it consisted of eight gentry, 11 professionals and only five tradesmen.

There seem to have been generally 12 councillors resident in Tewkesbury and 12 who were honorary appointments, of gentlemen or of the town's representatives in Parliament; they were not necessarily residents of the town. It is not clear whether the spate of resignations in 1833, when the Royal Commission was investigating the municipal corporations, was for this reason. Although the council contained its chartered 24 members, only about half normally conducted the business. It was rare for there to be controversy within the council or for a vote to be taken. The proposal to apply for an Act of Parliament to rebuild the Quay bridge was an exceptional occasion, when 15 councillors attended, and three opposed the motion.

The Parliamentary Franchise

A significant factor in the decline in economic importance of the freemen was the association with the parliamentary franchise. As freemen could certainly vote, the council was under a double pressure: to admit gentlemen in order that they could vote, and to make freemen in order to influence the result. Charles Hancock, one of the town's M.P.s and a member of the council, insisted in December 1700 on a meeting to make new freemen 'with a design as we apprehend to engage their votes . . . many of their fees being paid by him'. Reluctantly the council agreed, though protesting; Hancock was not re-elected.

Because of these pressures, there was a tendency in the early 18th century to admit freemen who did not live in the town. The council did try to resist, but gradually non-residence became accepted, aided perhaps by the fact that proprietors of freehold houses, who could also vote in parliamentary elections, were frequently non-resident. In 1831 there were at least 300 non-residents entitled to vote, and the Royal Commission found two years later there were 200 non-resident freemen.

From the beginning of the 18th century, all property-owning townsmen asserted their right to vote in parliamentary elections. Prior to 1708, only owners of front houses claimed the right; in the election that year for the first time all freeholders in the borough were polled. Atkins, writing soon after, accepted that there were 500 voters in Tewkesbury, 'freemen and all freeholders'. This, too, opened the way to fraudulent practices, as one of the Dowdeswell family quickly appreciated; the council deplored the 'scandalous practice to divide houses so as to create voters'. The bailiff, who was also the returning officer, was ordered not to admit voters created in this way. The same thing certainly happened again, for example in 1831, when property was apparently 'hastily conveyed' to try to influence the election. The Anti-Corn Law League was following a well-trodden path in its campaign to create voters in the 1840s. The freeholder franchise unfortunately encouraged 'Gentlemen and Traders to purchase the cottages in the borough' in order to secure votes, to the detriment of the humble who were rarely able to own their homes. The council became acquiescent or positively condoned these electoral practices. Aspiring or sitting members of parliament cultivated their support by subscribing generously to all town projects – roads, bridges, charities, schools, abbey and town hall.

Whenever there was great political excitement, the franchise was called in question, and Tewkesbury elections were quite often the subject of petitions to parliament disputing the results. The bailiffs could refuse votes in a partisan manner, and sometimes allowed 'great tumults and disorders in the town', as happened in 1717. The council in 1741 tried to prevent freeholders voting; in 1754 a defeated candidate protested at 'an illegal association of electors whose object was to sell their votes to mend the roads'. The handsome donations promised by the sitting members secured their re-election. Later in the century it was suggested that the Dowdeswell interest pursued 'their old schemes' and that £1,500 might be the sum necessary to secure one of the Tewkesbury seats.

About two hundred inhabitants in Tewkesbury could vote, a larger number than in many boroughs. From the late 18th century there was a nation-wide campaign to enlarge the franchise. The Geast Charity book writer noted without much sympathy the excitement in Tewkesbury and elsewhere in 1791, which led to Acts of Parliament being passed to keep 'the unruly' in 'awe':

> In the month of November this year the Principals of the French Revolution – namely what they call Liberty and Equality – having appeared in an alarming manner in many parts of England and many seditious publications being dispersed in various parts of the kingdom tending to inflame the mind, raise a spirit of disaffection and set all ranks of people against monarchical government . . .'

A Society for Political and Moral Information was founded in Tewkesbury, probably in 1792, which met monthly and subscribed to a periodical called *The Patriot* as well as to a local newspaper. Their aim was to protect the citizen's 'rights and liberties'. The London club called the Society of Friends of the People encouraged them, and the London Corresponding Society sent letters and pamphlets. Such groups were considered dangerously subversive, though the secretary of the Tewkesbury society admitted the 'smallness of our numbers'.

The latent radicalism of the town appeared in the 1796 election. There was a rush to apply for the freedom of the town; 'party feeling and animosity were carried to a very great excess'. One candidate had been courting popularity among the lower classes of freemen and others; another was Sir Philip Francis, who is supposed to have been the author, some 25 years earlier, of the inflammatory series of articles called the *Letters of Junius*. Over four hundred voted. The defeated radical candidates disputed the qualifications of some voters, and maintained their own supporters were excluded by the 'undisguised partiality' of the bailiffs. The Dowdeswell family member was a Tory, which no doubt added to the excitement, for until this time Tewkesbury had always returned two Whigs. From this date there was one Whig and one Tory sitting for Tewkesbury, who effectively neutralised each other.

In the 19th century the council was entirely Tory in sympathy, and secured the election of a Tory M.P. while popular pressure secured a Whig member. A Whig who failed to secure election spoke in 1812 of 'the torrents of corruption' and 'Wanton and lavish expenditure of the public money'. In June 1830 William Cobbett, 'that celebrated state quack', lectured in the theatre, and labourers' riots in the neighbourhood were attributed to his incendiary speeches and writings. There were riotous scenes in 1831, when reform of the franchise was under debate. The Tory, J. E. Dowdeswell, voted against the Reform Bill, and violent demonstrations were planned against him. A mob prevented the council eating its customary annual dinner at the *Swan*, the Riot Act was read, and the military had to be summoned from Gloucester.

The Reform Act was passed in 1832, and the new, uniform borough franchise throughout the country was a £10 rating qualification which excluded the non-resident voters. Dowdeswell's main support significantly had come from non-residents. In the election which followed the Reform Act, Tewkesbury returned two Whigs. The number of resident voters was slightly increased by the Act from about two hundred to three hundred and eighty-six. The old disputes over freemen and freeholders were no longer relevant. The victory of reform was celebrated with a 'substantial entertainment' for the poor.

Many small parliamentary boroughs lost the right to separate representation in 1832. As Bennett wryly noticed: 'it is well for the franchises of Tewkesbury, that since the census of 1801 the population of the borough has increased; as a slight diminution from the number of its inhabitants at that time must have placed it, in the Reform Bill, in Schedule B'. This would have involved it losing one of its two members. An Election Canto expressed it thus:

> Near was thy fate, O Tewkesbury!
> To hemiplegic Schedule B;
> But thy old Borough shall not yield,
> She shall take in the Oldbury Field,
> The man of loom, and man of lace,
> From Gloucester-Row to Hanbury Place.
> Thy census large, which Ricketts took,
> Runs round the Mythe and Swilgate brook,
> Within, without the the Borough's bound,
> And keeps awhile thy franchise sound.

Ricketts was the clerk to the Directors of the Poor. Enclosure of the Oldbury field, and consequent development, had saved Tewkesbury's M.P.s for the moment.

Reform of the Council

Tewkesbury council's financial position had deteriorated sharply in the previous 20 years. There were two main reasons: the erection of a new town hall left a debt of £1,200 (Sir William Codrington had 'given' the building only in the sense of lending the money) but, more serious, its principal source of income had ended. The council had never been rich, but tolls paid by traders in the market and on the quay had supplied a regular income. For years there had been attempts to evade these tolls. In 1757, 10 men, all maltsters and millers, had refused to pay, but the council brought a case in the Court of Chancery and the 10 conceded. Immediately following this case, the wheat market was moved to the Tolsey, and only barley was sold 'on the *Swan* door'. This move may have been made to facilitate the collection of tolls; it perhaps suggests that already by the mid-18th century corn was being sold by sample rather than in bulk loads in a cart or wagon. Less serious, but symptomatic, traders were avoiding tolls at the quay by landing coal or other goods higher up the Avon or even on the Mill Avon.

The issue flared up again in 1800. Corn factors complained of the tolls on the quay bridge. The council now commenced a ruinous series of legal actions. For them, it was a case of survival; the whole basis of the corporation rested on the charter and its grant of the right to collect tolls. It was a conflict of old and new, because a modern method of town government was being created by Act of Parliament, giving Paving Commissioners and Poor Law Directors power to collect rates. Tewkesbury council won a case in 1809 that selling corn by sample should not defraud them of tolls, but lost a case in 1812 that property could be seized if tolls were not paid, which meant an end to their power. At a public meeting at the *Cross Keys*, it was argued that the council's insistence on tolls was harming the corn market. Like the medieval guilds before it, the council was out of step with developing economic organisation.

Fighting the court cases bankrupted the council. They borrowed money but could not pay the interest, so that the debt steadily increased. Income from tolls had been about £160 a year at the beginning of the century; in 1833 it was £20. Insolvency was declared in 1828, by which date £6,000 was owed, and creditors wrote off two-thirds of the debt. All the council property was mortgaged to J. E. Dowdeswell, M.P. and Recorder of the town, who advanced £2,000 to make the necessary payments.

Despite its weak financial position, Tewkesbury successfully survived the inspection of the Royal Commission on Municipal Corporations, and following the Act of 1835 regulating the country's corporations, a new council of mayor, aldermen and councillors came into being. Tewkesbury borough survived because it had also just retained its status as a parliamentary borough. In the elections, the Tory councillors were all defeated, and a completely Whig council installed. Eight of the councillors were dissenters. Two Tories were chosen as aldermen in a gesture of conciliation.

The 1830s, nonetheless, marked a turning-point in Tewkesbury's story. From this time, it found itself more and more excluded from the development brought about by the railway. It became an old town amidst a rapidly altering and modernising age, and this is the subject of the last chapter.

The abbey cloister.

Chapter 8

The Modernisation of an Old Town: 1840-1940

For Tewkesbury, the start of Victoria's reign in 1837 marked a definite change in the town's fortunes. It had been an expanding economic centre until this time, but after 1841 the ten-yearly national census showed a static population well into the 20th century. Both the old parliamentary boroughs of Gloucestershire experienced the same relative decline, especially marked in the face of the thrusting growth of Cheltenham. In 1801 Cheltenham was smaller than either Tewkesbury or Cirencester; by 1811 it had overtaken both and equalled the county town in size. By 1901 Cheltenham was three times larger than Gloucester, which in turn was three times larger than Tewkesbury or Cirencester. Cheltenham therefore influenced the routing of the Midland railway line, and its need for water prompted the enterprise of the Water Company in constructing the Mythe works.

As the parliamentary system was brought more into line with the realities of population distribution, it was inevitable that both Tewkesbury and Cirencester would lose separate parliamentary representation. In 1867, both were reduced to one member; in 1885 they were merged into the county; subsequently both, together with a large rural area, form a constituency. Between the two world wars Tewkesbury's population declined quite significantly, but this was not entirely because of economic difficulties; it was also a reflection of rising living standards. New houses were built outside the borough boundary and the population in the town centre fell. The reorganisation of local government areas since the Second World War has led to a more practical boundary for Tewkesbury, which once more has an expanding population.

When the Midland Railway line between Gloucester and Birmingham was built through Ashchurch, with only a branch line connection with Tewkesbury, it was clear to the inhabitants that the town was left aside from an important main line of communication. The effects were seen immediately. The railway shattered the horse-drawn coaching network based on the town's inns and stables; within a year there were no stage coaches passing through Tewkesbury to Worcester, where before there had been 26 a day. The main hosiery business moved to Nottingham. Symptoms of decline are apparent in the 1841 census which shows 111 empty houses. In the 1860s Tewkesbury again unsuccessfully campaigned for a main line but had to be content with branch railways to Evesham and to Upton and Malvern.

The motor-car and charabanc in the 20th century restored a flow of traffic to Tewkesbury's main streets but transformed them from busy thoroughfares to a bottle-neck. A census in Gloucestershire in 1932 showed that, as far as the main roads were concerned, horse-drawn traffic had practically vanished; in 1945 nearly 13,000 tons of motorised traffic passed daily along the A38 north from Coombe Hill. The M5 motorway, which was planned during the Second World War, by-passed the town rather as the railway had done more than a century earlier, but with much more welcome results.

An important source for the history of Tewkesbury in the last 100 years is the local newspaper. Bennett had published an annual magazine from 1830 to 1849, called the *Tewkesbury Yearly Register and Magazine*, which summarised the local news. Tewkesbury did not have a newspaper until 1853, when John Garrison started publication of the *Monthly Record and General Advertiser*. The abolition of the newspaper duty by Gladstone, in 1855, encouraged a great expansion of the press; the Tewkesbury paper was enlarged and published weekly. Frederick Moore, of the Tewkesbury firm of solicitors, had a joint interest with Garrison, but quarrelled with him when Garrison became too radical in political sympathy. Moore then started his own newspaper, the *Tewkesbury Register and Agricultural Gazette*. Bennett had died in 1856, so Moore took up part of the older title. In his first issue of 31 July 1858, he wrote percipiently about the great power over the destinies of mankind which the cheap Press was going to have. His paper was not intended as a party political organ, but to 'instruct and amuse'. Its main function was to relay news and opinions on national and international affairs from the London papers; only a column or two was devoted to Tewkesbury news. However, Moore was clearly conservative in sympathy. The *Record* still continued to be published on Saturdays at a penny. It adopted a more light-hearted and pungent style of reporting and yielded respectable pre-eminence to its rival. Neither journal survived beyond 1930, though the *Register* title was taken on by the *Evesham Journal*.

59.   Frederick Moore (1832-1900) was 'very closely identified with most of the forward movements of the old borough'. He was founder, proprietor and editor of the *Tewkesbury Register*.

Moore used the *Tewkesbury Register* as a platform to campaign for improvements in the town; he became a councillor in 1872 and often seems to have fought outside when not making headway inside the council. He was a member of the Board of Guardians, caring for the poor of the district, and honorary secretary of the abbey restoration committee throughout the period of that work. In 1860 he helped establish the annual regatta, replacing the horse races which had been held on the Ham for many years, off and on, but had by then ceased. The regatta became an important social event in the life of the town. It continued for a few years after his death in 1900. In 1909, after 49 regattas had been held, its place on Bank Holiday Monday was taken by the 'working men's regatta, sports and flower show', which had been established about 1890. Moore deserves to be known as a considerable benefactor to the town.

The author of *The Portrait of Elmbury*, John Moore, was a member of the auctioneering branch of the same Tewkesbury family. He went into the auctioneer's office in 1924 but gave up the family trade three years later, when faced with the duty of selling a poor man's furniture – all but the bed – because the man was unable to pay the rent. He wrote his book in 1945, describing 20th-century Tewkesbury as he remembered it before he left in 1939. The pages of the *Register* show the closeness with which he described actual events and people.

In 1883 the *Register* looked back with satisfaction on its first 25 years of publication. Eight achievements of the period were picked out, and five stand today. Not all were Tewkesbury's own initiatives, like the first cited, 'The successful completion and opening of the great navigation works at the Upper Lode'. The opening of the new branch railway from Tewkesbury to Malvern was important at the time, but this railway was closed to passengers in 1961. Another achievement of the period, the construction of the Mythe waterworks, has proved to be of lasting importance. Local initiatives included the town's drainage system, the major restoration of the abbey, and the provision of the hospital in the town. The mid-Victorian period and particularly the decade of the 1860s was thus one of considerable enterprise to set against the apparent stagnation after 1841.

The *Register* might have included another major contribution to the town from the mid-19th century, the work of enterprising members of the Healing family. In the changing conditions of the corn milling trade, they built the Borough steam mills, which were amongst the largest in Gloucestershire; the mills continue to be an important feature of the town. A second area of achievement omitted by the *Register* was the result of the enterprise of a local builder, Thomas Collins. He was largely responsible for the restoration of the town's ancient timber-framed houses. More controversially, Collins was instrumental in the restoration of the abbey. His work coincided with the growing interest in archaeology and history, evident in the foundation of county archaeological societies throughout the country. The result was a new means of livelihood in Tewkesbury through tourism. As the 1885 guide said, the town 'abounded in characteristics and atmosphere of the dim and distant past'. In 1913 it was reported that the *Bell Hotel* and Bowling Green was 'much patronised by Americans on tour'.

Many of the improvements of the 19th century were achieved after battles between different sectional interests had been fought out in parliament. The amount of legislation passed increased enormously, much of it at local instigation. Gradually more general legislation imposed requirements on all municipal authorities, and the local council became an agent carrying out specified duties, in such areas as public health, education, inspection of nuisances, and regulations in case of cattle disease. In the early 20th century, Tewkesbury council's attention shifted from the general area of public health to the provision of housing. Although tourism had become an important economic interest, behind the picturesque front houses there were what councillors did not hesitate to call slums. They made considerable efforts in the years up to 1939 to tackle the problem, despite the difficult conditions of the period between the wars. Again, there was legislative encouragement.

Meantime the town participated in the facilities which technological inventiveness provided: electric light, telephone, wireless and cinema. The 1903 Town Guide reflected both the wish to encourage tourism and the new art of photography; many tradesmen had photographs to advertise their shops though the *Register* only inserted photographs on rare occasions until after the First World War. A photographic survey of the main streets was made soon after the Second World War which has fortunately been preserved in the borough council's records. It shows how little the appearance of the streets had changed since the beginning of the century. The 1960s was another decade of development, when the old town was modernised. Tewkesbury's special value was recognised in 1967 when the whole town centre was made a conservation area. It marked the development from restoration of notable structures to an appreciation of the overall shape and texture of the town.

The Railway Age

The construction of the Midland Railway line in the 1830s was a very significant event, bringing Tewkesbury quite early into the railway age, for good or ill. In *Portrait of Elmbury*, John Moore suggested that the townsfolk 'cold-shouldered' the railway, not wanting it to interfere with their amenities. This view was current in the 1860s, when a second railway scheme was being canvassed, and it obviously remained the general belief. The view was erroneous, as Frederick Moore pointed out in the *Register*; 'The only stand they made was to have the same railway accommodation as other towns'. Tewkesbury's inhabitants in fact wanted the railway to come through the town.

Bennett printed an account of Tewkesbury's battle for the Gloucester and Birmingham line in his *Yearly Register and Magazine*. When first projected, the line was planned to come close to the town. Then Tewkesbury learnt that 'in order to conciliate the inhabitants of Cheltenham' the route was to be farther to the east. Tewkesbury's inhabitants feared that 'an extensive and irreparable injury will be done to the traffic, trade and property of the town'. A petition to the House of Commons was quickly prepared, asking for a parliamentary surveyor and engineer to inspect each proposed route. Worcester likewise protested at being by-passed. The House of Commons did not respond and passed the Bill; attention then moved to the House of Lords. It seems the potential opposition of the peers was more formidable, so that 'the Railway Company adjusted their differences with the inhabitants of Tewkesbury'. The line was to come as near the town as practicable and, if no nearer than Ashchurch, a branch line was to be built to Tewkesbury and to the quay. The Act was passed in 1836. Tewkesbury petitioned both Houses of Parliament the following year in support of an amending Act carrying out the agreement. Worcester, too, secured a branch line in the amending Act; it was not built.

The station in High Street was completed by August 1839. It was a stone building, battlemented and with Gothic 'screen-work' and oriel windows, probably the first example of Victorian gothic-revival architecture in Tewkesbury. The company was more reluctant to extend the line to the quay but finally shared the expense with the council. The houses on one side of Quay Street were demolished and the extension built soon after. A steam engine and carriages opened the line to Ashchurch in June 1839 but for the first few years passengers were normally conveyed in a horse-drawn carriage, divided into two compartments for first and second class passengers, while third class passengers rode outside. Although the company's directors proudly announced that there was now rail communication all the way from Exeter to Newcastle, some 350 miles, there could be no through trains because of the different gauges: broad gauge to the south of Gloucester and narrow gauge to the north.

In presenting the Bill to parliament the promoters estimated that the annual traffic on the Gloucester and Birmingham line would amount to 70,000 tons of freight, mainly from the port of Gloucester 'whence Birmingham and its densely populated neighbourhood receive their chief supplies'. The estimated 400,000 passengers, on the other hand, would bring more revenue, hence the importance of Cheltenham. Tewkesbury hoped to supply Cheltenham with coal brought down the Severn from Shropshire and Staffordshire, drawing this trade away from the Coombe Hill canal, though the canal had already lost much trade to the Gloucester and Cheltenham tramway.

The Gloucester and Birmingham Railway was absorbed by the Midland in 1845. Within a year or so another line was being projected from Tewkesbury to Malvern, but was not agreed. The project was revived in 1859 by the Tewkesbury and Malvern Junction railway company. The *Register* greeted it enthusiastically, seeing the possibility of a long distance through route. 'This town has hitherto had no chance in the race of prosperity . . . with a line in existence from Cheltenham to Witney we may stand once again on the old direct London Road'. The hope for a connection between Cheltenham and Witney was premature; Witney was linked to Oxford in 1861, and to Fairford in 1873, but not to Cheltenham.

The council supported the Tewkesbury and Malvern Junction Company and the necessary Act of Parliament was passed in 1860. The anticipated freight was coal, iron, building and road-making materials, cotton and wool, implements, cereals and farm animals. The new line branched off the main line near Ashchurch, and crossed the Avon a short distance beyond King John's Bridge. A tunnel took the railway under Mythe Hill and it then ran on an embankment parallel to the old road and the Severn. Some of the embankment across the Avon Ham remains today. The railway took longer to complete than estimated; the Avon bridge was tested in 1864 with four engines on it, two on each line, and was opened three months later. The *Tewkesbury Register* reported:

> We announced last week that this line was to be opened on Monday last, but many persons, after so much disappointment, refused to believe that such would be the case. We can now positively assert that the railway communication between Tewkesbury and Malvern has actually been opened.

At this time the Midland took over the company. The line from Tewkesbury to Ashchurch was upgraded to double track, and a further railway from Ashchurch to Evesham also completed. From Evesham a connection was shortly completed to Redditch.

When first opened, there were four trains a day to Evesham and four to Malvern, though quite soon this service was reduced to three. Six trains a day made the connection at Ashchurch for Bristol and Birmingham, the journeys taking well over two hours in either direction. The *Register* optimistically foresaw Tewkesbury as a 'central and most important depot for the Midland Railway Company'. This hope was not realised, as Ashchurch was the natural depot and the Malvern line never escaped from being a branch line. This fact was appreciated by the council. A plea was put to the Midland to build a loop to Tewkesbury, from somewhere south of Ashchurch to somewhere north, at the same time obviating the need for a new passenger station, but it was disregarded.

Other proposed railway schemes impinged on the town at this time: one was Ross to Tewkesbury via Pauntley, Newent, Upleadon, Corse, Chaceley and Forthampton and another was Ledbury to Tewkesbury. Both projects would have linked existing railways. Tewkesbury did not favour either scheme, because an alternative proposal by the

60. The viaduct of 1864 across the Avon Ham, parallel with King John's Bridge and causeway, is the most obvious relic of the 100 years' existence of the Tewkesbury and Malvern railway.

61. The Upper Lode lock was built in 1858. Old barges were sunk to close the original channel which curved round the *Dowdeswell Arms*.

Northampton and Banbury Company to extend their line as far as Ross was seen as more advantageous. It would have brought a connection with the Midlands. None of these projects was in fact carried out.

In some ways the Malvern line was not an advantage to Tewkesbury. It involved the closure of the passenger station in High Street, though the rail to the quay continued to be used for freight. The new passenger station was some way out to the north-east. Even in 1961 it could be described as 'too far from town'. At this date the station and approach road were neglected, with sections in complete darkness and poorly paved, the waiting room was forlorn and it was not even possible to buy a railway timetable. The *Register* noted that 'The situation might be remedied by opening the old station in High Street'. A fruit canning factory had opened at Ashchurch in 1932 because of the useful rail connections with a market-gardening area, and as late as 1945 rail links in all directions had been presented as favouring expansion in this industry. The passenger services were withdrawn in 1961 because they were making heavy losses. The line was closed to freight a few years later and the track taken up.

The Severn Navigation

The growing skill in civil engineering which was the result of canal and road construction led also to consideration of how to improve the navigability of the river Severn. It was in some respects a more complicated undertaking: improvement in one section of the river affected the flow in another section, and might lead to flooding of the water meadows along the river's course. Locks and weirs would also affect the tidal nature of stretches of the river. The interests of some towns were better served by improvements than others. Gloucester, after many years of effort, had a canal to Sharpness Point which brought shipping to the canal basin on a much larger scale than to the old quayside. With a rail link to Birmingham from 1840 Gloucester was well-placed and so opposed improvement of the Severn. Tewkesbury was uncertain of where its best interests lay: some inhabitants were indifferent; some concentrated on the danger of flooding; the optimists thought Tewkesbury might gain from its situation at the confluence of the Severn and Avon and become once again a port for the towns along the Avon. Worcester, on the other hand, had canal communication inland but waterborne traffic down-river was limited by its shallowness in many places. Worcester entrepreneurs were therefore the main protagonists of Severn improvement. One supporter hopefully suggested the town could become a little Glasgow once the river were deepened and foresaw the use of steam vessels.

At the instigation of a group of Worcester men, plans had been made as early as 1784 for locks and weirs to deepen the navigation; they had failed to gain parliamentary approval, because of Gloucester's opposition. In 1835 another major attempt was made, frustrated this time not only by Gloucester, but by landowners fearing flooding, and by the Worcester and Birmingham canal company and Shropshire carriers fearing competition. Tewkesbury asked for improvement to the Old Avon between the Severn confluence and the quay to be included in the scheme and objected to the tolls on what had always been a free river. The scheme did not succeed this time but it foreshadowed to a large extent the improvements eventually carried out. A new steam dredging machine was to be used below Worcester and this was tried after 1842 when an Act of Parliament created a Severn Navigation Commission. Locks and weirs were constructed above Worcester as far as Stourport, rather higher up the river.

Although £140,000 was spent over the next few years, in the drought summer of 1847 the river was too shallow for navigation. For Tewkesbury the works so far were a disaster. The quay basin was 'almost as dry as the turnpike road' and it was 'utterly impossible to float even the smallest flat-bottomed boat' through the lock between the Old Avon and the Mill Avon. Trows and barges had to be unloaded at the Mythe or at Avon Mouth and cargoes taken in wagons and carts to the town. Tewkesbury urged that a significant improvement to navigability might be achieved with the construction of a lock and weir at the Upper Lode; it required the diversion of the river into a cut across the point of the Severn Ham, taking out one of the river's meanders. This is the course of the river today. The proposal was put to parliament several times over the next few years, before it was approved in 1853. Acceptance of the scheme had been delayed by the criticisms of Admiralty surveyors who had been given the responsibility to enquire into any modifications to harbours or navigations under a recent Act of Parliament. During the next five years this great engineering effort was accomplished. The weir is 500 feet (152 metres) long. Within a few years previous objectors admitted that their fears, particularly with respect to flooding, were groundless.

The river between Tewkesbury and Gloucester still remained unimproved. It was claimed that in this stetch 'the Severn is only just navigable', and Deerhurst shoal, where the river was only a little over a foot deep, was a particular obstacle. This was tackled between 1868 and 1871, with the construction of two more weirs. The canalisation of the river from Gloucester to Stourport was now completed. A depth of six feet was maintained until the 1890s when it was further deepened. No major improvements in navigation have been made since; vessels of 250 tons burthen reached Worcester in 1945. As far as Tewkesbury was concerned, the improvement of the Severn navigation did not keep the quay basin busy; the river carrying trade was reduced to 'very shadowy proportions compared with what it had formerly been', the *Town Guide* commented in 1895, a fact which it attributed, no doubt correctly, to the effect of the 'steam horse' and improved roads. Healing's mills continued to be supplied with corn by river for about a hundred years and their fleet of barges still lies at the quayside.

Public Health

Living conditions in the town deteriorated in the 19th century as more families pressed into the restricted built-up area. Population increase from 4,000 to just under 6,000 between 1801 and 1841 was rather less than many towns experienced, but everywhere housing and sanitation were too primitive to sustain these concentrations of people. A grim picture of life behind Tewkesbury's smarter frontages emerges from a report by T. W. Rammell, inspector of the national Board of Health, after his three-day enquiry in 1849. The poorer inhabitants were almost entirely without sanitation; as a result, 'the streets and alleys are much loaded with offensive filth'. Many inhabitants kept pigs as they had in past centuries; during the floods of the previous year pigs had been moved to upstairs rooms. Later, 30 people were reported for keeping pigs which were a nuisance to their neighbours. Jack, the rag-and-bone man in St Mary's Lane, kept his donkey in the kitchen. The houses were built so close together that they were 'back to back with those of their neighbours', so that ventilation was also poor. No wonder the editor of the *Tewkesbury Record*, on a walk through the town one evening early in September, described the 'frequent puffs of disagreeable odour' at many of the alley entrances.

Another visitor to the town, despite her interest in the picturesque, also observed the dark side. Dinah Mulock, later Mrs. Craik, visited Tewkesbury in 1852 before she wrote her novel *John Halifax, Gentleman*. She immediately saw in the town the setting for the story which she had been thinking about for some time. She sheltered from the rain in an alley which she describes at the very beginning of the story. It led out of High Street yet showed 'a glimmer of green field at the further end', perhaps Double Alley, as she noted the 'open house-doors on either side through which came the drowsy burr of many a stocking-loom, the prattle of children paddling in the gutter, and sailing thereon a fleet of potato parings'. A few pages later she seems to make use of her impressions again:

> I was less struck by the beauty of the picturesque old town than by the muddiness of its pathways, and the mingled noises of murmuring looms, scolding women, and squabbling children, that came up from the alleys which lay between the High Street and the Avon. In those alleys were hundreds of our poor folk living, huddled together in misery, rags and dirt.

Nearly a hundred people were registered in Double Alley on the night of the census of 1841, of whom a quarter were children under ten years old. On average, there were five people in each household, and there could be whole families living in one room. Double Alley was opposite the *Tudor House Hotel*; it is now the site of a new shopping area. Farther down the High Street, in Old Post Office Alley, there were 57 inhabitants; again a quarter were under ten years old. Bank Alley, off Church Street, which was behind the Old Hat Shop, contained 40 people, with three premises uninhabited. These three alleys were amongst 19, containing together about two hundred households, which were without any sanitary provision at all. There were more than one hundred alleys off the three main streets at this date.

Cholera in 1831 brought public attention to focus on the bad living conditions of the poor. Towns were recommended to set up Local Boards of Health and Tewkesbury followed this advice. Six doctors were amongst the first 28 members. Every alley and court was visited, cleanliness was encouraged, lime-wash was provided. Cholera reached Barton Street in July 1832 and, before it finished in September, 76 people had died; nearly half lived in alleys, and 16 lived in St Mary's Lane. The occupiers of the front houses escaped relatively unscathed. 'The destitute, the filthy and the dissolute were usually the first to be attacked.' The crisis passed, and with it the Board of Health.

The limitations of the Paving Commissioners' work were clearly seen at this time, but nothing was done until a second cholera epidemic threatened. In 1847 the numerous vacancies on the Commission were filled, and an effort was made to address Tewkesbury's problems, but the Commissioners found that their powers were inadequate, particularly in the amount of money they could raise. In 1848 an Act of Parliament provided a national framework for the setting up of local Boards of Health; the council decided to take up the proffered authority, which went much beyond the local Paving Act of 50 years earlier. It was bound to in any case. The death rate in the town between 1842 and 1847 was 28 per thousand, 'being in excess beyond the average rates presented by even the most crowded districts of large manufacturing towns, and denoting most unequivocally the existence of local circumstances strongly unfavourable to health'. With mortality over the limit specified by the 1848 Act, Tewkesbury was obliged to set up a Board. To make doubly sure, a petition signed by 163 ratepayers was presented, though not without voluble opposition. Before the local Board was formed in 1850, a second attack of cholera killed 54 people.

The Public Health Act seems to mark the first real intrusion of government into the regulation and inspection of private property. The Paving Commission had exercised some powers comparable with modern planning authorities, but they could only deal with obstruction on roads and pavements; the Board of Health could inspect private premises, enforce its requirements, and approve proposals for new buildings. It took over from the Paving Commission responsibility for roads. The members of the council constituted the Board whose work was, thereafter, the major part of the council's business.

Once in office, the board started to work on the most basic of Tewkesbury's problems, the provision of sewers and privies, albeit rather slowly. One privy per alley was considered adequate, but 200 properties lacked any access to even this level of amenity. A cottage sometimes had to be purchased for conversion, if the owner could not be persuaded to carry out the improvement. This was the case in Bank Alley for example. The front houses often did have either private sewers or connections with the street drains. The conservative editor of the *Tewkesbury Register* deplored the owners' lack of responsibility. 'The decency and comfort of the poorer classes have been very much promoted by the improvements of late years; but so utterly neglectful were formerly the owners of cottage property that much remains to be done before their tenants are properly accommodated.' Overcrowding of cottages was not tackled for another 50 years, since it involved embarking on a costly house-building programme.

The improvements led to further problems. Moore started a campaign in the *Register* in 1865, drawing attention to the 'filthy state' of the Swilgate, 'into which half the drainage of the town flowed, rendering its stench almost unbearable'. When brick drains had first been constructed, from 1824 onwards, they had chiefly taken surface water from the roads; there were three outlets on the Swilgate and five on the Avon. Now sewers taking waste farther from the town were needed. A scheme to relieve the Swilgate was prepared, with an outfall towards the Lower Lode. The following year Moore campaigned for similar action to be taken over the Avon: 'whilst the sewage of the Swilgate is being got rid of, the sewage of the Avon is being allowed to accumulate to the danger of the public health'. He said that when the Abbey mills were not working, the channel below the mill was nearly dry, so that the flow in the Mill Avon was not much better than in the Swilgate. The Board of Health needed some urging, but plans were prepared and works to drain High Street and Church Street commenced. The *Register* lamented in 1869 that the work was only 'half-finished'. The system provided then served Tewkesbury for nearly one hundred years, until after the Second World War.

The Waterworks

Mortality did not diminish much despite the improvements made by the Board of Health because water supply was the crucial element which the Board failed to tackle. The inhabitants drew their water from wells, or from the Avon. One pump per alley was often all there was, and not infrequently it was useless. The pump in Double Alley had been broken for three years when T. W. Rammell made his enquiry in 1849; the one in Townsend's Alley for seven years. There were only three public pumps in the town, so alley-dwellers without had to buy water or beg from a neighbour whose pump was working. The brewery used Severn water brought in casks by boat, an eloquent testimony to the state of the local water supply.

Tewkesbury finally gained a piped main water supply in 1870, but only because of Cheltenham's expanding requirement. A private water company had been formed in 1824 which supplied a few of Cheltenham's houses from a reservoir at Hewlett's on the eastern outskirts. As Cheltenham grew, there was a need for a supply to the poorer houses; it could not be left to private enterprise because the water company charged too much and was not interested in unprofitable public service. Cheltenham's new Improvement Commissioners applied for an Act to draw water from the springs at South Cerney; the water company applied for an Act to draw water from the River Severn near the Mythe. Out of this conflict, Tewkesbury gained a water supply. During 1863 surveyors were at work, planning the route to Cheltenham through Tewkesbury and Tredington, though the townsfolk were not aware of the scheme being considered; 'it has been a matter of much speculation as to what railway was coming through the town', the *Register* reported.

Early in 1864 the Cheltenham Waterworks Company asked for Tewkesbury council's support. Opinion was at first divided; some resented giving power over the town's streets to strangers and the proposed siting of the works on the Ham was not acceptable. Finally, in 1865, the council petitioned parliament in support of the company; it had agreed to give Tewkesbury a constant water supply in return for taking the pipes through the main streets, and to site the works at the Mythe. The clauses of the bill relating to the supply of water to Cheltenham were rejected in the House of Lords through the pressure of Cheltenham's Improvement Commissioners; the Act was passed only with respect to Tewkesbury. In the end, the water company lost its fight to supply Cheltenham because the Borough Council bought it out. It had been right about the eventual source of Cheltenham's water, though not until 1894 did the town draw from the Mythe works.

Preparations for the new water works started slowly. Land in Brick Kiln meadow and Pear Tree orchard was purchased. A new footpath was constructed, giving access to the Tute; the company was not allowed to stop the path along the Severn bank and underneath the Mythe bridge. Building started in 1869; pride was evident in the Gothic style of the pumping station combined with the engine-man's residence, built of red and black bricks with Bath stone dressings. The building still exists, on the left-hand side of the approach road to the Mythe bridge, though partly obscured by later extensions. On the other side of the road an ornamental brick tower provided sufficient head of water, it was said, to supply the tops of the highest houses in Tewkesbury. The foundation stone was laid in June 1869, with a procession of Tewkesbury and Cheltenham town dignitaries, mace bearers and a brass band. After the ceremony there was a celebration lunch in the town hall. The tower was replaced 20 years later by one higher up on Mythe hill, built to provide a greater head of water. The first tower was demolished in 1930 and the bricks used to build the houses on the same site; the second tower is now a private house. From the beginning, the Waterworks Company thought on a grand scale. The Act authorised 3,000,000 gallons a day to be extracted from the Severn, an amount greatly in excess of what was actually extracted; two double-acting steam engines were commissioned to pump a mere 12,000 gallons a day. Even in 1937 only 2,000,000 gallons were being drawn.

62. At the side of the approach road to Mythe Bridge, Cheltenham Waterworks Company in 1870 built a brick residence for the engine and the engineman.

63. About the same date, 1872, the Rural Hospital was built in the Oldbury. The right-hand end is an extension of 1892.

The company was investing a large sum of money speculatively – it built with Cheltenham in mind – and was in danger of having no Tewkesbury subscribers at all. A public meeting in February 1870 protested at the company's proposed scale of charges. It was accused of trying to recover the £8,000-£10,000 spent fighting for parliamentary sanction. To frighten the company, it was suggested that Tewkesbury's wells were quite adequate, even though the previous summer they had been dry. Fortunately, satisfactory rates were agreed, and by March 1870 the pipes were filled.

The process of extending the supply to houses, cottages and alleys was slow. The Board of Health used the water to clean the streets, and it was piped to the Tewkesbury Union workhouse. The *Register* reported with satisfaction in May 1871 how quickly a fire had been extinguished using the piped supply. Soon the benefits for the health of the town were appreciated. When the parliamentary battle to supply Cheltenham was renewed in 1878, a Tewkesbury witness supported the company in evidence to the Select Committee. He pointed to the marked fall in the death rate since 1870, from 26 to 16 per thousand. Households with piped water were no longer the victims of typhus infections. Yet 50 years after installing the main, a quarter of the houses were still not connected.

From the first there was argument over the purity of Severn water. One advantage the Waterworks Company saw in supplying Tewkesbury from the Severn was to dispel Cheltenham's prejudice. In evidence to the House of Commons, a spokesman from Gloucester, opposing the company, pointed to the number of large towns above Tewkesbury which discharged their waste into the river. 'Moreover, there were situated on its banks, on both sides, brickyards, tanyards, chemical and various other manufactories, all of which pour their abominations into the stream.' The company's supporters said the Severn was purer than the Thames above Teddington Lock, which was probably true but not necessarily comforting. Worcester, they said, used Severn water not only for general domestic purposes, 'but frequently for drinking', a reminder that drinking water, for many, came in the form of beer, and had been boiled. The company managed to convince the parliamentary referees that the water was safe to drink, at any rate after some simple filtering had been done. The water went first into settling tanks, and then through slow sand filters before being pumped up to the water tower. Enough water was stored to be able to avoid drawing from the Severn for several weeks if necessary. Nonetheless at flood times there were recurring complaints about cloudiness and the slow sand filters were inadequate. In 1911 the company installed perhaps the first example of a new type of filter which has since become universal. Chlorination was introduced at the same time.

Quite soon after the Mythe works were opened, unusually severe weather threatened their operation. In 1881, there was one of the rare occasions when the Severn was completely frozen and the water filters were covered with over a foot of ice; a similar cold spell occurred in 1940. A few years after the freeze of 1881, Tewkesbury experienced one of the 'great floods' in its history. The town was completely surrounded by water, as it had been in 1814 and in 1770. The town clerk in 1770 had sailed right round the town in an excise boat, from the rivers Carrant to Swilgate to Mill Avon and back over King John's bridge; on the way he had rescued a doctor, found sitting astride his garden wall topped with broken glass, after his boat had sunk. In the 1886 flood, 'scores' of houses were partly submerged. The water rose so suddenly that people were caught unawares and had no time to rescue carpets and furniture from downstairs rooms. Only the top rail of the fence along the Mythe road was visible. After the long spell of cold weather in 1947 there was an even greater flood; it was estimated that more than 17,000 million gallons of water per day passed the Severn intake. It perhaps equalled the famous flood of 1483, 'Buckingham's water', so-called because the Duke of Buckingham was prevented from crossing with a rebel army from Wales by the sudden and enormous rush of water, which, it was said, drowned many people as well as animals. The Water Company state that the supply of water has never been interrupted.

The Cemetery and the Hospital

One suggested way of reducing the dangers to health in 19th-century towns was to provide burial grounds away from built-up areas. The graveyards round the churches seemed uncomfortably close during outbreaks of cholera, and special arrangements were made in Tewkesbury to bury victims in the grounds of the workhouse. Beyond the workhouse was open ground; in 1857 a cemetery was opened there and in 1880 it was enlarged.

Medical care was another area of public initiative. A Dispensary was established in the Oldbury in 1815, supported by subscriptions and donations from public-spirited and better-off inhabitants. It gave medical advice and medicine to the poor. Some people thought that a regular contribution of a penny a week would serve the poor better: more money would be raised, and the poor would not be deterred from calling the doctor – medical attention would be given earlier, when it might cost less. This suggestion was not adopted. The Dispensary was still in existence when the *Register* discussed the merits of establishing a 'rural hospital' to serve the 14,000 inhabitants of the Tewkesbury Union, particularly in cases of accident. Like the Dispensary it would rely on voluntary contributions. Subscribers would 'recommend' patients, who would contribute according to their means.

Hospitals had been provided on this principle for many years. Recently, Bourton-on-the-Water had established one, which a party of three gentlemen visited. They recommended that Tewkesbury's hospital should be on exactly the same scale. There was opposition on the grounds that Tewkesbury was surrounded with hospitals at Gloucester, Worcester and Cheltenham. Moore campaigned for amalgamation with the Dispensary, but this logical move was even more strongly opposed. Three of the town's doctors refused cooperation, but a fourth, Dr. Devereux, became Medical Officer and served in this capacity for many years.

Although the Tewkesbury Union was described as 'a poor district' by the opponents of the rural hospital, 'hearty and liberal support' was forthcoming. Two cottages were adapted and within a short time six patients were being treated. The *Register* wrote enthusiastically that 'the great expectations of the success of the institution have been more than realised'. A year later the governors could report 60 patients admitted, paying from 1s. 0d. to 7s. 6d. (5p to 37.5p) per week. After six years, the hospital had treated 480 patients, the majority surgical cases, and some the victims of serious accidents in the town.

In 1871 a purpose-built hospital was designed by a Cheltenham architect and built by Collins & Cullis. It was domestic in appearance, and had space for 10 beds. It was later extended to 26 beds but otherwise continued unaltered until 1934. Medical standards had changed by then, and the hospital seemed gloomy and inconvenient. Moreover, the number of patients treated each year was three times as many as in 1871, mainly, it was suggested, because of motor accidents. Funds were raised to buy a new site, Orchard House off Barton Street, where a new 22-bed hospital was built. The Dispensary treated several hundred out-patients every year, and both charitable institutions continued in parallel until after the Second World War. The Tewkesbury council purchased the old hospital, and the ground floor rooms were made into a free library in 1936. The library has now moved into the former grammar school next to the *Bell Hotel*.

Electricity

Electricity was the last major public utility to be available in Tewkesbury. Councillor Jones, an important coal merchant in the town, first raised the question in 1889, and again in 1892. Councillor Jackson tried in 1891. National legislation of 1882 and 1888 had created the general framework for municipal electric lighting schemes, giving local authorities a measure of control over private companies. With local authority consent, the Board of Trade could issue an order which allowed an electric company to dig up the streets or erect overhead wires. The council considered the matter at length in 1900, aware that the North British Electrical Supply Company was going to apply for a provisional order from the Board of Trade. Members were inclined to think electricity should be a municipal undertaking; their experience of the Gas Company led them to a view which was shared elsewhere, that such companies made too much profit. Relations with the Gas Company were not always smooth; as a result of trying to negotiate better rates for the supply to the street lights, the town had been in darkness for months. Two members of the council had an 'interest' in the Gas Company, and it was unsuccessfully urged that they should withdraw from discussions of the electricity question.

A report was commissioned from Christy Brothers of London; at first it was kept confidential, but eventually a summary was published in the *Register*. Christy's anticipated that electricity would be used not only for lighting of streets, business and private premises, but also for a 'refuse destructor' and a pump to provide river water to flush the sewers. The works were to be along Lower Lode Lane. The council was alarmed by the cost, as its income was limited and the town was already in debt. For the moment the question was shelved.

Healings were generating electricity to light their mills in 1891, which the town guide noted as 'a great desideratum in the interests of health' and by 1903 the Eagle shirt factory also had its own generator. In 1904 the question of a town supply was raised again. The Chepstow and Ross Electric Company and the Southern District Electric Corporation both notified the council of their intention to apply for a provisional order; the local Gas Company recognised the danger and also entered the lists. Councillor Jones hoped competition might make the Gas Company reduce its prices. He foresaw that lighting alone was not likely to be profitable, but that 'electricity would come in more generally for power and heating purposes'. He also spoke of a possibility of electrically-driven cars. In order to frustrate the initiative of the other contenders, the council obtained a provisional order in 1905, which was valid for two years, so effectively postponing discussion.

When the Board of Trade was asked to extend the order, a somewhat tart letter demanded to know what the council had done in the interim. It was clear the initiative could be lost for 42 years because of the 1888 Act, if a private company was granted an order. A way out was found by transferring the council's existing permission to a private company on conditions determined by the council. In this way private enterprise bore the costs and the risk. Mr. J. Parker, a civil engineer and borough surveyor of Hereford, had been instrumental in the Chepstow and Ross Company, which had been interested in Tewkesbury a few years before. He now formed the Tewkesbury Electric Light Company Limited. Two members of the council had an interest in this enterprise. It later became a subsidiary of the Shropshire, Worcestershire and Staffordsire Electric Power Company.

The works were erected in St Mary's Lane, and the company set about laying cable, mainly under the streets, but some overhead. Optimistically, the Gas Company's contract to light the streets was not renewed, but it had stout supporters in the council; they objected to the cost of buying new electric light lamp standards, particularly as only the front streets would be lit by electricity and the back streets would be dependent on gas lights. After much argument about the time span of the contract, the Gas Company agreed to continue for one year, and this decision in practice gave it another eight years. Some businesses, like the *Royal Hop Pole Hotel* and the Empire Meat Company, made their own arrangements to place electric lights outside their premises. During the First World War the question was raised occasionally, but for some time there were lighting restrictions in force and only three gas lamps were lit. In 1917 an experimental electric light was hung over Church Street. A general electric scheme was prepared in 1920 and the council began to replace the gas lamps, a few at a time. Both systems continued in operation together until after the Second World War; in 1962 there were still 40 gas lights in use in the town.

Restoration and Conservation

(i) *Houses*. Dyde had considered Tewkesbury a modern, brick-built town in the 1790s; 50 years later it was being appreciated as a store of ancient timber-framed houses. The third congress of the British Archaeological Association met in Gloucester in 1846, and visited Tewkesbury; as well as seeing the abbey, the members were shown the old houses and were given a lecture on them by John Britton, F.S.A. He was the first to suggest that the undercroft of the house on the corner of St Mary's Lane was not a church but part of a 13th-century inn. The writer of the town guide was not inclined to accept his suggestion, though respecting the 'great antiquary and archaeologist', but modern opinion supports Mr. Britton. Other archaeological societies visited the town in the next few decades. Interest was mainly concentrated on a small number of unusual and picturesque houses, like the Nodding Gables or the Hat Shop; Rowe, a Cheltenham printer, had made a series of lithographs of these particular buildings in his *Old Houses of Tewkesbury* in 1839. A review at the time said he had 'rescued these fast vanishing remnants of what the town was, from the oblivion which otherwise awaits them'.

The Bristol and Gloucester Archaeological Society was founded in 1876. Its first summer meeting was held in Gloucester, and the programme included visits to Tewkesbury and Deerhurst. In 1885 the society met in Tewkesbury. On this occasion Mr. Frederick Moore read a paper on Tewkesbury's old houses and conducted a party round the town. Subsequently, with his brother, H. P. Moore, he expanded the paper and it was printed by North in 1886, and included as a supplement to the town guide of 1895.

About 1860 there was a 'change in feeling with respect to conservation'. The local builder, Thomas Collins, is given the credit in North's guide of 1895, where it is suggested that but for his work all the old houses would 'very probably' have gone, with the single exception of the Nodding Gables which many wished to see preserved. North said that the change had come just in time. Many old buildings had gone, to make way for modern shops and dwelling-houses. Those that had so far survived were 'in a very dilapidated state, and irremediable decay was fast over-spreading them'. Collins purchased a number in order to preserve them, 'reconstructing parts which had gone too far in dilapidation'.

The first house which Collins restored in 1860 was opposite the *Hop Pole*; in the 1980s it was gutted by fire. In 1865 he restored the Cross House, where he removed the roughcast from front and side. This became his own home. The front range of windows on the *Berkeley Arms* with the carved tracery was uncovered in 1877. The property next door, including Lilly's Alley, was found to have similar windows in 1895. Collins removed the roughcast from the *Bell* and from the house next to the *Black Bear* in High Street. Other characterful houses which he restored included the Nodding Gables, the Wheatsheaf and Clarence House in High Street, and the Old Hat Shop in Church Street. Before he died in 1900 he had the satisfaction of seeing these old houses appreciated as 'archaeological treasures'.

The obituary in the *Tewkesbury Register* described Collins' progress from a working stone-mason who had served a seven-year apprenticeship to mayor of the borough and in 1897 honorary freeman. Collins was born in Tewkesbury; there were bricklayers and masons of the same name who were freemen of the town in the 18th century. About 1859 he formed a partnership with William Cullis, bricklayer and plasterer; each had been working on his own and had employed four men in 1851. Collins and Cullis took another partner, W. H. James of Cirencester, who seems to have handled large building contracts like the erection of the Borough mills in 1865. James retired, and the Collins and Cullis partnership was dissolved in 1877. Thereafter a nephew, Francis William Godfrey, managed the business and became a partner in 1895. Collins said he was employing 400 men in 1881. After Collins' death, Godfrey occupied the Cross House. In 1939 the 'extensive works' of the firm of Collins and Godfrey were described as 'widely known for ecclesiastical and school work'. During the Second World War the business of the joinery workshops contracted, it was suggested because of the 'introduction of imported, ready-made joinery and the replacement of wood by metal for window frames'. The name of Collins and Godfrey is recorded on many humble iron gratings in the town and the firm was responsible for a number of public buildings and many houses in the neighbourhood. It disappeared in the 1970s.

(ii) *The Abbey church.* Thomas Collins' major work was in the restoration of Worcester, Gloucester and Hereford cathedrals, and Tewkesbury Abbey. In 1864 an article appeared in the *Gloucester Chronicle* proposing that now the three great cathedrals were being cared for, it was time to turn attention to Tewkesbury. Moore frequently wrote in the *Register* about the subject of restoration – it had been discussed, he said, 'more or less for the last twenty years'. Indeed, major work had been planned 30 years earlier

64. The abbey monument to Thomas Collins (1819-1900) records that he was five times mayor and that he was 'zealous in preserving the ancient beauty of his native town'. A new development on the site of his builder's yard is called Collins Court.

but left undone for lack of funds. Moore hoped that a start was being made in 1860 when a new window was placed in the east end; on this occasion Sir George Gilbert Scott had visited the abbey and given advice. In May 1864 a public meeting was held at the town hall to consider ways and means. In company with Thomas Collins, Scott examined the abbey and in August gave his opinion on the 'best mode of effecting the restoration'.

The *Register* printed Scott's report. 'In restoring a church, one is apt to suppose that the object is to bring it back to the state in which it was at some former period.' Scott said it was clearly impossible to bring the abbey back to the Norman style of its first construction. On the other hand, he went on:

'In your church, the Norman structure still remains – subject to more or less alteration – as the nucleus of the entire building, and in many parts almost unaltered, especially the noble central tower, which is one of the most majestic which remain to us, and is, throughout, a Norman structure'.

The purpose of the restoration, he said, should be to make it again 'substantial' and to fit it for use by the Church of England. Structurally, he found the abbey

in a much better state of repair than you generally find a similar church to be. Happily the building itself has suffered less from time and mutilation than is the common lot of ancient structures. The walls seem to have been very firmly built, and, in the main, continue sound and strong. The south transept is an exception to this, and requires considerable reparation, including the careful underpinning of its foundations.

The report must have pleased Tewkesbury townsfolk, who had many times carried out repairs to their church, most recently between 1824 and 1830, when the exterior of the tower and the foundations generally had been extensively renovated. Even so, the interior was apparently very damp; the *Register* later spoke of 'the walls streaming with moisture and the continuous damp and musty atmosphere which pervaded the whole building'.

Following the report, a fund was opened, and £4,000 was promised provided the work was not started until adequate funds were available to complete it. As a result, nothing further was done for some years. Then Thomas Collins, at his own expense, offered to restore the misericords, or 'monks pews', to the choir, which involved removing some of the existing seating. The following year he offered to continue the work by clearing all the 18th-century wooden galleries from the transepts and eastern two bays of the nave, and repairing the stone piers of the tower which had been cut into when the pews had been fitted. This offer created the impetus for restoration to be vigorously pursued. In 1874, Sir George Gilbert Scott was invited to prepare plans and to instruct Collins and Cullis to start work.

Restoration of the choir, transepts and chapels began, while services were held in the main part of the nave. Fittings considered unsightly, such as pews, pulpit and organ gallery, and also monuments, were removed. For the first time in centuries, the whole length of Tewkesbury Abbey would be seen, with the removal of the screen which had cut off part of the nave and all the eastern end of the church, where the monks had worshipped, from the rest of the nave. The organ screen was relatively modern, though in the original position. New fittings were designed and made through the generosity of local inhabitants. The floors, which were a hotch-potch of different materials, brick, stone, tiles and wood, were relaid, and gravestones either removed or laid flat. The stone-work was cleaned, repaired and repointed, which meant undoing the restoration work of a generation earlier, when the stone had been scraped and then covered with a stone-coloured distemper. The roof was coloured by a London firm. The motif of the suns in the choir was copied and used in the tower ceiling.

As the work proceeded, it became something of an archaeological investigation. When the floors were taken up, the opportunity was seized to excavate all the notable burials of the abbey's early days. A detailed account of this work was included in Kelly's *Directory*. New tiles were commissioned to the same heraldic designs as ancient tiles which were found. In the past, one floor had been laid on another; now the original levels of the nave were restored, including the step where the screen had been. As a result, the bases of the pillars were revealed.

Thomas Collins was interested in archaeology; he was to discover the Saxon chapel at Deerhurst in 1885. At Tewkesbury, he had a particular opportunity for investigation in the chapels on the north side of the abbey. For centuries they had been the grammar school, but had been abandoned because of extreme dilapidation. Collins progressively stripped off the alterations and accumulations of the past. He found the original floor four feet below the existing level; the steps outside indicate the depth to which rubbish had accumulated. He also found the pillars which had once separated the building from another to the west. The roof was supported with posts to prevent it falling in; Scott designed a new one based on study of what remained together with features of later date, making an odd re-creation of historic development. The Freemasons paid for part of the work. These chapels are now the book shop and a choir room.

Outside, the roofs of the chapels at the eastern end were repaired and drainage was provided on three sides. The approach to the abbey was much improved by the excavation of soil so that the path and porch were on the same level. Previously there were nine steps down to the porch and another into the aisle. The porch was repaired and the gates moved to the street, where they are today.

The abbey was opened in September 1879 with considerable ceremony. Scott had died the previous year, only two weeks after inspecting the work at Tewkesbury. Collins gave a celebratory dinner in the *Swan Hotel* for all his workpeople, after a boat trip to Worcester and a special 'workmen's service' in the abbey. The *Guardian* reported that it was 'a true restoration . . . All that is really beautiful has been preserved: only the disfigurements of an age which cared nothing for historic associations and architectural grandeur have been swept away'.

Not everyone agreed; it depended on a religious rather than an architectural viewpoint. The arrangements which the restoration committee had swept away had been designed for listening to sermons. The area beyond the screen had been a smaller church within the abbey, with the pews arranged crossways in the choir, a wine-glass pulpit and sounding board against one of the tower pillars, and pews and galleries in the transepts facing inwards. Everyone who mattered sat in this part of the church. In the new arrangement, the ancient misericords were placed lengthways for choir and clergy, and pulpit and seats were put in the nave for the congregation; now the choir's voices would be heard a little distanced from the congregation, and an atmosphere of beauty and holiness created. With the abbey's restoration, the long tradition of Puritanism in the town had come to an end. The Puritans had placed emphasis on preaching; Scott was associated with the high church or Anglo-Catholic revival in the Church of England, which placed emphasis on ritual.

William Morris gave forceful expression to the architectural viewpoint on restoration, in a letter of March 1877 to the London journal, *The Athenaeum*. A meeting had been held in Lambeth Palace to launch a national appeal for funds and the report in the paper caught Morris's eye. 'On looking closer, I saw that this time it is nothing less

65. The gates to the churchyard, given in 1750 by Viscount Gage, M.P., were moved in the Victorian restoration from the top of the steps leading to the porch.

than the minster of Tewkesbury that is to be destroyed by Sir Gilbert Scott.' In his letter, Morris proposed a Society for the Protection of Ancient Buildings, to keep watch on old monuments 'to protest against all restoration that means more than keeping out wind and weather, and by all means, literary and other, to awaken a feeling that our ancient monuments are not mere ecclesiastical toys, but sacred monuments of the nation's growth and hope'.

In the Manifesto for the Society he wrote of the 'strange idea of restoration which implies that it is possible to strip from a building this, that and the other part of its history – of its life that is – and then to stay the hand at some arbitrary point, and leave it still historical, living, and even as it once was'. Morris gathered a notable committee which included a number of well-known artists and writers, and the society exists today, giving technical advice and support to anyone attempting to 'conserve' an ancient building.

The news of Morris's intervention eventually reached Tewkesbury. An article in the *Birmingham Post*, repeating one from the *Art Journal*, was spotted in September. The editor of the *Register*, as honorary secretary of the restoration committee, was naturally offended. 'Who is Mr. Morris?' he asked. Morris had by this date established himself as a designer and craftsman, and successful manufacturer since 1861. The *Register* suggested he was 'known to a small circle of admirers as a poet'. The following week a letter was published suggesting Morris was not well-informed; he evidently had no knowledge of the careful archaeological work and discoveries nor of the mutilation of the tower pillars by 'churchwarden restorers of the Georgian era'. The editor added: 'We have never heard of any visit paid to the abbey by Mr. Morris; on the contrary we have reason to believe he has never seen it'. The correspondence in the national press continued in lively vein off and on for 20 years, as the conservationists attacked the continuing restoration.

As far as Tewkesbury was concerned, not all the work planned was completed when the abbey was reopened; some items were postponed, though as much for lack of money as because of disapproval. 'The restoration of Tewkesbury abbey has of course not progressed, nor will it continue to do so, without providing a theme for cavillers', Moore wrote in 1882. 'The abbey restoration will go on all the same.' The external repair of the main roofs was still to be done, and was certainly necessary. The nave roof and bosses were coloured by Gambier Parry of

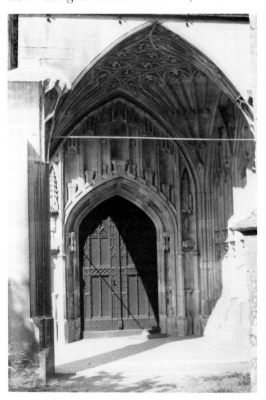

66. The porchway over the re-opened south doorway of the church, constructed in 1900, was based on the remaining traces of the cloister vaulting.

Highnam Court, near Gloucester, but more discreetly than the choir decorations which had been done by a London firm. A new west window was planned; the perpendicular-style window had been built in 1686, replacing one which was blown down. Scott had discovered that originally there had been a seventh arch in the west end, almost certainly destroyed in inserting the first perpendicular window in the 15th century. There may have been discussions in the restoration committee about restoring the arch, and rebuilding the west end with small windows in the Norman style. A hint reached S.P.A.B. which campaigned vigorously against the work. Only the stonework of the window as it existed was finally repaired.

Later, again at his own expense, Collins set about one of the most interesting ideas, that of restoring the cloister. There was no public way round the south side of the abbey, which belonged with the Abbey House to a private owner. When John Martin of Upper Hall, Ledbury, died, his property was auctioned. The restoration committee raised a special subscription and was able to purchase the house in July 1883, with land round the abbey and the abbot's gateway which Martin had restored. This action aroused considerable national interest, and was the subject of a supportive resolution by the Society of Antiquaries of London. The house became the vicarage, a striking benefaction to the town. A path was opened at the back of the abbey, together with the blocked doorway to the cloister, in 1893. Collins was reconstructing one bay of the cloister at the time of his death and his nephew, F. W. Godfrey, completed it. No more was done, though it could have been a most imaginative improvement to the abbey surroundings. Collins and Moore both died within ten days of each other in January 1900. A monument to Collins, which was said to be a most life-like portrait, was erected in the abbey by public subscription.

Collins has been criticised for his restoration work, much of which he paid for himself although he was not a very wealthy man, leaving £18,000 at his death. At the celebratory dinner after the opening of the abbey in 1879 he spoke of his great love for the building. 'Some of his first impulses and aspirations were gained from the abbey church. As a young man he had studied in that school of art and tried to understand the principles that moved the builders of that noble pile. He had in a very humble way tried to light his taper at the torch of those noble builders'.

Each generation has had to make its contribution to the maintenance of so ancient a structure. The 800th anniversary of the consecration of the church was commemorated in 1923 by the restoration of the seven choir windows. Important repairs were necessary because of the serious infestation of death-watch beetle, first discovered in the tower in 1933 and then in the whole structure in 1956. The tower was repaired on the outside between 1935 and 1939. National and international appeals have been made. Whatever Morris may have argued about historical authenticity, the work of Scott, Collins, Moore and the other citizens of that time ensured that the abbey remained esteemed by the townsfolk whose predecessors had purchased it from Henry VIII.

Victorian Industries

The first large-scale ordnance map of Tewkesbury was published in 1886, based on a survey made in 1883. It can be used as an interesting guide to the Victorian industries of the town, especially when put with a rating list and census returns of similar date. A variety of small-scale enterprises, in textiles, building, brewing, milling, shoe manufacture and engineering are indicated by the larger blocks of shading on the map.

A walk round the town might start with the oldest of the traditional industries, the Abbey corn mills, which were still in use, despite the presence of the much larger Borough Mills at the quay; both these buildings may be seen today. At the end of Mill Bank and along St Mary's Lane there was a tannery; although the tanning of leather had been an important traditional industry, the tan pits were disused when the map was being made. Dinah Mulock had seen the tannery and it was part of the setting for *John Halifax, Gentleman*. Subsequently, a shoe factory used part of the tannery, and in the early 20th century a firm of ironmongers, Thomas B. Milner and Company. This firm seems to have been the first to use the name 'Halifax Works'. The monument to Dinah Mulock had been put in the abbey in 1890, so impressing the book on Tewkesbury's consciousness. The Electricity Company also used part of the tannery for its works. A few of the tannery buildings still remain.

At the end of St Mary's Lane the map shows a chemical works which produced manures and cattle food. Near the Cross, and reached by a narrow lane called Post Office Lane, there was a shoe factory. Established in 1860 by Knight and May, boot and shoe wholesalers, it was called the 'Eagle' works, and showed an attempt to introduce a larger scale of production to one of the traditional crafts in the town, at a time of general expansion. At first, about ninety men were employed, but the factory was not successful; after some interruptions to production, including a strike in 1863, it closed in 1870. The map indicates that the factory was disused in 1883.

From the Cross, a walk down Tolsey Lane would pass the extensive builder's yard of Thomas Collins. Only Tolsey House remains today, in later years the office, where the clerk also lived. It has a mock-Tudor front, recalling Collins' interest in timber framing. Then there was Nailors Square, an indication of a trade which Bennett had described, in 1830, as one of the staple industries of the town. It lasted for some time longer; Price & Robinson, ironmongers, nail manufacturers and tin plate workers, were listed in the 1856 directory, and there were nailors in the 1881 census. Near the Borough mills were two breweries, Abbey brewery, which stretched all along Smith's Lane, and the Tewkesbury brewery on Quay Street of Blizard, Colman and Company. The name can be seen on a building now used by the Borough mills and the medallions of a hand holding a sheaf of corn are most distinctive. At the top of High Street, between the *Black Bear* and King John's Bridge, stood another brewery and distillery, which had existed since 1770. Beyond the bridge was Bathurst's boat-building yard.

By this date, the Oldbury had quite a number of houses and industrial premises, including engineering works. One engineer, James Savory, had come to Tewkesbury in 1841 and had set up the Ne Plus Ultra pin factory; he built new premises near the High Street station in 1855 and in 1881 described himself as an 'engineer, civil and practical'; another, James Pickering, was recorded in 1885 as a 'machinist'. In Station Street a very large malthouse had been built, where all the children had been feasted in 1863 when the Prince of Wales was married. Tewkesbury had had many small malt houses in the past but most were probably disused by this date, and are not marked on the 1886 map. The most notable industrial building in the Oldbury was the textile factory in East Street, since converted into houses. A silk mill and a shirt factory were also in the area.

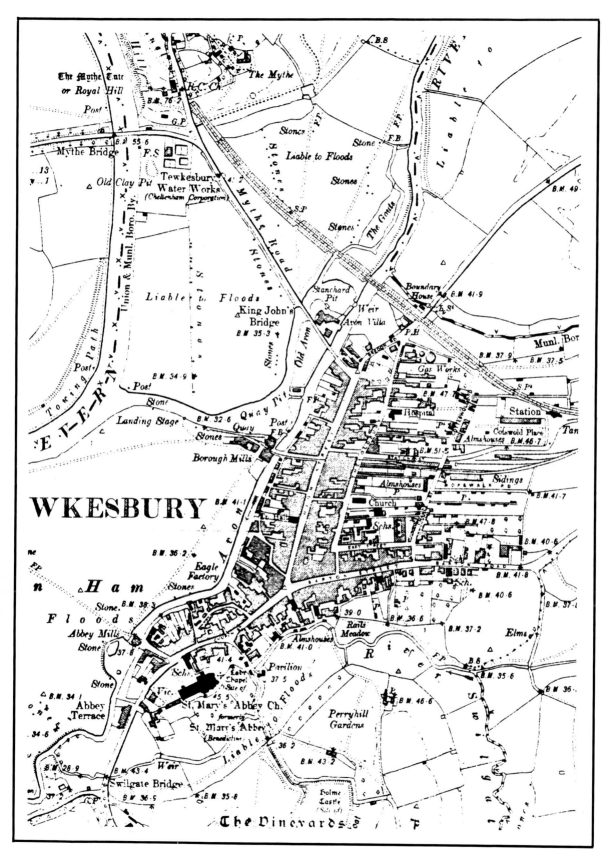

ORDNANCE SURVEY MAP SURVEYED 1882-3
published 1886; 2nd edition 1903

Textile Manufacture

The East Street factory was from the beginning designed for textile production. It had been built by George Freeman in 1825-6, as a cotton lace factory. Freeman, with two others, had patented a new machine for the manufacture of 'bobbin lace' or 'twist net'. He had left Nottingham and come to Tewkesbury after an attempt to start a business in Warwick. When the first block of the building was complete, 37 lace machines were installed; 37 lace makers, mostly women, were recorded in the 1851 census. In the 1830s, he was employing about one hundred and fifty people altogether, and had installed a steam engine. The factory worked until Freeman retired, about 1853, and then seems to have been empty for several years, until an effort was made to revive the hosiery business.

From the time of the general depression in the frame-work knitting trade in the 1840s, stocking makers had drifted away from Tewkesbury; most significant, two hosiers had moved, James Hooke to Exeter and James Blount Lewis to Nottingham, 'to take advantage of better power and transport facilities'. Nonetheless, in 1851 there were still 225 stocking knitters in the Tewkesbury area, and none in any other part of the county. A few years later the *Register* wrote gloomily of the 'depressed, we might also say, extinguished condition of the stocking trade', and the *Record* of 'the disappearance of the lace trade from our factories, the transfer of our trade to rival towns'. The attempt in the 1860s to revive the hosiery trade, and the East Street lace factory, was therefore warmly welcomed. The Patent Renewable Hosiery Company extended and re-equipped the East Street premises and opened in festive spirit. Barton Street and Chance Street were decorated with bunting, and a banner across the street proclaimed 'Prosperity to the Manufactory of Tewkesbury and plenty to the Poor'. An article, with a picture of machines in the factory, appeared in the *Illustrated Times* in November 1860. One hundred hands were taken on, and there were optimistic predictions that it would soon be six hundred. Four months later disaster struck – the owner had died and the two hosiers, Owen and Uglow, had been declared bankrupt. Owen had invented and patented a 'renewable' stocking, which could have a new heel inserted when the first one was worn out. It was the intention to manufacture to this patent in Tewkesbury, but disagreements prevented it; the *Register* presumed that the new stockings 'have therefore been made since at Nottingham'.

Two local men, one a solicitor and the other a doctor, restarted the factory as the Tewkesbury Hosiery Company Limited. It took on 103 people in October 1862, all out-of-work knitters, and manufactured in wool. The trade faltered, as the hopes for army contracts did not materialise. An impressive number of stockings was made in the 15 months of operation, about one thousand pairs a week. A new product, seamless shirts knitted on a circular frame, was tried. Just under a year later, the factory closed. At that time, it included three main workshops on the ground floor and three on the first floor, a smith's and a carpenter's shop, bleaching and dyeing houses, trimming shop, warehouse, a 14 h.p. steam engine, and seven cottages fronting Chance Street. Another partnership resumed production until 1870. Then G. & C. Iliffe bought the premises, and converted them to silk throwing, which continued until 1878 when Iliffe's moved to Coventry with all the equipment.

Silk throwing (or spinning) had already been introduced into Tewkesbury. A building behind the fives court and the Wheatsheaf, formerly a theatre, was converted to a silk mill by Humphrey Brown in 1847. As he was elected one of the two members of parliament for Tewkesbury in the same year, the silk mill enterprise seems to have been a way of securing Tewkesbury votes; he was a local man, a merchant and carrier, and had also been active in promoting the Birmingham and Gloucester railway. The first silk business probably did not last for many years; it restarted in 1858 when advertisements for some two hundred operatives appeared in the *Register*, 'and until this gap is filled up, we do not see clearly how parents possessing a quiverful of children are entitled to complain of destitution'. Three years later, the mill employed 160 'hands' but the business had closed before 1870. Thomas Walker, an agricultural engineer, set up in business here in 1871; the old silk looms were still in the building. Walker moved to new premises in Oldbury Street about 1882; when the building was destroyed by fire in 1908, it was reported that the business had been on those premises for 26 years.

Another silk business, Avonside Silk Mills, occupied the Eagle shoe factory for a year or so, employing 120 women and children. It was succeeded in 1874 by a more long-lasting textile venture, the Tewkesbury Manufacturing Company, which had started in Barton Street six years earlier. The company employed about ninety making collars, cuffs and shirts. By 1900, about two hundred were working there, and by 1915 perhaps as many as three hundred, but the factory had closed by 1919. Today, much of the site has been cleared, while a small tie factory occupies a part, so continuing the textile traditions of Tewkesbury. Although there was quite a lot of enterprise in the mid-Victorian period, it was apparently not easy to establish a manufacturing business, despite the labour available in the town.

The failures of the hosiery factories in the 1860s and of silk throwing in the 1870s meant that very few framework knitters could find work; there were at most fifty left, the *Register* estimated in 1878. The final blow seemed to be struck that year when James Hooke died. After his move to Exeter in the 1840s, Hooke had gone on buying Tewkesbury's knitted stockings, but the progress of mechanisation in the north soon completely displaced the hand frames. North thought in 1895 that the peak of the trade in Tewkesbury had been passed as long ago as 1810, and he identified technical change in the design of the looms as the critical factor. A vestige of the hosiery business survived until the turn of the century; three people used the description 'hosier' in 1902. Joseph Williams, who occupied the Old Hat Shop, called himself a hosier up to and after the First World War. He was a general draper and sold carpets as his successor does today. In addition, he was a glover, which makes an interesting link with the glover Bartholomew Read, who occupied the same premises in Church Street in the 17th century. The occupants of Bank Alley behind the Hat Shop probably worked for Williams; in 1881 they included two stocking-makers, a shirt-maker, a sewing machinist and two collar-makers. The alleys may often have provided accommodation for workers employed in the front houses. Charles James Wilkes was perhaps the last active hosier in the town. He tried to continue Hooke's business. His daughter recalled selling his stocking frames as scrap meal in 1902.

At its peak, in 1841, framework-knitting had employed a quarter of the working men of Tewkesbury, as well as their wives and children. No major area of employment replaced the hosiery industry.

Corn Milling

Until the Healing family built the Borough Mills at the quay, in 1865, the Abbey Mills had been important locally. Originally there were two separate water mills on the Abbey Mills site, as 19th-century records made clear, the upper mill which in 1807 had six pairs of stones, and the lower mill which had four pairs. The two mills were the Abbey and Town Mills from medieval times, and in the early 19th century were still known by both names. The mills were separated by a pathway into the Ham until about 1854, when it was diverted round the side. The mills were sold in 1823 with a block of property in that area of Tewkesbury, including the *Bell Hotel*, the bowling green, the large malthouse, cottages on Millbank, and land in the Ham. Four water-wheels drove the sets of grindstones. There was also a malt mill in 1823 with steel rollers, a means of grinding which foreshadows later developments for flour milling. A wages book of 1854 shows the miller employing 17 men and 13 women. The Abbey Mills continued to work into the 20th century; a new 80 h.p. turbine was installed and two water-wheels were still in use to drive eight pairs of stones, and to produce the mill's electric lighting. There was said to be a local demand for stone ground meal, which William Rice and Company supplied. Before 1933 the mills had become a luncheon and tea room.

67. Samuel Healing (1799-1883), maltster and miller, with his two sons built the flour mills on the quay in 1865. In the first borough council election in 1835 he topped the poll.

In the *Register* of 12 December 1863 there was an item headed 'Board of Health. Proposed Improvements on the Quay' and it continued:

Mr. Lewis (of the firm of Moore, Lewis and Moore) said he attended on behalf of Messrs. Healing, to submit to the notice of the Board, a work of great public improvement and importance. Messrs. Healing proposed to erect on the site of the warehouse, lately in the occupation of Messrs. Rice, just over the Quay Bridge, and leading towards the Locks, a large steam mill.

Samuel Healing, the founder of the firm, was in his mid-sixties and was one of the leading townsmen of Tewkesbury. He had been in business both as miller and malt-ster, and had owned or occupied several other mills, including a mill at Strensham, north of Tewkesbury; he lived in Church Street since at least 1841. His sons, William and Alfred, were in their early thirties and their names appear on an indenture of 1864, as taking possession of the site of the new mill from William and Michael Procter. The warehouse used by Messrs. Rice was probably only a small part of the site. As shown by the Poor Relief Book there was already a steam flour mill at the Quay, owned by Thomas Bluck and occupied by

Richard Procter, called the Quay mills in Kelly's 1856 *Directory*. According to T. W. Hibbard, writing in 1897, Samuel Healing took over the Abbey Mills in 1858 and at the same time also had the Quay Mills. Later, this smaller steam-powered mill was occupied by Rice. Healings' new Borough flour mills represented a major development, not only by their size and importance in 1865 but, notably, for the technical improvements incorporated subsequently.

Early in 1866 the paper reported that

> Messrs. Samuel Healing and Sons' Borough Flour Mills are now completed and in operation. The mill building is 80 ft. by 40 ft., and contains 7 floors, all of good height. The whole of the works have been executed by Mr. W. H. James of Tewkesbury, who has furnished the designs and has had the sole charge and superintendence throughout. The mill contains 12 pairs of stones and the most approved description of machinery for elevating and cleansing the wheat and dressing the flour.

A flour mill with 12 pairs of millstones could have supplied a substantial market. For instance, with 2 pairs idle for stone dressing and the mill running for only 40 hours per week, enough flour could have been produced to supply 11,000 people at the rate of 5 lbs. of flour per person per week. As the population of Tewkesbury was a little less than 6,000 in 1851 and 1861, with a drop by 1871, the new mill had sufficient capacity to supply not only the whole town, but an extensive additional market.

Healings' site at Tewkesbury placed them in the category of 'country millers', compared with the increasingly important firms at the large ports, even though Tewkesbury did have a small quay. Economic milling became partly a problem of transport costs, so improved river navigation and the best possible rail links were vital, to allow flexible trading strategies in wheat buying and flour selling. During the 1860s the pattern of wheat supply for the British milling industry was changing. In the later 1850s nearly three-quarters of the wheat available for consumption was produced at home, and just over a quarter came from a growing number of overseas suppliers. In the early and mid 1860s 40 per cent. of the wheat supply was imported and the trend continued, spurred by rapid technical change in the milling industry, so that in the later 1880s imported wheat made up nearly 70 per cent. of the total. Much of the foreign wheat was harder than English; the home-grown varieties produced bread of superior taste, but the foreign wheats gave stronger flours and bolder, well-piled loaves. The popular criteria had become appearance and economy.

Radical changes in British milling practice began in the late 1870s with successful experiments by Henry Simon of Manchester who became the leader in the development of milling engineering; next in prominence as consultant and contractor was Harrison Carter. New kinds of machinery were introduced into many mills, particularly between 1883 and 1885, with another major phase of mill development around 1890. Hard wheats could not be milled effectively by millstones, without producing large quantities of bran fragments. The problem was overcome by using roller mills, with pairs of chilled, cast iron, fluted rolls to break open the grain. Smooth iron rolls were used to reduce the interior of the grain to flour and numerous designs of sieving and purifying machine were developed to separate components and eliminate the bran. In the early and mid 1880s millstones were gradually replaced and in the early 1890s they became obsolescent.

In 1885 Healings introduced Carter's automatic roller system into the Borough mills, thereby associating themselves with the more progressive millers in the country. There was a major extension to the wheat storage buildings in 1889 and probably improvements in the main mill at the same time. By 1892 the Borough mills were stated to have a productive capacity of 25 sacks per hour or 3,500 sacks per week. In comparison, J.-Reynolds and Company's Albert flour mill at Gloucester then had a capacity of 20 sacks of flour per hour and Priday Metford's City flour mills could produce 15 sacks per hour. A sack was 280 lbs. of flour. These were the three principal mills in the area. Small provincial firms were severely affected by continually intensifying competition as large imports of American flour threatened the viability of the British milling industry during the mid- and late 1880s, but Reynolds and Healings were able to extend their trading areas in South Wales and parts of the Midlands.

Referring to the decay of the country water mills, that had previously supplied the smaller towns and rural communities, T. W. Hibbard, principal of J. Reynolds and Company, observed in 1897 that 'there is scarcely one now making flour for sale'. Whereas the small mills either stopped or survived on provender trade, Healings' business prospered and the tall brick buildings still dominate the view along the Mill Avon. In 1961 the business was acquired by Allied Mills Limited and in the mid-1970s the mill was again remodelled, with the installation of a large new milling plant of the latest modern design.

20th-Century Industries

The principal industries established in the Victorian period lasted also through the first half of the 20th century. G. E. Payne, the former county planning officer, in a review in 1944 listed three large businesses: Collins and Godfrey, building contractors, employing 300, Healings' Borough flour mills, employing 120, and Bathurst's, building yachts, launches and small ships, employing one hundred. All were established well before the end of the 19th century; William Bathurst was building boats in the area called Hammocks beyond King John's Bridge before 1852; the Collins and Cullis partnership was formed about 1859; Healings built the Borough mills in 1865. Payne also noted some smaller enterprises, including malting, a small cattle cake manufacturer, and an agricultural engineering works. A review of Tewkesbury's industries prepared in 1915 for a visit to the town by the Cotteswold Club is remarkably similar. It mentioned the building firm, the Borough mills, maltsters (Downing and Company, still in business in 1939) and two engineering firms. Though these two firms had disappeared by 1939, Walker's premises had been taken over by another agricultural engineering firm, F. T. Raggatt and Sons.

More generally, the pattern of occupation in Tewkesbury in the first half of the 20th century displayed no special characteristics and the main employments remained the same between 1911 and 1951: food processing and retailing, building, transport and the distributive trades. Many found work as general labourers. The openings for school leavers were limited. Out of 70 boys leaving school in 1915, only three went to learn a trade. Five became clerks, four motor mechanics, two mill hands; some went into the armed forces. Most, it was·said, were errand boys for a few years, and then drifted into unskilled work. The girls worked in the shops or went into domestic service. In 1944 the largest opportunity for women was working in a milk depot.

Efforts were made to attract industry. A full-page advertisement was inserted in a brochure on Gloucestershire industries, published in 1904, and another in 1920, describ-

68. & 69.   The Borough Mills on the Quay were powered by steam from their start in 1865. The nearest building is the original mill and beyond the bridge is the first warehouse of 1874. Healings' mills extended beyond the original edge of the Quay. The Old Avon here flows round a wide curve and into the Severn.

ing the facilities of the town, and the 'ample labour skilled in engineering, wood and stone working, milling, shirt-making etc.' While the brochures contained descriptions of particular firms in Gloucester, Stroud and elsewhere, there were none of Tewkesbury, so far outside the mainstream of the county's industries was the town. Thomas Walker and Sons were the subject of an article in the *Gloucester Chronicle* in 1924, on unusual industries in the county. The firm was one of only three in England manufacturing fairground equipment. They were said to make every part themselves, down. to the smallest bolt, and had a large staff of wood carvers, amongst other trades. They complained of unfair German and American competition, because of those countries' tariffs, and shortly after this date did go out of business.

The inter-war period was one of general depression, so it is not surprising that it is not marked by any surge of enterprise comparable with the late 1850s and 1860s. The general strike of 1926 was symptomatic. It was called to support the miners in their protest against a reduction in wages. As Tewkesbury had mainly small enterprises and shops, it was not very strongly unionised. Only Collins & Godfrey was large enough to be organised and on the first day they voted not to strike 'as yet'. Men tried to report for work on the railway at Ashchurch on the first day but found no trains running. The *Register* gives the impression that Tewkesbury was unaffected, but 300 strikers did try to prevent Healings' corn barges leaving the quay, and they were likely to have been local men. There were some local newspapers despite the strike, and a few copies of the government's news sheet, the *British Gazette*, reached Tewkesbury. Further attempts were made to draw industry to the area. A Chamber of Commerce was founded in 1926, working closely with the Severn Development Association which advertised on the continent. Enquiries from Austria, Belgium and Germany came to nothing, when it was realised that there was no development grant available.

Unemployment in Tewkesbury reached nearly three hundred in 1932, 31 per cent. of the insurable population, and after a despairing deputation to the council had represented the case of the town's unemployed, the council did put in hand a small programme of public works. Wyatt's meadow on the southern approach to the town was levelled and turned into a car park. The house-building programme was also resumed. The basic problems remained until 1939. Quite early in the war, post-war plans were being formulated and an industrial and housing advisor was appointed. The council was sure that 'Tewkesbury must have industries'. Since the Second World War, the area has seen considerable industrial development, aided by quick access to the motorway.

20th-Century Housing Schemes

Now that sanitation and water supply had been dealt with, the council's attention became focused on the housing problem. Municipal enterprise in this area was first encouraged by legislation in 1875 but was not very widely undertaken until after the First World War, when central government grants were available. The question of houses for artisans was raised in Tewkesbury about 1900. The council moved slowly to a decision; in 1913 it was agreed that there was need and plans were drawn up for 30 or 32 two- or three-bedroomed houses, to be erected on a site between the cemetery and Gloucester Road, convenient for main services of light, water and drains. The site was called Prior's Park and there was ample room for further development. The houses were to be brick on the lower storey and roughcast on the upper; the larger ones were estimated to cost £177 each to build. The Local Government Board agreed to make a loan. At this time the medical officer considered 30 houses were unfit for habitation, but they could not be demolished without alternative accommodation being made available. It was decided to proceed initially with the construction of twelve. The First World War had started before the council was able to inspect the first completed block.

Once the war was over, a much larger scheme was formulated, for 122 new houses, all with three bedrooms but some with a parlour and some with only a living room and scullery. Now it was estimated that 120 of the 1,000 or more 'workers' dwellings' in Tewkesbury were unfit for habitation, and 400 were unfit but capable of conversion and repair. Altogether 1,240 houses were enumerated in the town. Not surprisingly, the *Register* asked if the present scheme was adequate. Immediately 12 houses were started, built by Collins and Godfrey, and occupied by 1921; there were three times as many applicants as houses. They were let for 5s. 6d. a week (27.5p), which was beyond the means of the average alley-dweller who earned about £1 a week. It was suggested that the building programme would not touch the very class for whom it was intended, though it was hoped that there might be a ripple of moves towards the new houses, the alley-dwellers taking up the places vacated by those moving to the new estate. In time, this was seen not to be the case. In 1931 there were 98 empty houses in the town, but they did not help to relieve the overcrowding. The council houses were occupied by the skilled artisan rather than the unskilled labourer. Nonetheless, gradually the alley houses became vacant and were closed and demolished.

Building continued until the financial difficulties of the years after 1929 made the council less willing to go on borrowing money. Members were pressed to continue, in order to make work for the unemployed in Tewkesbury. Courageously, despite its indebtedness, the council agreed. A survey of 1936 showed that the town had made a substantial inroad on the problem of overcrowding, which was by no means as bad as in some other Gloucestershire towns. Between 1931 and 1943, 155 new houses were built to replace slum clearances. There was also some private building in Prior's Park and a building society which had been formed in Tewkesbury about the beginning of the century helped some private house owners.

The need for more slum clearance was still keenly felt. Post-war planning started in 1943, when the County was informed that Tewkesbury needed 250 more houses and flats; the Planning Officer thought twice the number was needed, and he was eventually proved right. In 1955 there were still 197 houses scheduled for clearance, and in 1960 there were 240 sub-standard houses. After the war, a large development took place in Prior's Park, and gradually the density of occupation in the town centre was relieved.

The Modernisation of Everyday Life

The First World War is often presented as the end of an era, but it was not a turning point in many respects. There was serious loss of life: 148 names were recorded on the war memorial in the abbey and a stone cross was put at the junction of the three streets where once the Tolsey had stood. On the same site a Crimean War cannon had briefly been placed as a memorial in 1858, but had been moved to the cemetery in 1865 and thence to the Jubilee Gardens in 1901. During the war, the *Register* was full of the military events; it recorded also the domestic struggle to maintain food supplies, and the frequent voluntary fund-raising. During the German submarine campaign of 1917 and 1918, the shortage of food became acute. Allotments were started to encourage people to grow their own vegetables, particularly potatoes, and an 'Eat less bread' campaign started. Everyone was allowed four pounds of bread a week; the average consumption in Tewkesbury in July 1917 was 4.3 pounds. The weekly butter ration was two ounces per person. Certain hoteliers refused to cooperate with bureaucratic enquiries about amounts of food consumed. Great efforts were made to raise money for the war. 'Aeroplane week', in March 1918, set a target of five planes or £12,500 from Tewkesbury and district. Double the amount was raised. The local committee distributed circulars and made many personal visits. An aeroplane showered the town with leaflets and showed off some stunts. This was not the first aeroplane at Tewkesbury; several had landed on the Ham the previous December and had been unable to leave for some days because of fog and engine trouble.

After the war was over, everyday life was not substantially altered. Many features typical of the 20th century in fact pre-date the war, like telephones and the cinema, though not the radio. The first telegraph posts had been installed between the Hermitage turnpike gate and the Mythe in 1862. In 1914 there were about 148 telephone numbers on the Tewkesbury exchange, which included Forthampton, Chaceley, Tredington and Shuthonger. The Borough mills had number two. In 1939 the numbers had reached 239; a firm of solicitors had 'Tewkesbury 1'.

The first cinema, the Picture Palace, had been built in 1912, on the site vacated by Walker's engineering works. It was severely damaged by fire in 1932. The Sabrina cinema replaced it and had all the most up-to-date equipment for 'talkies'. A High Street shop was demolished to create an open space in front. The Sabrina closed in 1963 and has been replaced with the new Roses Theatre. Photography, too, was a popular hobby before the end of the 19th century; the town guide shows this with advertisements by two chemists for photographic materials and a jeweller for cameras, while a drug store not only sold cameras but also made a dark-room available free to customers. A photographer in the Abbey Studio made lantern slides.

The bicycle and the motor car were beginning to give people greater freedom and mobility before 1914. The bicycle was popular well before the end of the 19th century; in the 1903 town guide hoteliers advertised accommodation suited to cyclists. 'At the abbey entrance gates there is usually a bicycle attendant who will, for the modest sum of one penny, keep his eye on the visitor's machine', the guide reported. There were both agents and a cycle manufacturer in the town. J. S. Osborne was also a motor car agent and was one of the small number of authorised dealers for Ford cars in Gloucestershire. Three issues of the *Register* in 1915 carried advertisements for the range of Ford cars and a van – each illustrated by a silhouette. The model 'T' had been produced in Manchester four years earlier.

In the 1930s it seemed to some that multiple shops were invading the town; It was a matter for comment in *Portrait of Elmbury*. The Chamber of Commerce discussed the difficulties of the small trader in 1942. There was then a feeling that the day of the shop in the front room of the house was over, and 'that the tentacles of the multiple trade have intensified their stranglehold upon the individual trader'. Five well-known multiple stores had shops in Tewkesbury: Boots the Chemists, the International Tea Company's Stores Limited, the London Central Meat Company Limited, W. H. Smith &

Son at the station, and the Gloucester Cooperative and Industrial Society Limited. All but Boots were in the town before 1914. A Tewkesbury Cooperative and Industrial Society had existed in 1885; the International was trading in Tewkesbury by 1902. Similarly, three national banks were established by 1939, Lloyds, the Midland and the National Provincial; Lloyds was already there by 1914 and the Midland by 1923, absorbing the local banks of the previous century.

Directories seem to chart a substantial reduction in the number of small craftsmen by 1914 in comparison with the mid-19th century. In Pigot's Directory of 1842, well over half the people named were craftsmen: blacksmiths and whitesmiths; cutlers and nailors; shoemakers, curriers and tanners; bricklayers, plumbers and stonemasons; cabinet and chair-makers; carpenters, wheelwrights and coopers; tailors, milliners and straw-hat makers; framesmiths, stocking and lace manufacturers. Kelly's Directory for 1914 lists far fewer in those trades – only a fifth of the people named, and in 1939 only a seventh. The change was almost certainly real, because the railway had facilitated the transport of manufactured goods from every part of England and the self-sufficiency of a small town had gone.

Tourism

A rapid increase in the number of visitors coming to Tewkesbury was noticed towards the end of the 19th century. It encouraged the town's two printers to vie with each other in producing town guides. Bennett had published an abridgement of his History in 1835 and 1848, for the convenience of the 'numerous strangers who visit the abbey church'. This served for the next 23 years; then William North, printer of the Register, published his first guide book. North also published in 1886 'A Short Account of the Old Houses of Tewkesbury with a detailed list of the more interesting of those still extant', by H. P. and F. Moore. Gardner, the printer of the Record, produced a Visitors' Guide in 1891, which also adopted the format of a walk round the town. North expanded his guide in 1895. Photographs accompanied the advertisements in Gardner's 1903 Guide, which had the town council approval.

The town council claimed in 1904 that 80,000 visitors a year were coming to the abbey, and consequently there was 'much to be done in catering for them'. Kelly's Directory in 1914 listed seven hotels, three inns, two refreshment rooms, two coffee houses and a restaurant, as well as 13 public houses and 10 beer shops. Some of the eight confectioners may also have kept cafes, like Palmiro Barsanti, whose tea gardens were behind the Abbey Cottages. A few of the old timber-framed houses were being used to cater for tourists: Prince Edward's House at 102 Church Street, supposedly where the prince was murdered after the battle of Tewkesbury, and the Coffee House at the Cross, today only a facade to the Cooperative Store, are two examples. After the First World War, the Tudor House, where John Moore lived as a child, joined the Bell, the Royal Hop Pole and the Swan as one of Tewkesbury's principal hotels. Gupshill Manor became a hotel before 1933; the 'Ancient Grudge', which in 1914 had been occupied by a plumber, and the Abbey mills, became cafes. Number 73, Church Street, identified with Sally Watkin's cottage in John Halifax, Gentleman, became a restaurant more recently.

It was possibly to encourage tourists that in 1908 the council started marking sites of historic interest, including Bloody Meadow, and an enquiry was made into old roads and footpaths in danger of disappearing. Perhaps an awareness of its history prompted the council in 1918 to buy back again the remaining rights of the manor of Tewkesbury, which had been sold after the reorganisation of the council in 1835. This meant the council controlled the Avon fishery and shared with trustees control over the Severn Ham. The townsmen's common rights were exercised by selling the value of the grazing every year, and distributing the proceeds amongst the burgesses – 345 people received 1s. 6d. (7½p) each in 1932; the responsibility for the Ham has now passed to the new borough council. In 1929 the council purchased the Vineyards, and erected a monument recalling important aspects of Tewkesbury's history: its charters, its manor house called Holm Castle, the lordship of the Earls of Gloucester, and the town's purchases of the abbey church and the manor.

Conclusion

The history of Tewkesbury in the 19th and early 20th centuries is typical of urban experience, even though Tewkesbury was so very small compared with the developing conurbations of the time. (The town had been offended when it was deemed too small to be included in Gladstone's list for his first Post Office Savings Banks in 1861.) It suffered the same parliamentary regulation of its affairs, faced the same problems, discussed the same issues as other councils, large or small.

One of the most striking themes of the period is the increase in state control over local affairs. It started in the 1830s, with the Poor Law Amendment Act which required the formation of groups of parishes into unions, and the Municipal Corporations Act which imposed an elective framework on the council. Elections widened the social composition of the council and totally changed its political complexion. 'All classes but the operative are represented in our council', the *Register* said in 1858; 'it comprises tradesmen as well as merchants and professional men'. The 1848 Public Health Act required a Board of Health to be set up, transformed by later legislation into an urban sanitary authority and then into an urban district council. Tewkesbury was also the centre of a rural sanitary district, based on the poor law union, whose meetings were held in the workhouse. The rural district was amalgamated with Cheltenham rural district in 1935, much to Tewkesbury's dismay.

All these statutory bodies had clerks and other officers and so were a discernible influence on the occupational structure of the town. The Registration of Births, Marriages and Deaths was required by Act of Parliament in 1836, in areas based on the poor law unions; the registrar's office was therefore in Tewkesbury. There was a clerk to the Burial Board, which had been set up in 1856 to open a new cemetery and close the old one; the sanitary authorities appointed medical officers of health and inspectors of nuisances and after 1892 also surveyors of the highways. Not until 1944 was Tewkesbury's own town clerk made a full-time officer.

Legislation permitted the formation of a local police force in 1835; its headquarters were at the town hall. It became part of the county constabulary in 1869 and in 1883 moved to the former borough gaol in the Bredon Road. Tewkesbury's Quarter Sessions were abolished in 1949. Legislation also encouraged and regulated municipal enterprise in the areas of public utilities and in the provision of housing. Every council found itself, like Tewkesbury's, faced with the awkward relation between rating income and expenditure which frequently inhibited action.

Tewkesbury was able to avoid a School Board after the Education Act of 1870 because

70. The former Grammar School was built in 1907; now it houses the library and past volumes of the *Tewkesbury Register*.

71. The Abbey Mills and Mill Bank are often painted and photographed. The scene epitomises three important aspects of Tewkesbury's character – timber-framing, riverside activity, and the great Norman abbey tower.

the town had an adequate number of school places, but from 1876 there had to be a school attendance officer and committee, to see that all children under the age of 10 were receiving schooling. The *Register* observed that dread of this officer was not strong enough to draw the boys of the town from fishing when the Abbey mill pond was being emptied in 1894, after one of the water-wheels had collapsed. The 1902 Education Act transferred responsibility for education to the elected county councils which had been set up some fourteen years previously. The county council purchased the house in which the grammar school met and in 1906 built new premises next door; the site of the house is now a car park for the *Bell Hotel*. The grammar school building today houses the library with its local collection, including the bound volumes of the *Tewkesbury Register and Agricultural Gazette* from its first publication in 1858.

In 1974 Tewkesbury regained its historic position as the administrative centre of a large surrounding area, under a new district council with the title 'Borough Council'. In some ways history has come full circle back to the manor of Tewkesbury controlled by the Saxon Brictric 900 years before and by the Norman Earls of Gloucester. The council's headquarters built on Windmill Hill may even be on or near the site of the former manor house of Holm Castle. The traditional town council was also able to preserve its historic role by accepting the status of parish council, and has its headquarters in the town hall in High Street. With an industrial area at Ashchurch, an agricultural area of 172 square miles and a shopping centre in Tewkesbury, the district has an economic basis which preserves and revitalises its long history. Whatever the changes in future concerning municipal organisation and the life of this town, it is hoped that the interpretation in these pages will be an interesting and perhaps useful record.

Old door at the side of the nonconformist academy.

References

Sources quoted in the text or from which particular points of information have been drawn are listed under each section heading. Books and articles are indicated by the author's surname followed by the date of publication; a full list of the titles is given in the consolidated bibliography. Manuscript sources are always listed last.

Abbreviations
G.C.L. Gloucester City Library.
G.R.O. Gloucester Record Office. P329 Tewkesbury parish records. TBR Tewkesbury Borough records.
P.P. Parliamentary Papers.
S.P.A.B. Society for the Protection of Ancient Buildings.
T.Y.R. & M. Tewkesbury Yearly Register and Magazine.
T.B.G.A.S. Transactions of the Bristol and Gloucestershire Archaeological Society.
V.C.H. The Victoria History of the Counties of England: A History of Gloucestershire.

Chapter 1
RIVERS AND ROADS
Fowler (1977), 44.
Hannan (1973), 18-21.
Hooke (1985), 102.
Rawes (1972), 9.
Smith (1964-5), (2), 68.
V.C.H. (1968), 110.

EARLIEST SETTLEMENTS
Finberg (1957), 53-5.
Fowler (1977), 40-5.
Hannan (1973), 20.
Hooke (1985), 213.
Hurst (1976), 64.
Leech (1981), 90-3.
Margary (1957), 21-2.
Marshall (1976), 30.
Miles & Fowler (1972), 7.2 and 7.3.
Richmond & Crawford (1949), 1, 5, 23, 49.
Sanders & Webster (1960), 41-4.
Smith (1964-5), (1), 19; (2), 62.

THE SAXON PERIOD
Annales Monastici (1), 43.
Atkins (1712).
Bede (1955), 66, 222.
Branigan (1976), 120-1.
Finberg (1951), 57.
Gelling (1974), 68-9.
Gelling (1984), 28, 41, 51, 68-9, 167, 249.
Hooke (1985), 3-20, 38, 84, 164.

Smith (1964-5), (1), 13; (4), 37, 42-3.
Taylor (1957), 17-48.
G.R.O.: TBR/A14/15.

THE ORGANISATION OF THE CHRISTIAN CHURCH
Annales Monastici (1), 43.
Atkins (1712), 725-37.
Bede (1955), 222.
Blunt (1975), 16.
Finberg (1957), 33; (1972), 35, 44.
V.C.H. (1907), 2.
V.C.H. (1968), 154-5.

INVASIONS OF DANES AND NORMANS
Atkins (1712), 726.
Bennett (1830), 267.
Domesday Book (ed. Morris 1982), 1.24-39.
Freeman (1869-70) (2), 673; (4), 178.
Giles (1848), 31.
Smith & Ralph (1972), 26.
Taylor (1957), 244.
English Historical Documents (1953) (2), 430.

Chapter 2
THE NORMAN INFLUENCE
Bennett (1830), 321-5.
Finberg (1957), 61, 73, 81.
Rowley (1983), 87.
V.C.H. (1968), 110, 121-2, 137-8, 140-1, 146-7, 158, 184, 235.
Wakeman (1859), 319.
William of Malmesbury's Chronicle (1847), 432.
G.C.L.: Hockaday 368 (1279), 369 (1540).
G.R.O.: D592; P329/MI/1.

THE DEVELOPMENT OF THE TOWN PLAN
Aston & Bond (1976), 98.
Smith (1964-5) (2), 63.
V.C.H. (1968), 110, 126.
G.C.L.: Hockaday 369 (1502).
G.R.O.: Q/RI 141.

TEWKESBURY'S LORDS
Bennett (1830), 19, 23, 74, 282.
Blyth (1961), 109-10.
Dyde (1798), 96.
Hannan (1975), 9-11.
North (1891), 46-8.
Poole (1951), 84.
Rackham (1986), 47, 361-2.
Rowley (1984), 208-10.
Smith (1964-5), 68.
V.C.H. (1968), 112, 114-5, 131-3, 138.
Verey (1980), 366.
G.C.L.: Hockaday 369 (1519).
G.R.O.: TBR/A1/1; TBR/D6/1; D592; D2957(83); P329/MI/1.

THE EARLY MEDIEVAL ECONOMY
Glasscock (1975), 90-3.
Phillips (1856), 37.

Chapter 3
In Chapter 3 and Chapter 5, material on the timber-framed houses of Tewkesbury has been drawn particularly from S. R. Jones' section in V.C.H. (1968), 126-31, together with personal observation. The list of buildings of special architectural or historic interest compiled by the Department of the Environment under the Town and Country Planning Act 1971 has also been most useful; the loan of the list by Mr. Malcolm Foster is here gratefully acknowledged. It is also available in the Tewkesbury library.

V.C.H. (1968), 131.

THE BATTLE OF TEWKESBURY
Blyth (1961), 99-120.
Hammond *et al.* (1971).
Smith (1964) (2), 69.
G.C.L.: Hockaday 369 (1514).
Moore (1985), 456.

THE ECONOMY OF THE TOWN IN THE LATE MEDIEVAL PERIOD
Bennett (1830), 379-80.
Bennett (1830), 201; 411.
Gray (1984), 167.
Commons Debates (1935) (2), 129-30.
V.C.H. (1968), 143.

THE PUBLIC WAYS TO THE TOWN
Bennett (1830), 379-80.
Bennett, T. Y. R. & M. (2), 411.
G.C.L.: Hockaday 368-9.
Rogers (1972), 114.
V.C.H. (1968), 115.

THE DISSOLUTION OF THE MONASTERIES
Atkins (1712), 224-6, 590, 724-5, 787, 795.
Bennett (1830), 114, 146-7, 341-2.
Bennett, T. Y. R. & M. (1), 145-6, 411; (2), 450.
Courtney & Linnell (1984), 200.
Irvine Gray (personal communication: notes from the vicar's commonplace book).
G.C.L.: Hockaday 369 (1535).
Harris (1980).
Hoskins (1976), 128-9.
Leland (1889-90), 276-7.
Machin (1977), 49-50.
Pepin (1980), 95-7.
Register, 26.6.1897.
Savine (1909), 221, 225-6, 250.
Valor Ecclesiasticus (2), 471-86.
V.C.H. (1907), 61-5, 435.
V.C.H. (1968), 165-7.
G.R.O.: P329/MI/1.

Chapter 4
Much information in both Chapter 4 and Chapter 5 has been drawn from the first council minute books, deposited in G.R.O.: TBR/A1/1 and TBR/A1/2, and also from the Geast charity book, G.R.O.: D2688. These two sources are not separately itemised in each section. The section on the Civil War is based largely on the Geast charity book and includes some extracts from this contemporary account of the Civil War. Bennett (1830), 47-71, printed much contemporary evidence from political news sheets, and is also drawn on throughout.

Bennett (1830), 209, 378.
Hector (1980), 22-3.
Rogers (1972), 17.

1575: THE BOROUGH INCORPORATED
Bennett (1830), 199, 244, 309, 379.
Clark & Slack (1976), 115, 128.
Hilton (1985), 18.
V.C.H. (1968), 118, 142-3, 152-3.
G.R.O.: P329/MI/1; P329/CW2/1.

THE PORT
Bennett (1830), 43-4.
V.C.H. (1968), 140, 146.

EXTENSION OF THE BOROUGH'S POWERS
Beecham (1978), 171.
Bennett (1830), 208, 245, 383.
Clark & Slack (1976), 119, 126-39.
Commons Debates (1935) (3), 171-2; (4), 307 and 390.
Holman (1977), 92.
V.C.H. (1968), 146, 153.
Willcox (1940), 31.
G.R.O.: D760/36.

THE CIVIL WAR
Bennett (1830), 181, 185, 247-8, 309, 419-20.
Tewkesbury Official Guide, 21.
Willcox (1940), 31.
Williams (1898), 241.
V.C.H. (1968), 153.
G.R.O.: P329/CW2/1; TBR/A1/3.

RESTORATION POLITICS
Percival (1972), supplement.
Bennett (1830), 185, 187, 252, 254.
Bennett, T. Y. R. & M. (1), 38.
V.C.H. (1968), 149.

Chapter 5
Considerable use has been made of surviving inventories, which were made to accompany wills. Many were preserved in the Diocesan records, and are now deposited in G.R.O. They are bundled by years, and are referred to by year and number within the bundle. The council minute books, G.R.O.: TBR/A1/1 and A1/2 and the Geast charity book, D2688 have been drawn on in every section and are not separately itemised.

Percival (1972).

SOCIAL STRUCTURE AND OCCUPATIONS

Clark & Slack (1976), 115.
Clarkson (1971), 88-9.
Fiennes (1982), 54.
Harrison (1877), Chapter 5.
Men and Armour (1902), 114-27.
Tawney (1934), 28.
Willcox (1940), 164.
Wyatt (1976), 6-10.
V.C.H. (1968), 120, 128, 142.
G.C.L.: Hockaday Abstracts, 370.
G.R.O.: Inventory 1675/48 (Clarke).

NEW TRADES

Awdrey (1973), 25.
Beckinsale (1980), 319.
Gray (1965), 106.
Rolt (1973), 148.
Thirsk (1984), 239-55.
V.C.H. (1968), 114.
Willcox (1940), 151, 158, 161.
G.R.O.: D421.

PLAGUE AND THE POOR

Bennett (1830), 306-11.
Ripley (1972), 203.
Willcox (1940), 135, 139.
Wrigley & Schofield (1981), 332-3.

THE STREETS

Bennett (1830), 255.
Dyde (1798), 81.
Steer (1950).
Willcox (1940), 222.
V.C.H. (1968), 130.
G.R.O.: Inventories: 1662/9 (Higgens); 1663/58 (Mopp; will 187); 1664/95 (Crumpe; will 136); 1676/68 (Lane); 1678/86 (Pritchett); 1681/15 (Reade; will 16); 1685/46 (Mayo); 1685/161 (Later); 1685/160 (Tandy); TBR/B3.

THE HOUSES

Bennett, T. Y. R. & M. (1), 322.
Moore (1886), 11-12.
V.C.H. (1968), 128.
G.R.O.: TRB/B3.

HOUSE PLANS

Alldridge (1983), 24, 28.
V.C.H. (1968), 124.
G.R.O.: Inventories: 1587/61 (Underhill; will 245); 1622/8 (Arpen); 1662/9 (Higgens); 1663/58 (Mopp; will 187); 1673/13 1681/26 (Wakeman); 1685/24 (Nanfan).
G.R.O.: D383 (copy of hearth tax).

FURNISHINGS

Inventories and wills as in previous section. In addition:
G.R.O.: Inventory: 1675/48 (Clarke).

SOCIAL RELATIONSHIPS
Ibid., in addition:
G.R.O.: Will 1664/136 (Crumpe); inventory 1673/13 (Warren: will 105); will 1706/189 (Jaynes).

Chapter 6
Sources of particular importance for both Chapters 6 and 7 are: (1) the letters of Mary Yorke from Forthampton Court. Selections were published in the *Tewkesbury Register* between 18 November 1950 and 24 February 1951 by E. A. B. Barnard; cuttings exist in the G.R.O., PE/11 and also a typescript of some letters, D1137/2 and 3. Modernised punctuation and spelling have been used in extracts printed here, and contractions have been expanded. References are given to the date of publication in the *Register*, where relevant. (2) the notebooks of the auctioneering firm of Moore and Sons. They are in the G.R.O., D2080 and the volume numbers are given in the references.

Cobbett (1973), 126.
Defoe (1971), 366-8.
Gentleman's Magazine, 61, 53.
Moore (1966), 66.
Tewkesbury Official Guide, 59.
Warner (1802), 45.
Bodleian Library, Oxford, Gough/Glos. 9.
G.R.O.: P 329/CW2/2; D2688.

GEORGE III IN TEWKESBURY
Bennett (1930), 12, 313.
Bennett, T. Y. R. & M. (2), 105-10.
Gentleman's Magazine, 58 (ii), 758.
V.C.H. (1968), 175.
Yorke, *Register* 30.12.1950.

TURNPIKES
Bayes & Roberts (1971), 82.
Bennett (1830), 278-81, 292.
Bennett, T. Y. R. & M. (1), 132, 140, 237, 287; (2), 476.
Cossons (n.d.), 1, 3.
Gloucester Turnpike Roads, G.R.O. 'Signal' teaching aid (1973), 6, 7.
Herbert (1985), 135.
G.C.L.: R292.85.
G.R.O.: TBR/E/1; TBR/D6/1; QT/8/R4; D2080/465; D2688; D592.

STAGES AND POSTING HOUSES
Bennett (1830), 203.
Copeland (1968), 160.
Herbert (1985), 30, 46, 71-5.
Yorke, *Register*, 9.12.1950, 20.1.1951, 17.2.1951.
G.R.O.: D2080/64, 114, 196; D2688.

SEVERN AND AVON
Bennett (1830), 288-90, 320, 445.
Bennett, T. Y. R. & M. (1), 21, 237.
Cossons & Trinder (1979), 106-7.
Gell & Bradshaw's Directory (1820).
PP 1850 XLIX, 373-3.
Rolt (1969), xi, 71-2, 120, 136, 149.
Universal British Directory (1800).
Waters (1947), 21.

V.C.H. (1968), 115.
Yorke, *Register*, 18.11.1950, 27.1.1951, 10.2.1951, 24.2.1951.
G.R.O.: D2866; D2079 I/79.

PAVING THE TOWN
Bennett (1830), 197.
Bennett, T. Y. R. & M. (1), 127; (2) 485.
Copeland (1968), 64.
Corfield (1982), 157-8.
Cossons & Trinder (1979), 92, 96.
Dyde (1798), 78, 84.
Lyon-Smith (1985), 9-11.
G.C.L.: RF302.2 (26 Geo. III c. 39).
G.R.O.: TBR/A1/8; TBR/A7/1; D2866.

Chapter 7
Dyde (1798), 78.
Yorke, *Register*, 20.1.1951.

THE WORKHOUSE
Bennett (1830), 219-21.
Smith (1971), 21.
V.C.H. (1968), 150.
Yorke, *Register*, 6.1.1951.
PP 1834 XXX-XXXV; see particularly queries 7.22.50.
G.R.O.: TBR/E1 (32 Geo. III); P329/CW2/2; P329/21; D2688.

POVERTY AND CHARITY
Bennett (1830), 316-8.
Bennett, T. Y. R. & M. (1), 180.
Yorke, *Register*, 6.1.1951; 20.1.1951; 27.1.1951.
G.R.O.: P329/VE2/1; P329/VE3/2; D2688; QT/S(II).

REBUILDING AND REFURBISHMENT
Byard (1974), 176.
Corfield (1982), 174-5.
Bennett (1830), 151.
Bennett, T. Y. R. & M. (1), 107, 157.
Dyde (1798), 77, 84.
Gentleman's Magazine, 58 (ii), 758.
G.R.O.: TBR/A1/7; D2688.

NEW SCHOOLS
Bennett (1830), 113, 219, 226-7.
Bennett, T. Y. R. & M. (1), 150, 394; (2), 119.
Gentleman's Magazine, 88 (i), 634.
Gray (1984), 168.
Platts & Hainton (1954), 58-9.
PP 1818 I, 314; 1835 XV, 265; 1842 XV, 314, 325.
V.C.H. (1968), 166.
Yorke, *Register*, 10.2.1951.
G.R.O.: P329/SC1/1; P329/IN1/9; P329/IN1/11; P329/52.

ENCLOSURE OF THE OLDBURY
G.R.O., D2080/88.

TRADES AND PROFESSIONS
Bennett (1830), 201.
Bennett, T. Y. R. & M. (1), 21-3.
G.R.O.: D2080/23, 180, 181, 501; TBR/A6/1.

TEWKESBURY MANUFACTURE
Adcock (1973), 7-8, 20.
Atkins (1712), 725.
Bennett (1830), 202-3.
Bennett, T. Y. R. & M. (1), 200; (2), 483.
Chapman (1967), 18-19; 48; (1972), 25.
Fiennes (1982), 190.
Henson (1831), 165, 237, 360, 363-4.
PP 1834 XXX-XXXV, queries 11 & 12; PP 1845 XV.
Rath (1976), 143-4.
Yorke, *Register*, 25.11.1950; 10.2.1951.
G.R.O.: TBR/A1/6; TBR/B105a; P329/VE2/1; D2688; D2080/20, 108; D214/F1/193; Inventory 1767 (1).

THE DECLINE OF THE COUNCIL
G.R.O.: TBR/A1/4; A4/1.

THE PARLIAMENTARY FRANCHISE
Atkins (1712), 723.
Bennett (1830), 255, 259, 261, 267.
Bennett, T. Y. R. &. M. (1), 52-3, 64, 74-5, 77, 87, 257.
PP 1834 XXX-XXXV, query 16 & 17; query 53 see Twyning; 1853 XXIII
G.C.L.: R302.214.
G.R.O.: D2688; TBR/A1/5, A1/6; A1/8.

REFORM OF THE COUNCIL
Bennett, T. Y. R. & M. (1), 256-7.
Dyde (1798), 218.
PP 1835 XXIII.
G.R.O.: TBR/A1/7; A1/8.

Chapter 8
Much of the material in this chapter has been drawn from the weekly newspaper, the *Tewkesbury Register and Agricultural Gazette*, deposited in the Tewkesbury branch of the Gloucestershire County Library. A few copies of the earlier newspaper, the *Record*, have been preserved in the Gloucester City Library. County Directories which have been used are listed in the Bibliography. The enumerators' books for the national censuses in 1841, 1851, 1861, 1871 and 1881 have been consulted on microfilm in Gloucester City Library.

Register, 4.8.1883; 10.9.1932.
Moore (1966), 112.
Payne (1946), 286.
Williams (1898), 258-9.

THE RAILWAY AGE
Register, 5.11.1859; 20.2.1864; 21.5.1864; 20.1.1866; 17.2.1866; 30.12.1960.
Beckinsale (1980), 262-7.
Bennett, T. Y. R. & M. (1), 289-91, 347-8, 440; (2), 29-30, 45, 392.
Christiansen (1981), 58, 101.
Maggs (1986), 12-15.
Moore (1966), 22, 181.
Payne (1946), 161.

Stimpson (1981), 16.
V.C.H. (1968), 61.

THE SEVERN NAVIGATION
Bennett, T. Y. R. & M. (1), 252-5, 292-4, 345-7; (2), 28, 68-9, 101, 299-300, 393-4, 398-406.
Payne (1946), 238.
North (1895), 13.
Richardson (1964), 5.

PUBLIC HEALTH
Register, 9.4.1859; 7.10.1865; 28.7.1866; 21.9.1867; 6.2.1969.
Bennett, T. Y. R. & M. (1) 103-9; (2), 395-8.
Lyon-Smith (1982), 27, 34.
Mulock (1912), viii, 2, 27.
Rammell (1850).
V.C.H. (1968), 151.

THE WATERWORKS
Register, 21.11.1863; 12.12.1863; 5.3.1864; 1.4.1865; 2.9.1865; 28.11.1868; 10.4.1869; 19.2.1870; 8.10.1870;
23.5.1871; 9.3.1878.
Bennett (1830), 305, 317.
Bennett, T. Y. R. & M. (1), 140-2.
Hart (1965), 302.
Henderson & Bradley (1969).
North (1895), 7.
Rammell (1850), 16.
G.R.O.: TBR A/1/10.

CEMETERY AND HOSPITAL
Register, 17.12.1864; 11.2.1865; 18.3.1865; 8.4.1865; 1.7.1865; 30.6.1866; 3.8.1872; 1.4.1931.
Bennett, T. Y. R. & M. (1), 105.
North (1895), 3.
Burrow (1941), 31.
G.R.O.: P329/52/13.

ELECTRICITY
Register, 22.1.1900; 8.9.1900; 22.10.1904; 13.7.1907; 9.2.1962.
Gardner (1891), 68-9.
Gardner (1903).

RESTORATION AND CONSERVATION: HOUSES
Register, 2.1.1900.
Bennett, T. Y. R. & M. (2), 261.
Blake (1982), 49.
Moore (1886), 15.
McGrath & Cannon (1976), 40.
North (1895).
Payne (1946), 161.
T.B.G.A.S., 10, 144.

RESTORATION AND CONSERVATION: THE ABBEY
Register, 26.5.1860; 30.4.1864; 14.5.1864; 6.8.1864; 20.5.1865; 27.9.1879; 30.9.1882; 21.7.1883; 9.9.1933.
Bennett (1830), 138, 145, 148, 152-3.
Gough (1959), 10.
S.P.A.B. Manifesto (1878); (1982).
G.R.O.: P329/CW2/4; CW4/2; CW4/3.

TEXTILE MANUFACTURE
Record, 11.8.1855.
Register, 11.9.1858; 16.2.1861; 18.10.1862; 6.2.1864; 13.2.1864; 28.1.1865; 20.8.1870; 19.1.1878; 21.6.1884; 10.12.1932.
Adcock (1973).
Bennett, T. Y. R. & M. (2), 381.
North (1895), 13.
Rath (1976).
Williams (1898), 356.
G.R.O.: P329/OV/1/15 (1881); D2080/1867.

CORN MILLING
Register, 12.12.1863; 31.3.1866; 5.4.1894.
Burrow (1933).
Milling, July 1909, 80; June 1928, 697-70.
The Engineer, November 1887, 404.
The Miller, June 1885, supplement; June 1892, 144-6; May 1897, 190; August 1899, 376-7; May 1906, 159; April 1935, 394-5.
Lawes & Gilbert (1893), 77-131.
The Story of a Country Mill
North (1874), 21.
G.R.O.: D1080/40, 271, 303, 311, 313, 327; P329/OV/1/13; TBR/A/14/15; TBR/D7/9.

 20TH-CENTURY INDUSTRIES
Register, 8.5.1926; 16.5.1926; 22.3.1928; 21.10.1931; 24.6.1944.
Gloucester Chronicle, 22.3.1928.
Burrow (1933), 39.
Chance & Bland (1904), 78.
Proceedings of the Cotteswold Naturalists Field Club, 19.
Transactions of the Worcestershire Naturalists Club, 7.

20TH-CENTURY HOUSING SCHEMES
Register, 21.7.1900; 23.9.1901; 29.12.1917; 22.3.1919; 15.11.1919; 23.7.1932; 20.2.1943; 11.3.1960.
Payne (1946), 298.

THE MODERNISATION OF EVERYDAY LIFE
Register, 19.4.1862; 23.9.1901; 13.1.1917; 21.4.1917; 6.12.1917; 24.12.1917; 10.12.1932; 3.6.1933; 20.3.1942.

TOURISM
Register, 11.7.1908; 1.6.1918; 14.5.1932.
Chance & Bland (1904), 78.
Elrington (1976).

CONCLUSION
Register, 30.10.1858; 31.8.1861; 5.4.1894.
V.C.H. (1968), 150, 152.

Bibliography

WORKS OF PARTICULAR RELEVANCE
Atkins, Sir R., *The Ancient and Present State of Glostershire* (1712, reprinted Gloucester 1974).
Bennett, J., *The History of Tewkesbury* (1830, reprinted Gloucester 1976, with introduction by C. E. Elrington).
– *The Tewkesbury Yearly Register and Magazine* (1), (1840) and (2), (1850).
Blunt, J. H., *Tewkesbury Abbey and its Associations* (1875).
Dyde, W., *The History and Antiquities of Tewkesbury* (1st ed. 1790; 2nd ed. 1798).
Moore, H. P. & F., *A Short Account of the Old Houses of Tewkesbury* (1886).
Victoria County History of Gloucester, 2, ed. W. Page (1907); 8, ed. C. R. Elrington (1968).

GUIDES TO EXPLORATION
Clifton-Taylor, A., *Six English Towns* (1978).
Foster, M., *A Walk Round Tewkesbury* (n.d.).
Gough, L., *A Short Guide to the Abbey Church of St Mary the Virgin at Tewkesbury* (Tewkesbury, 1959).
Hilton, C., *Tewkesbury in Old Picture Postcards* (Netherlands, 1982).
The Old Baptist Chapel, Tewkesbury Borough Council (n.d.).
Tewkesbury Official Guide, published by the Town Council (revised 1983).
The Official Guide to Tewkesbury Borough, Published by Tewkesbury Borough Council (n.d.).

GENERAL BIBLIOGRAPHY
A Cursory Disquisition on the Conventual Church of Tewkesbury (published E. Redell, Tewkesbury, 1818).
Annales Monastici, 1, ed. H. R. Luard (1857).
Aston, M. & Bond, J., *The Landscape of Towns* (1976).
Awdrew, Rev. W., ed., *Industrial Archaeology in Gloucestershire* (1973).
Beckinsale, R. & M., *The English Heartland* (1980).
Bede's History of the English Church and People, translated L. Sherley-Price (1955).
Beecham, K. J., *History of Cirencester* (1887, reprinted Gloucester 1978).
Branigan, K. & Fowler, P. J., eds., *The Roman West Country* (1976).
Buchanan, C. A. & R. A., *Central Southern England* (Batsford Guide to Industrial Archaeology, 1980).
Chapman, S. D., *The Early Factory Masters* (1967).
– *The Cotton Industry in the Industrial Revolution* (1972).
Christiansen, R., *Regional History of the Railways of Great Britain* (1981).
Clark, P. & Slack, P., *English Towns in Transition 1500-1700* (Oxford, 1976).
Clarkson, A. H., *The Pre-Industrial Economy in England 1500-1750* (1971).
Cobbett, W., *Rural Rides* (1830, reprinted 1973).
Commons Debates 1621, ed. Notestein, W., Reef, F. H. & Simpson, H. (U.S.A. 1935).
Copeland, J., *Roads and Their Traffic 1750-1850* (Newton Abbot, 1968).
Corfield, P. J., *The Impact of English Towns* (Oxford, 1982).
Cossons, N. & Trinder, B., *The Iron Bridge* (Bradford-on-Avon, 1979).
Defoe, D., *A Tour through the Whole Island of Great Britain* (1724-6, reprinted 1971).
Domesday Book: Gloucestershire, ed. J. Morris (Chichester, 1982).
Dyde, R., *The Antiquities of Tewkesbury Church to which is added particulars of the battle of Tewkesbury* (Tewkesbury, 1787).
English Historical Documents, 2, ed. D. C. Douglas & G. W. Greenaway (1953).
Fiennes, C., *The Illustrated Journeys 1685-c. 1712*, ed. C. Morris (1982).
Finberg, H. P. R., ed., *Gloucestershire Studies* (Leicester, 1957).
– *The Early Charters of the West Midlands* (Leicester, 1972).

Freeman, E. A., *The History of the Norman Conquest of England* (Oxford 1869-70).

Gelling, M., *Place-Names in the Landscape* (1984).

Giles, J. A., ed., *Six Old English Chronicles* (1848).

– *William of Malmesbury's Chronicle* (1847).

Glasscock, R. E., *The Lay Subsidy of 1334* (Oxford, 1975).

Harrison's Description of England 1577, ed. F. J. Furnivall (1877).

Hart, G., *A History of Cheltenham* (Leicester, 1965).

Hector, L. C., *The Handwriting of English Documents* (Dorking, 1980).

Henson, G., *History of the Framework Knitters* (1831, reprinted 1970).

Herbert, N., *Road Travel and Transport in Gloucestershire* (Gloucester, 1985).

Hooke, D., *The Anglo-Saxon Landscape: the Kingdom of the Hwicce* (Manchester, 1985).

Hoskins, W. G., *The Age of Plunder: King Henry's England 1500-1547* (1976).

Leech, R., *Historic Towns in Gloucestershire* (C.R.A.A.G.S., 1981).

Maggs, C., *The Birmingham Gloucester Line* (Cheltenham 1986).

Margary, I. D., *Roman Roads in Britain* (1957).

McGrath, P. & Cannon, J., eds., *Essays in Bristol and Gloucestershire History* (B.G.A.S., 1976).

Men and Armour for Gloucestershire in 1608 (1902, reprinted Gloucester 1980).

Miles, D. & Fowler, P. J., *Tewkesbury: the Archaeological Implications of Development* (1972).

Moore, J., *The Portrait of Elmbury* (1946, reprinted 1966).

Mulock, D. M., *John Halifax, Gentleman* (1856, reprinted 1912).

Ogilby's Road Maps of England and Wales (1675, reprinted Reading 1971).

Payne, G. E., *Gloucestershire, A Survey: a physical, social and economic survey and plan* (1946).

Phillipps, Sir T., *The Gloucestershire Subsidy Roll, 1 Ed. III 1327* (1856).

Platts, A. & Hainton, G. H., *Education in Gloucestershire, a short history* (Gloucester, 1954).

Poole, A. L., *Domesday Book to Magna Carta* (Oxford 1951).

Rackham, O., *The History of the Countryside* (1986).

Restoration of Tewkesbury Abbey: Report of a meeting held at Lambeth Palace on Saturday, 3 March, 1877 (Tewkesbury, 1877).

Reynolds, S., *English Medieval Towns* (Oxford 1977).

Richardson, L., *The River Severn* (privately printed, 1964).

Rogers, A., *This Was Their World* (1972).

Rolt, L. T. C., *Navigable Waterways* (1969).

– *Thomas Telford* (1969).

Rowley, T., *The Norman Heritage 1066-1200* (1969).

Rudder, S., *A New History of Gloucestershire* (1779).

Savine, A., *English Monasteries on the Eve of the Dissolution* (Oxford, 1909).

Smith, A. H., *Place-Names of Gloucestershire* (E.P.N.S. 39) (4 vols., Cambridge, 1964-5).

Smith, B. & Ralph, E., *A History of Bristol and Gloucestershire* (Beaconsfield, 1972).

Steer, F. W., *Farm and Cottage Inventories of Mid-Essex 1635-1749* (Chelmsford, 1950).

Thirsk, J., *The Rural Economy of England* (1984).

Valor Ecclesiasticus (Records Commission, 1817).

Verey, D., *Gloucestershire: the Vale and the Forest of Dean* (*The Buildings of England*, ed. Pevsner, 1980).

Waller, P. T., *Town, City and Nation* (Oxford, 1983).

Warner, Rev. R., *A Tour Through the Northern Counties of England and the Borders of Scotland* (1802).

Waters, B., *Severn Tide* (1947).

Willcox, W. B., *Gloucestershire, a Study in Local Government 1590-1640* (1940).

Williams, W. R., *The Parliamentary History of the County of Gloucester, 1213-1898* (Hereford, 1898).

Wrigley, A. & Schofield, R., *The Population History of England, 1541-1871* (Cambridge, 1981).

ARTICLES, PAMPHLETS AND THESES

Adcock, J. A., *The Tewkesbury Hosiery Industry 1760-1900* (1973). G.R.O.: IN 36.

Alldridge, N., ed., *The Hearth Tax: Problems and Possibilities* (C.O.R.A.L. 1983).

Bayes, J. F. & Roberts, J., 'Turnpike Roads from Gloucester to Cheltenham and Tewkesbury', *Journal of the Gloucestershire Society of Industrial Archaeologists*, 1971. (Also *Gloucestershire Historical Studies*, 3, 1969).

Bazeley, Rev. Canon, 'The Battle of Tewkesbury 1471', *T.B.G.A.S.*, 26 (1903).

Blake, S., *George Rowe, Artist and Lithographer* (Cheltenham Art Gallery and Museum, 1982).

Blyth, J. D., 'The Battle of Tewkesbury 1471', *T.B.G.A.S.*, 80 (1961).

Branigan, K., 'Villa Settlement in the West Country', Branigan & Fowler (1976).

Byard, H., 'The Historic Organs of Bristol and Gloucestershire', *T.B.G.A.S.* 93 (1974).

Cave, C. J. P., *Roof Bosses in the Nave of Tewkesbury Abbey* (Oxford, 1929).

Chapman, S. D., *The Cotton Industry in the Industrial Revolution* (1972).

Cossons, A., *The Tewkesbury and Cheltenham Roads*, Schedule of Turnpike Acts relating to Gloucestershire (n.d.). (G.R.O.: ROL.G4).

Courney, T. & Linnell, E., 'Old Bowling Green Site, Tewkesbury: Salvage Observations 1983', *T.B.G.A.S.*, 102 (1984).

Finberg, H. P. R., 'The Genesis of the Gloucestershire Towns', ed. Finberg (Leicester, 1957).

Fowler, P. J., 'Archaeology and the M5 Motorway: Gloucestershire 1969-75: A Summary and Assessment', *T.B.G.A.S.*, 95 (1977).

Gelling, M., 'Some Notes on Warwickshire Place Names', *Transactions of the Birmingham and Warwickshire Archaeological Society*, 86 (1974).

Gentleman's Magazine: 58 (ii) (1788); 61 (i) (1791); 88 (i) (1818).

Gough, H., *Itinerary of Edward I* (Paisley, 1900).

Gray, I. E., 'Some 17th century token issues', *T.B.G.A.S.*, 84 (1965).

– 'Records of Four Tewkesbury Vicars, *c.* 1685-1769', *T.B.G.A.S.*, 102 (1984).

Hammond, P. W., Shearring, H. G. & Wheeler, G., *Battle of Tewkesbury 4th May 1471* (Tewkesbury, 1971).

Hannan, A., 'Tewkesbury 1972: an interim report', *Glevensis*, 7 (1973).

– 'Holm Castle, Tewkesbury, an excavation during 1974', *Glevensis*, 9 (1975).

· – 'Holm Castle', *Glevensis*, 10 (1976).

Harris, M., *Alan of Tewkesbury 1186-1202* (Tewkesbury, 1980).

Henderson, J. & Bradley, J. D., *A Short History of the Mythe Waterworks* (North-West Gloucestershire Water Board, 1969).

Hilton, R. H., 'Medieval Market Towns and Simple Commodity Production', *Past and Present*, 109 (November, 1985).

Holman, J. R., 'Some Aspects of Higher Education in Bristol and Gloucestershire, *c.* 1650-1750', *T.B.G.A.S.*, 95 (1977).

Hurst, H., 'Gloucester (Glevum): A Colonia in the West Country', Branigan & Fowler (1976).

Industrial Gloucestershire (Chance and Bland, Gloucester, 1904).

Lawes, J. B. & Gilbert, J. H., 'Home produce, imports, consumption and price of wheat, over forty harvests 1852-53 to 1891-92', *Journal of the Royal Agricultural Society*, (1893).

'Leland in Gloucestershire', ed. Latimer, J., *T.B.G.A.S.*, 14 (1889-90).

Lyon-Smith, R. J., 'Tewkesbury Local Board of Health 1848-1855', *Gloucestershire Historical Studies*, 13 (1982).

– 'The Lighting of Tewkesbury Streets', *Local History Bulletin*, 51 (1985).

Machin, R., 'The great rebuilding: a reassessment', *Past and Present*, 77 (November, 1977).

Map of Great Britain, c. A.D. 1360, known as the Gough map (Oxford 1958).

Marples, M. J., *The Founders of Tewkesbury Abbey* (Tewkesbury, 1982).

Marshall, A., 'A Romano-British Settlement at Southwick Park, Tewkesbury', *Glevensis*, 10 (1976).

Ordnance Survey sheet 60, first one inch map (sheet 44, 1828) (reprinted Newton Abbot, 1970).

Percival, A., 'Gloucestershire Village Populations', *Local Population Studies*, 8 (1978).

Proceedings of the Cotteswold Naturalists Field Club, 19 (1915-17).

Rammell, T. W., *Report to the General Board of Health* (1850).

Rath, T., 'The Tewkesbury Hosiery Industry', *Textile History*, 7 (1976).

Pepin, P., 'Monasticon Anglicanum and the History of Tewkesbury Abbey', *T.B.G.A.S.*, 98 (1980).

Richmond, I. A. & Crawford, O. G. S., 'The British section of the Ravenna Cosmography', *Archaeologia*, 93 (1949).

Ripley, P., 'Parish register evidence for the population of Gloucester 1562-1641', *T.B.G.A.S.*, 91 (1972).

Rushforth, G. McN., Lancastrian notables 'The Burials of in Tewkesbury abbey after the battle of Tewkesbury 1471', *T.B.G.A.S.*, 47 (1925).

Sanders, M. G. & Webster, G., 'A section across the Roman road between Tewkesbury and Worcester on Shuthonger Common', *Transactions of the Worcester Archaeological Society*, 37 (1960).

Smith, B. S., *Tewkesbury and Gloucestershire History*, Exhibition at the Fitz Hamon Art Centre (Tewkesbury, 1971).

Stimpson, M., *The History of Gloucester Docks* (1981).

Society for the Protection of Ancient Buildings, *A School of Rational Builders* (1982).

– First Annual Report of the Committee, 21 June 1878.

– *Manifesto*.

Tawney, A. J. & R. H., 'An occupational census of the 17th century', *Economic History Review*, 5 (1934).

Taylor, C. S., 'The origin of the Mercian shires', ed. Finberg (1957).

The Story of a County Mill: Healings of Tewkesbury (n.d.).

Thirsk, J., 'The fantastical folly of fashion: the English stocking knitting industry 1500-1700', in Thirsk, ed. (1984).

Transactions of the Worcestershire Naturalists Club, 7 (1918-22).

Wakeman, T., 'On the kitchener's roll of Tewkesbury abbey', *Journal of the British Archaeological Association*, 15 (1859).

Wyatt, J. W., 'Trades and occupations in Gloucester, Tewkesbury and Cirencester in 1608', *Gloucestershire Historical Studies*, 7 (1976).

GUIDE BOOKS AND DIRECTORIES

1. Guide Books

(Note: listed in chronological order; when not dated an estimated date is given; place of publication Tewkesbury. Located in G.C.L., G.R.O. and Abbey library).

North, W., *A Guide to Tewkesbury and Neighbourhood* (1874).

Gardner, W. J., *Visitor's Guide* (1891).

North, W., *New Handbook and Guide to Tewkesbury Abbey Church* (c. 1893).

– *Notes on Old Tewkesbury, past and present, with comprehensive history and description of Tewkesbury abbey church* (c.1895).

– *A Handbook and Guide to Places of Special Interest in Tewkesbury and the Surrounding Neighbourhood* (c. 1895).

Gardner, W. J., *Official Guide to Tewkesbury*, by W. Davies (1903).

North's Guide to Tewkesbury, its history and attractions – the official guide (published Ed. J. Burrow, Cheltenham and London, c. 1916).

Idem (c. 1922).

Burrow, Ed. J., *Official Guide to Tewkesbury*, (c. 1930; c. 1933 and c. 1941).

2. Directories

(Note: located in G.C.L., G.R.O., and Cheltenham library).

Bailey's British (1784).

British Universal (1800).

Gell and Bradshaw (1820).

Pigot (1822-3).

Idem (1842).

Slater's Royal National and Commercial Directory and Topography (1852-3).

Kelly's Post Office: 1856, 1870, 1885, 1902, 1906, 1914, 1923, 1939.

ACTS AND PARLIAMENTARY PAPERS

1726: 12 Geo. I c. 18 (Turnpike).

1751: 24 Geo. II c. 39 (Avon Navigation).

1755-6: 29 Geo. II c. 51 (Turnpike).

1786: 26 Geo. III c. 17 (Paving).

1792: 32 Geo. III (Poor Relief).

1808: 48 Geo. III (Key Bridge and Enclosure).

1812-13: 53 Geo. III (Gaol).

1823: 4 Geo. IV c. 2 (Mythe Bridge).

1826: 7 Geo. IV c. 78 (Turnpike).

1860: 23 Vict. c. 72 (Railway).

PP 1834 XXX-XXXV: Replies to Urban Queries from Commissioners on the Poor Laws.

PP 1835 XXIII: Reports from Commissioners on Municipal Corporations in England and Wales. (Pages 263-6 reproduced in Bennett, T. Y. R. & M. (1), 188 ff.).

PP 1842 XV: Digest of schools and charities for education presented by Commissioners for inquiring into charities.

PP 1845 XV: Report of the Commissioner appointed to enquire into the condition of the framework-knitters.

PP 1850 XLIX: Reports on Turnpike Trusts.

Index